MARKETING OF FINANCIAL SERVICES

A Thesis Submitted to

The Maharaja Sayajirao University of Baroda

for

The Award of the Degree of

Doctor of Philosophy

in Business Administration

By
Umesh R. Dangarwala

Under the guidance of
Prof. B. S. Patel

Department of Commerce including Business Administration

Faculty of Commerce

The Maharaja Sayajirao University of Baroda,

Vadodara

September 1999

P/Th
9043

CERTIFICATE

Certified that the work incorporated in the thesis titled "MARKETING OF FINANCIAL SERVICES" submitted by Mr. Umesh R. Dangarwala comprises the results of independent and original investigations carried out by him under my supervision. The material that has been obtained and used from other sources has been duly acknowledged in the thesis.

Place : Vadodara
Date : September 3, 1999

Prof. B. S. Patel
Research Guide

DEDICATED

TO

LATE SHRI LATESH A. DANGARWALA

- MY COUSIN -

ACKNOWLEDGEMENTS

This Research Project was undertaken under the able guidance of Professor B. S. Patel, Former Dean and Head, Department of Commerce including Business Administration, Maharaja Sayajirao University of Baroda. I am highly indebted to him for his continuous and invaluable efforts in going through the manuscript of my thesis and in suggesting the proper methods to be followed for the betterment of the work. I express my heartfelt thanks to him for the guidance provided to me in the midst of his busy schedule.

I have given a word of honour to the Management of the responding organizations not to disclose their identity. I am happy to gratefully acknowledge their full support, personal as well as administrative, in collecting data from their personnel. To the Top Management of the Organization who besides giving me the permission provided total back-up facilities to me, and the respondents who spared time to respond to my lengthy questionnaires, meticulously, I owe not nearly formal thanks but a grateful acknowledgement of their outright obligation to me.

I also express gratitude towards the respected Librarians of all the under mentioned libraries for the kind permissions they have granted to use the materials of their respective Libraries, viz., Smt. Hansa Mehta Library of The Maharaja Sayajirao University of Baroda, Library of Indian Institute of Management, Ahmedabad, Library of Sardar Patel University of Vallabh Vidhyanagar, Library of Institute of Chartered Accountants of India, Mumbai, Library of Institute of Chartered Financial Analyst of India, Hyderabad, Library of Indian Institute of Bankers, Mumbai.

Professor I. P. Vyas, Former Head of the Department of Commerce including Business Administration has been a perennial source of personal encouragement to me since the commencement of my work. I place on record my hearty thanks to him for all that he did for me, expertly and selflessly.

I take this opportunity of putting on record my deep gratitude to Professor K. M. Joshi, Faculty of Management Studies, The Maharaja Sayajirao University of Baroda for his affectionate and expert counselling that proved to be immense help to me at every stage of my work.

Dr. A. R. Hingorani, Head, Department of Commerce including Business Administration, silently and subtly observed the progress of my work and engaged in academic discussions from which I got very useful hints for improving my work. I place on record my heartfelt thanks to him.

Professor A. G. Sandhe, Former Head of the Department of Commerce including Business Administration and Shri Pragnesh B. Shah, Faculty colleague and a friend, did not allow me to forget my work and rest. Their constant reminders kept almost on the run. To them, I owe a special debt of gratitude.

My sincere thanks are to my faculty colleagues Prof. S. K. Singh, Prof. J. R. Khedkar, Prof. D. S. Pathak, Prof. M. D. Mohite, Prof. Sanjeev Joshi, Shri M. R. Vyas, Dr. Samir Joshi, Dr. Sharad Bansal, Dr. P. M. Shah, Shri G. S. Patel, Shri Y. N. Parikh, Shri Kalpesh Shah and Dr. Amit Pandya who actively assisted me in various phases and aspects of my work. But for the devoted assistance, I could not have completed my work at all.

Mr. Shamal A. Pradhan, my departmental colleague, provided two-fold service of organizing my data-files, intelligently and doing the necessary referential work during report writing. I heartily record his very useful contribution in my efforts.

I express my special thanks to Vishal Patel, Alpit Patel and Sheetal Patel, students of the Faculty for helping me in collecting and analyzing the data and for their kind cooperation.

I will be failing in my duty if I do not mention, if not for thanks, at least for record, the immense concern and emotional involvement of my wife, my children and parents. I do not thank them but recollect the experience of their deep affection for me, even now.

Mr. Rahul D. Joshi and Mr. Hiral G. Kansara who laboriously and meticulously typed the thesis promptly and diligently, deserve special thanks.

Umesh R. Dangarwala

CONTENTS

ACKNOWLEDGEMENTS	*i*
CONTENTS	*iv*
LIST OF TABLES	*viii*

CHAPTER – I
INTRODUCTION — 01

1.1	MARKETING & ECONOMIC DEVELOPMENT	02
1.2	DEVELOPMENTS IN MARKETING	10
1.3	SERVICES MARKETING	21
1.4	NATURE & SCOPE OF THE STUDY	43
1.5	LIMITATIONS OF THE STUDY	44
1.6	ORGANIZATION OF THE STUDY – CHAPTERIZATION	45

CHAPTER – II
LITERATURE REVIEW AND A RATIONALE OF THE STUDY — 50

2.1	INTRODUCTION	53
2.2	A RATIONALE OF THE STUDY	57

CHAPTER – III
FINANCIAL SERVICES MARKETING — 60

3.1	INTRODUCTION	60
3.2	FINANCIAL SERVICES IN THE INDIAN CONTEXT	60
3.3	SPECIAL CHARACTERISTICS OF FINANCIAL SERVICES	62
3.4	THE MARKETING AND COMPETITIVE ENVIRONMENT	69
3.5	THE FINANCIAL SERVICES MARKETING MIX	73
3.6	FINANCIAL PRODUCTS (SERVICES) - THE OPTIONS AVAILABLE	78
3.7	TECHNOLOGY POWER FOR FINANCIAL PRODUCTS	93
3.8	FINANCIAL SERVICES REGULATION AND LEGISLATION: IMPACT ON FINANCIAL SERVICES	93

CHAPTER - IV
METHODOLOGY 96

4.1	INTRODUCTION	96
(a)	Statement of Problem :	
(b)	Research Objectives	
(c)	Focus of research	
4.2	SAMPLING	99
(a)	Sample Frame	
(b)	Sample Size :	
(c)	Sampling Technique	
(d)	Sample Selection	
4.3	INSTRUMENTATION – QUESTIONNAIRE	100
4.4	SCORING TECHNIQUE	102
4.5	DATA COLLECTION	104
4.6	DATA ANALYSIS	105
4.7	CLASSIFICATION OF RESPONDENTS ORGANIZATIONS	106
4.8	VARIABLES IN THE PRESENT STUDY	111

CHAPTER - V
ANALYSIS AND INTERPRETATION OF DATA:
COMPARISON AND DIFFERENTIATION OF GROUPS 114

5.1	INTRODUCTION	114
Section – I		
5.2	PERFORMANCE OF THE SAMPLE ON DIFFERENT MARKETING PRACTICES	115
5.3	RISK TAKER GROUP COMPARED WITH SAFE PLAYER GROUP IN TERMS OF ADOPTION OF MARKETING PRACTICES	116
5.4	PROFESSIONALLY MANAGED GROUP COMPARED WITH TRADITIONALLY MANAGED GROUP IN TERMS OF ADOPTION OF MARKETING PRACTICES	123
5.5	FUND BASED SERVICES GROUP COMPARED WITH FEE BASED/ADVISORY SERVICES GROUP IN TERMS OF ADOPTION OF MARKETING PRACTICES.	129

5.6	PRIVATE ORGANIZATIONS GROUP COMPARED WITH NATIONALIZED ORGANIZATIONS GROUP IN TERMS OF ADOPTION OF MARKETING PRACTICES.	134
5.7	CONCLUDING REMARKS IN SECTION I	138

Section – II

5.8	INTRODUCTION	142
5.9	THE MARKET ORIENTED AND SAFE PLAYER GROUPS DIFFERENTIATED ON VARIOUS MARKETING PRACTICES	143
5.10	THE PROFESSIONALLY MANAGED AND TRADITIONALLY MANAGED GROUPS DIFFERENTIATED ON VARIOUS MARKETING PRACTICES	155
5.11	FUND BASED SERVICES GROUP AND FEE BASED/ADVISORY SERVICES GROUP DIFFERENTIATED ON VARIOUS MARKETING PRACTICES	162
5 12	PRIVATE ORGANIZATIONS AND NATIONALIZED ORGANIZATIONS GROUPS DIFFERENTIATE ON VARIOUS MARKETING PRACTICES	163
5.13	CONCLUDING REMARKS	165

CHAPTER VI
ANALYSIS AND INTERPRETATION OF DATA: ASSOCIATION BETWEEN GROWTH RATES AND MARKETING PRACTICES 168

6.1	INTRODUCTION	168

Section – I

6.2	STEPWISE REGRESSION APPLIED ON ENTIRE SAMPLE	171
a)	Correlation of all variables	
b)	Regression of Variable 1 (growth rate) on variable 2 (CDP)	
c)	Regression of Variable 1 (growth rate) on variable 2 (CDP) & 6 (PMP)	
d)	Regression of Variable 1 (growth rate) on variables 5 (PRP), 3(PDP) & 4 (NPP)	
e)	Interpretation of regression results for the entire samples	
6.3	DISCUSSION ON VARIABLE 2 (CDP)	178
6.4	DISCUSSION ON VARIABLE : 6 (PMP)	183

Section – Ii

6.5	REGRESSION ANALYSIS – CONTRIBUTION OF SIGNIFICANT VARIABLES 2 AND 4 IN THE DIFFERENT GROUPS OF CLASSIFICATION.	188

- a) Introduction
- b) Risk Taker Group
- c) Safe Player Group
- d) Professionally Managed Group
- e) Traditionally Managed Group
- f) Fund Based Services Group
- g) Fee Based / Advisory Group
- h) Private Organization Group
- i) Nationalized Organization Group
- j) Concluding Remarks on Section – II

CHAPTER VII
SUMMARY, IMPORTANT FINDINGS AND THEIR IMPLICATIONS — 207

7.1	SUMMARY OF THE STUDY:	207
7.2	FINDINGS AND THEIR IMPLICATIONS.	209
7.3	SUGGESTIONS FOR IMPROVING MARKETING OF FINANCIAL SERVICES	213
7.4	DIRECTION FOR FURTHER RESEARCH	217

BIBLIOGRAPHY — 219

APPENDIX-I QUESTIONNAIRE ON "MARKETING OF FINANCIAL SERVICES" — 234

APPENDIX – II Major Recommendations of Selected Committees (1985-95) — 253

APPENDIX-III COMMITTEE ON TRADE FINANCIAL SERVICES [GATs] — 283

LIST OF TABLES

Table No.	Title	Page No.
Table I-1	Coordinated Marketing System, Developed versus less Developed countries.	8
Table I-2	List of Selected Services	25
Table I-3	Reasons for Growth of Service Industries	26
Table I-4	Implication of Service Characteristics and Ways of Overcoming Them	36
Table II-1	List of related studies / research	56
Table IV-1	Composition of "Risk Taker" Group and "Safe Player" Group in the sample.	107
Table IV-2	Composition of Professionally Managed Group and Traditionally Managed Group in the sample.	108
Table IV-3	Composition of "Fund Based Services" Group (FBSG) – "Fee Based/Advisory Services" Group (ABSG) in the sample.	109
Table IV-4	Composition of Private Organizations Group and Nationalized organizations Group in the sample.	110
Table IV-5	Composition of Consumer Finance Organizations and Industrial Finance Organizations in the sample.	111
Table V-1	Performance of the entire sample on different Marketing Practices	115
Table V-2	Comparison of RTG-SPG groups on different Marketing Practices	117
Table V-3	Comparison of PROF.MG. -TRAD.MG. groups on different Marketing Practices	125
Table V-4	Comparison of FBSG – ABSG groups on different Marketing Practices	130
Table V-5	Comparison of POG – NOG groups on different marketing practices	135

Table No.	Title	Page No.
Table VI-4	Regression of Variable 1 (Growth rate) on Variable 2 (CDP)	174
Table VI-5	Contribution of Variables 2 (CDP) and 6 (PMP)	175
Table VI-6	Regression of Variable 1 (Growth rate) on Variable 2 and 6 (CDP and PMP)	176
Table VI-7	Identification of the Target Market	179
Table VI-8	Estimate and forecast of total Market Demand and Market Share	180
Table VI-9	Information on Competitors	182
Table VI-10	Promotional Aspects	184
Table VI-11	Response Sought through Communication	186
Table VI-12	Simple Correlation in the Risk Taker Group (n = 34)	189
Table VI-13	Regression of Variable 1 on Variable 2 and 6 in the Risk Taker Group	190
Table VI-14	Simple Correlation in the Safe Player Group (SPG)	191
Table VI-15	Regression of Variable 1 on Variable 2 and 6 the safe player group	192
Table VI-16	Simple Correlation in the Professionally Managed group (n=35)	193
Table VI-17	Regression of Variable 1 on Variables 2 and 6 in the Professionally Managed Group	194
Table VI-18	Simple Correlation in the Traditionally Managed Group (n=17)	195
Table VI-19	Regression of Variable 1 on Variable 2 and 6 in the Traditionally Managed Group	196
Table VI-20	Simple Correlation in the FBSG Group (n = 23)	197
Table VI-21	Regression of Variable 1 on Variable 2 and 6 in the FBSG Group	197
Table VI-22	Simple Correlation in the ABSG Group (n = 29)	199
Table VI-23	Regression of variable 1 on Variables 2 and 6 in ABSG Group	200
Table VI-24	Simple Correlation in the Private organizations Group (n=11)	202
Table VI-25	Regression of variable 1 on Variables 2 and 6 in the POG	203
Table VI-26	Simple Correlation in the Nationalized organizations Group (n=41)	204
Table VI-27	Regression of Variable 1 on Variable 2 and 6 in NOG	205
Table VII-1	Major Findings	210

CHAPTER – I
INTRODUCTION

CHAPTER – I

INTRODUCTION

Today 75 million Americans are employed in the service sector and as much as 70 per cent of the US economy is service-oriented.[1]

A recent FICCI paper avers that the service sector can contribute more than 50 per cent to the national GDP by AD 2000 provided it grows at a rate of 5.3 per cent annually.[2] If this works out, the projected growth in this sector is going to surpass the growth in the agricultural and industrial sectors.

Services occupy a place of significant importance in the Indian economy. The service trade accounts for almost 46 per cent of the total GDP in India. According to the Seventh Plan document, it is expected that its share would increase to 58 % by the end of the century.[3] It employs nearly a fourth more than the people employed in the manufacturing sector in India.

Finance plays an important role in shaping the economy of a country. The present study is concerned with the marketing practices of the financial service organizations. A review of the existing literature on the subject reveals that the marketing problem of the financial service organizations has remained a fairly unmapped area. The purpose of this study is to investigate to what extent the financial service organizations adopt the marketing concept in their marketing decisions, for the marketing concept holds, that, the key to achieving organizational goals consists in determining the needs and wants of target markets and delivering the desired satisfactions more effectively and efficiently than competitors.

In the present chapter, to begin with, a discussion on "Marketing and Economic Development" is undertaken. This is followed by "Developments in Marketing" and "Service Marketing". In the latter half of the chapter, the Nature and Scope, Limitations and Organization of the thesis are given.

1.1 MARKETING & ECONOMIC DEVELOPMENT

Marketing has a key role to play in the economic development of a country through its potential contribution to the process of economic development. Economic growth implies rise in gross National product through generation of additional income in various sectors of an economy such as agriculture, mining, industry and trade. [4]

It may be noted that literature on Economic Development[5] prior to world war II, laid heavy emphasis on industrial expansion as the key to induced economic growth. In the early 1950's, literature on economic development suggested that the agriculture sector should be developed first, followed by the industrial sector. But in the last two decades, the importance of balanced growth between rural and urban areas has been well understood and acted upon.

In general the process of economic development involves the transformation of agriculturally based rural economies into industrially based urban economies and a harmony is established between the two sectors in satisfying each other's needs. Increased specialization of labour, the adoption of more scientific technologies and the geographic separation of production and consumption are necessarily accompanied by the development of a more complex marketing system. Thus, marketing is considered to be a set of techniques and procedures aimed at facilitating the flow of goods and **services** from procedures to consumers in a given economy.[6]

1.1.1 ROLE OF MARKETING IN ECONOMIC DEVELOPMENT

The role of marketing in the economic development of a country is described below:

(i) Marketing helps in stimulating potential aggregate demand.

(ii) If accelerates the process of monetizing the economy.

(iii) It gives rise to the concept of a national market.

(iv) Marketing also helps in sustaining the existing levels of employment.

(v) The enlargement of the market size results in two distinct advantages. The oft experienced shortage of capital resources can be met partly through a more rational use of inventory.

Secondly, the growth of market institution helps in the discovery of entrepreneurial talent. In the words of Peter Drucker "Marketing is also the most easily accessible 'multipliers' of managers and entrepreneurs in an under – developed growth area".[7]

(vi) An enlarged market makes economically feasible, the various economies of scale. There can be economies of scales both in production and distribution of goods and services.[8]

(vii) The welding of small markets which can be achieved through marketing makes possible the movement of such factors of production as, labour and capital over a wider area where, they can be most efficiently used. In the hitherto independent markets which are now joined, there tends to be closer correspondence in the price of various commodities. This helps to reduce price fluctuations and possibly works towards lowering the cost of living.[9]

(viii) More generally, growth in marketing can help disseminate new ideas favourable to economic growth, new patterns of consumption, possibly new techniques and new ideas of social relations.[10]

1.1.2 THE CONCEPT A NATIONAL MARKET[11] IN DEVELOPING ECONOMIES

Rostow noted that the marketing system can play a critical role in the balanced growth of rural and urban sectors in a Less Developed country. Many developing nations are characterized by a build up in social capital and are not yet at a point where significant structural distribution exist to hinder economic growth. Such structural distortions develop from the following conditions:

- There is some industrial capacity usually developed to substitute for the import of certain kinds of common goods;

- the market for most of these manufactured goods is thin (textile being an exception);

- although some development is taking place in every less developed country, the gap between the rural and urban life is widening at an accelerated rate;

- as a result of this imbalance men and women migrate from the rural areas to the cities, where there are insufficient industrial opportunities to provide full employment.

Rostow maintains that the way to achieve a take off into sustained growth for nations experiencing such conditions is to breakdown these structural distortions, to produce self-re-inforcing agricultural and industrial expansions and create truly national markets within these countries.

1.1.3 ROLE OF MARKETING FUNCTIONS IN ECONOMIC DEVELOPMENT

The lack of real marketing mentality is deplorably apparent in developing countries resulting in the consequence of waste of irreplaceable resources, more hunger and even death. [12]

Lack of co-ordination between marketing and production hampers development more so where resources are limited and where every effort should be devoted in obtaining optimum use of capital, manpower, land and energy.

The proper user of marketing research techniques (such as forecasting sales) can reduce the differences between a country's productive capacity and the demand for its production. [13] No doubt the techniques must be tailored especially to bring structural changes in the markets.

Management have come to rely on advertising as a tool to speed up the demand, making the investment in new enterprises or expansions of established houses worthwhile.[14] Knech comments that in developing countries there is a general overestimation of advertising as a means of marketing communication.

Distribution is an important factor that caters to the economic development of a country. In the developing countries, the conventional channels, which are riddled with parasitic middlemen, are being shaken and are now getting shorter.[15] (This has particular relevance to the Indian situation). Further, effective distribution bridges the gap between the manufacturer and the consumer.

1.1.4 COORDINATED MARKETING SYSTEMS

Conditions that have influenced the growth of coordinated marketing system in the developed countries also seem to be present in the less developed countries. Comparative conditions conducive to growth of coordinated marketing systems in developed versus less developed countries are shown in Table I-1. Although conditions similar to those described in Table I-1 exist in less developed countries, they are relatively much less sophisticated than conditions in developed countries, and their influences on achieving channel co-ordination would be tempered by the attitudes and behaviour of existing middlemen and policy makers.

Table I-1

Coordinated Marketing System, Developed versus Less Developed Countries.

Prevailing growth conditions in Developed countries	Relevance to Less – Developed countries
The need for assured volume encouraged the growth of centrally coordinated marketing systems.	Most companies have low and unpredictable sales and have a definite need to develop an assured sales volume to avoid price fluctuations and spoilage.
Relative profitability declined as a result of growing competition therefore, new approaches such as vertical integration and co-ordination were adopted by firms to ameliorate these pressures.	Most stores seem to have relatively new levels of profitability, partly because of atomistic competition and partly because of duplication and un-coordinated activities at different levels.
The changing nature of the environment and the growing complexity of marketing processes and markets increased the need for affiliation. Expansion and re-location of markets also contributed to the growth of centrally coordinated markets.	Overall, growth in markets has been slower. However, substantial growth in market process is visible in some of the larger urban centers. There is an acute disparity between rural and urban markets.
There is opportunity to capitalize on potential economies and savings that resulted from scheduling, simplifying, and repositioning marketing activities, and economies of scale at each stage of the centrally coordinated total business system.	Chances for potential economic saving exist. However, these opportunities are hard to comprehend by the current core of marketeers and policy makers.

Source : Bert C. McCannon, "The emergence and growth of contractually integrated channel is in the American Economy", in Marketing and Economic Development edited by Peter D. Bennett, American Marketing Association, Chicago, 1966.

1.1.5 MARKETING AND ECONOMIC DEVELOPMENT – ITS RELEVANCE TO THE SERVICE ORGANIZATIONS IN INDIA

If a case in favour of service organizations is taken, then how they promote 'marketing and economic development' is discussed below.

(i) Promotion of service organization would have two immediate catalytic benefits on the national economy [16]:

- increased employment would increase buying power which is needed for the expansion of consumer markets. That is, they spread the total income generated more widely over the population.

- the growth of service organizations would provide the nation with a vast pool of providers of various services.

This would help in the progressive diffusion of fruits of modern science and technology.

(ii) The growth and productivity of service organizations scattered throughout the nation provide the basic services that are needed for economic development.

(iii) The perception spreading in the policy circles is that the next phase of development should be on the making of efficient national markets and from this widened base, move on to the generation of new lines of diversified exports. These diversified exports alleviate pressures on the nations credit situation and generate foreign currency reserves which can be used for economic development in other spheres of industrial growth. Historically it had been found that export of goods & **services** had usually followed or paralleled the development of a national market. [17]

(iv) Growth in the market can reduce the community's need for working capital. The capital, which is released, can be used for increased consumption, further economic growth or a combination of the two. [18]

1.2 DEVELOPMENTS IN MARKETING

Prior to the time of the Industrial Revolution, virtually all trade and exchange processes involved some personal contact between suppliers and their customers. This meant that individual producers could cater to the needs of their, customers, and most of the trade was very local in nature. The increase in overseas trading and the advent of the industrial revolution heralded the start of new types of trading practices, and the introduction of some of the processes which are part of marketing today.

Initially, producers and manufacturers were concerned mainly with logistical issues – transporting and selling goods to widespread markets, often located far away from the point of production. The focus here was on production, with consumption and consumers being seen as the end result of a production and distribution chain. For as long as demand outstripped supply, which was generally the case as western counties started to go through periods of dramatic growth in economic activity and technological change, producers could all exist profitably simply by producing more efficiently and cutting costs. Little attention was given to the role of the consumer in exchange processes.

In the early twentieth century the realization that marketing was, in itself, an important part of the business process led to the founding of the American Marketing Association and the development of the earliest aspects of marketing theory and practice. It was much later, however, that the need for a marketing orientation was recognized, with a clear focus on the needs of the consumer.

1.2.1 MARKETING THEORY DEVELOPMENTS

The greatly increased production of goods which arose out of mechanization following the industrial revolution was matched by increased levels of demand in the mass market. The problem for producers lay in getting their products to the market. Manufacturers were investing heavily in premises and machinery in pursuit of better and cheaper production. They did not want to be involved in the distribution of the products. A distribution trade grew up to serve every industry.

a)   **First Generation Marketing**

Wholesalers opened warehouses in major cities and bought products in bulk from the manufacturers. They stored the products and organized their distribution to retailers and other smaller organizations throughout markets. This was the development of channels of distribution, still crucial to successful marketing today, and is recognized as first generation marketing. At this stage the main concern was getting the product to market – selling all that was produced.

b)   Second Generation Marketing

It was only during the second half of the twentieth century that the focus began to shift towards the notion that producers should look at what consumers actually wanted – produce what can be sold to the market, rather than try to sell what is produced. This was the start of second generation marketing. The early stages of the second generation saw the development of the idea that firms should take on a marketing orientation – marketing should become the integrated focus of their business policy. Firms should seek to satisfy their profit needs by identifying and satisfying consumer needs.

New ideas in the 1960s also pressed the need for a broader orientation with a focus on consumer needs and criticized firms which were still too product orientated. By defining their business in terms of their products, firms could constrict their own growth and development – even survival – as consumer needs and technologies were changing rapidly. The essential task for firms was to analyze their business from the consumer's perspective – to look at their market offerings in terms of the needs satisfied, rather than the products offered. Thus the Hollywood film industry, for example needed to focus on it business as 'entertainment' rather than 'making movies' if it was to enjoy continued profitability and success in the face of increasing competition from television.

c) Third Generation Marketing

From the mid – 1960s onwards, marketing thought grew and matured. There was increasing awareness of the role that marketing played, not only in business but through its influence and impact on consumers and society as a whole. Marketing began to be seen as something, which was not only relevant to commercial organizations, actively seeking profits at the end of the day. Marketing could be equally important for organizations and services which were not necessarily traditional, profit-led businesses. Schools, health programs, charities and other types of not-for-profit organizations could benefit from a marketing orientation. Even political parties could employ marketing programs to win voters. Marketing was viewed as being applicable across a very broad spectrum of commercial and social activity.

From this realization came the emergence of third generation marketing. This hinged on the idea of a broader application of marketing within society, across all types of organizations, and for greater benefit to society. Society's needs should be considered in line with those of consumers, and profits should not be sought at an unacceptable cost to society. This has led to a call for firms to engage in ethical marketing practices and, increasingly, to adopt environment sound, 'green' policies.

In moving towards the development of a body of marketing theory, much has been drawn from other academic disciplines. This is especially true of the behavioral sciences, economics and management science. A debate exists as to how much actual marketing theory has been established to date. What is generally accepted, however, is that marketing is evolving as a discipline with a wide base of knowledge, concepts and techniques and areas of theory which may ultimately come together to provide an integrated base of marketing theory.

1.2.2 THE MARKETING ENVIRONMENT

All organizations operate within the marketing environment. This consists of the micro-environment which relates to the organization itself – its own internal environment – and the external or macro- environment which will affect all organizations to a lesser or greater degree. Environmental analysis is vital for marketing success as organizations must be able to understand (and predict where possible) those factors which may impact upon their marketing strategies.

Environmental analysis plays a key role in strategic planning, both at a corporate and functional level. Essentially, the key steps involved are as follows:
- Identifying influences (positive and negative).
- Control those, which can be controlled.
- Use those which can contribute to competitive advantage.
- Overcome, or defend against, potentially damaging influences.

The Micro-environment is the internal environment of the organization. Its influence, therefore, will be specific to a particular organization. The factors to be analyzed in the internal environment will include the following:

a. The company itself – management structure, strong points, distinctive competencies, failings, finances
b. Customers
c. Suppliers
d. Channel members
e. Competitors
f. Other publics which may include:

Government or political bodies
Pressure groups
Financial institutions
Shareholders
Influencer market

In effect, any person or organization which can influence the company's marketing activities – and marketing success – in any way should be included here. This list is not absolutely comprehensive as individual organizations may need to consider special influences.

The macro – environment is the wider, external environment in which all firms operate. The organization should study the macro – environment factors relevant to their business or operational activities – in other words, in their competitive domain. The types of influence likely to have an impact on present and future activities can be broken down into several main areas.

Political / legal factors
Economic factors
Socio-cultural factors
Technological factors

These analyses, when completed in detail, will from the basis of the SWOT analysis, used in the planning process. SWOT (strengths, weaknesses, opportunities and threats) represents a way of categorizing the environmental analysis in a way which can help organizations in determining appropriate strategic action. The internal factors can be divided into those which are strengths and those which are weaknesses, while the external factors can be similarly categorized as either opportunities or threats.

Sometimes this is not quite so simple as it sounds. For example, the single European market may represent a substantial opportunity for many organizations. Equally, it can also be a threat, due to the possible increased competition from other member countries. Similarly, the innovative entrepreneurship of the head of the organization might be its outstanding strength, whilst also being a weakness if too much of the organization's success rested on that one individual as they could go elsewhere, or become unable to work for some reason.

However, organizations should undertake the analysis regularly to help them decide on future courses of action. Organizations should:

Build on their strengths

Attempt to overcome weaknesses

Exploit opportunities

Defend against threats.

1.2.3 MARKETING ORGANIZATIONS

A marketing organization has marketing as its key focus. It is organized around marketing and is customer – led or market – led. It anticipates and responds to the needs of the market in designing it current and future strategy. The idea of a marketing oriented organization can be made clearer by comparing it with other organizational philosophies which have been identified.

Firms which are production oriented focus on production as the key to success. In their view, the market will always seek products which are both cheaper and widely available. The organization's main task therefore, is continually to improve and refine production efficiency, thereby producing greater numbers of goods at lower prices. This approach does hold some credibility, especially in situations where demand is relatively high, and could increase with lower prices. This is the case in areas such as home electronics where color televisions and CD players, for example, have become far more popular as supply increased and prices fell. In the extreme, however, it ignores the customer viewpoint and will not succeed once markets have become saturated.

Some companies are product oriented, believing that consumers will seek products, which are innovative or technologically superior in the marketplace. They constantly strive to develop new products, which stand out. This is a high-risk approach with significant chances of failure, as seen by the number of 'flops' in the market. This approach can work successfully but it needs to take into account consumer tastes and wants. Without doing this, firms can fall into the trap of becoming too narrowly constrained, by viewing their business in terms of 'products' rather than in terms of customer needs and satisfactions. Both a production and a product orientation could equally apply to service providers, where there is too much attention focused on the service and the service provisions, rather than on the customers.

A selling orientation is where the focus of the firm's attention is on the 'hard sell'; heavy promotion, advertising and sales tactics to get rid of whatever is produced. This technique is evident today, particularly in the area of unsought goods – goods which do not fulfil specific consumer needs, but which are heavily promoted, frequently with deferred payment terms and pressurized sales tactics. A good example of this approach is in the selling of timeshare holidays which usually employs all the tactics outlined above – and often leads to unhappy consumers who claim they were pressurized or misled into signing a sales agreement. This approach can be lucrative in the short – term, but is unlikely to succeed in the long – term.

An organization, which is marketing oriented, as indicated previously, aims to achieve it organizational objectives by anticipating and satisfying the needs and wants of its consumers. Long-term customer satisfaction is a key goal, and the organization is committed to attracting and retaining customers. The business is defined in terms of need satisfaction rather than specific service or product areas, and as those needs change, this should be reflected in the organization's activities. Additionally, organizations may adhere to a societal marketing orientation, where attention is given to the long – term good of society, as well as consumers. This is becoming more and more evident in today's environmentally conscious marketplace.

1.2.4 MARKETING TODAY

No doubt, the developments within marketing which have led to what we know as marketing today, but, it is external factors in the political, social and business world which have shaped the role and development of marketing. Some of the influences which have an impact on the development of marketing are as follows:

a)   **Political / Legal**

Changes in government policy towards business enterprise.
The growth of global trade and the impact of trade barriers and currency agreements, for example:
Privatization
De-regulation of advertising for the professions.

Legislation on environmental issues.

Consumerism and the power of consumer pressure groups.

b) **Economic**

World economic trends.

Levels of consumer affluence, spending power.

The imposition or relaxation of price controls.

Inflation levels.

Attitudes to, and increases in, consumer borrowing.

The importance of the service economy.

The opening of the single European market.

c) **Socio-cultural**

Increased numbers of women in the workplace.

Cross-cultural issues in international marketing.

Increased leisure time, and the wide scale pursuit of leisure interests.

Growth in consumer travel and tourism.

d) **Technological**

The impact of technology on business processes; the use of scanning systems (EPOS) in retailing and use of automatic cash dispensers (ATMs) in banking, for example.

Technological developments in consumer products.

Telecommunications impacts on business and society through developments such as telesales, telemarketing, teleworking.

Awareness and use of technology in the home.

The above lists are example of the factors which have impacted on the development of marketing today. New modes of marketing have come about because of social and technological changes, such as dramatic growth of direct marketing, which can be very finely tuned to customer wants through the use of sophisticated databases. Teleshopping via dedicated satellite TV channels is another new concept. Marketing education is increasing, and the recognition of marketing as a profession is growing, underpinned by the award of Chartered status to the Institute of Marketing, for example. The role and influence of marketing in almost every sphere of society today should not be underestimated.

1.3 SERVICES MARKETING

There can be little argument, however, that the differences between the marketing of physical products and services marketing, the underlying concepts and management decisions are much the same:

- Marketing – driven organizations, whether in the manufacturing or service sectors, must have an intimate knowledge of the market in order to identify unfulfilled market needs and provide a marketing offering which will meet those needs, thereby satisfying both the customer, and the organization's objectives.

- Market research, marketing planning, and the development of a set of marketing mix tools are equally important in services marketing and the marketing of physical goods.

1.3.1 THE CONCEPT OF SERVICE

There are many definitions of marketing laid down but the basic marketing concept is concerned with:
Identifying and satisfying the needs and wants of consumers by providing a market offering to fulfil those needs and wants through exchange processes, profitably.

Some important points must be emphasized here:

- Consumer of goods or services may be individuals or organizations, or other groups; for example, voters supporting a political candidate.
- The term 'marketing offering' is used deliberately as this can mean a physical good, or a service, or a combination of the two, or it can be extended to cover other entities to which the marketing concept may be applied; for example, political figures and ideas, 'pop' music and charitable causes.
- The idea that an organization will seek to fulfill consumer needs profitably is not restricted to financially profitable goals as not all organizations aim to make profits as such; for example non-profit making concerns such as medical and educational institutions, or groups such as the Scouts organization, may adopt marketing

principles, but their end objective may be counted in ways other than cash profit.

Organizations involved in marketing are not necessarily corporations or commercial firms.

Services marketing embrace the marketing concept, and yet the nature of services marketing is complex, and service organizations may fall into various categories:

- Service organizations may be profit orientated or non-profit (sometimes called 'non-for-profit') concerns.
- They may provide personal services to individual consumers, or business services, or both.

The key issue is that organizations who want to be close to the market and close to their customers – in other words, marketing – driven – must adopt the marketing concept. A marketing – driven organization will first of all communicate with its market(s); in contrast, a non – marketing organization will provide what it believes will sell, not what the market wants.

According to Kotler[19], "A service is any activity or benefit that one party can offer to another that is essentially intangible and does not result in the ownership of anything. Its production may or may not be tied to a physical product."

W.J.Stanton[20] views services as fulfilling certain wants and states, that, "services are those separately identifiable, essentially intangible activities which provide want satisfaction, and are not necessarily tied to the sale of a product or another service. To produce a service may or may not require the use of tangible goods. However, when such use is required, there is no transfer of title (permanent ownership) to these tangible goods.

As in the case of a product, in the case of services also the starting point for understanding the marketing dynamics is the want satisfaction of the customers. It is important to correctly identify the particular want(s) which your service is fulfilling, since this will provide the clue for designating the most appropriate marketing strategy.

To be successful, organizations have to firstly, identify the basic need which is being fulfilled by your service, and secondly, find ways and means to differentiate it from that of the competitors so that they can increase their number of customers and also command their loyalty. Table I-2 gives the list of selected services.

Table I-2

List of Selected Services

Utilities	Insurance, Banking, Finance
Electricity	Banks
Water Supply	Share & Stock Brokers
Law Enforcing, Civil, Administrative and Defense Services	**Business, Professional & Scientific Activities**
Police	Advertising
Army	Marketing Research
Air Force	Consultancy
Navy	Accountancy
Judiciary	Legal
Civil Administration	Medical
Municipal Services	Educational
	Research
(Sewage, disposal of corpses maintenance of roads, parks & public buildings)	Maintenance & Repairs (of plants, machinery & equipment) Leasing Computer Programming Employment Agencies
Transport & Communication	**Leisure, Recreation**
Railways (passenger & freight)	Cinema, Theatre
Air Transport (passenger & Freight)	clubs, Gymnasiums
Post & Telegraph	Restaurants, Hotels
Telephone & Telecommunication	Video Game Parlours
Broadcasting (All India Radio)	Casinos
Telecasting (Doordarshan)	Self-improvement Courses
Distributive Trades	**Miscellaneous**
Wholesale Distribution	Beauty Parlours
Retail Distribution	Health Clubs
Dealers, Agents	Domestic Help
	Dry-cleaning
	Matrimonial Service

Source: Adapted from Donald Cowell, "The Marketing of Services", Heinemann, Lonodn.

1.3.2 REASONS FOR GROWTH OF THE SERVICE SECTOR

Manufacturing industries grew because they produced tangible goods which satisfied man's physiological needs of food, shelter and clothing. As the basic need was fulfilled there was demand for improved satisfaction, and this led to a proliferation of variations of the same product and number of companies involved in its manufacture. The growth of service industries can be traced to the economic development of society and the socio-cultural changes that have accompanied it. Following Table I-3 presents the reasons for growth of service industries.

Table I-3

Reasons for Growth of Service Industries

1. Increasing affluence	Greater demand for services (activities which consumers used to perform themselves) such as interior decoration, laundry, care of household products such as carpets, care of garden etc.
2. More leisure time	Greater demand for recreation and entertainment
3. Higher percentage of women in the labour force	Greater demand for creches, baby sitting, household domestic help
4. Greater life expectancy	Greater demand for nursing homes and health care services.
5. Greater complexity of product	Greater demand for skilled specialists to provide maintenance for complex products such as air-conditioners, car, home computers.
6. Increasing complexity of life	Greater demand for specialists in income-tax, labour laws, legal affairs, marriage counselling employment services.
7. Greater concern about ecology and resource scarcity	Grater demand for purchased or leased services, car rental, travel, resort to time sharing rather than ownership basis.
8. Increasing number of new products	The computer-sparked development of such service industries as programming repair and time sharing.

Source: Schoell, K. F. and J. T. Ivy, 1981 "Marketing: Contemporary Concept and Practices", Allyn and Bacon; Boston.

Sometimes, the growth of a specific service industry is the result of a combination of several reasons. Increasing affluence coupled with desire to utilize leisure time for leisure rather than for dong odd repair jobs in the house had led to the growing tribe of plumbers and electricians. Increasing affluence combined with increasing complexity of life and increasing insecurity has led to the phenomenon of credit cards and travelers cheques which have proved to be almost perfect substitutes for money. These credit cards provide convenience and safety. In fact, convenience is proving to be a key concept in the provision of services.

1.3.3 MARKETING MIX

In order to be able to satisfy the needs and wants of the market, in a way which suits the organization's objectives, the organization needs to design a market offering and present it to the market for consumption. The way in which this is achieved is by means of a set of marketing tools – the marketing mix.

There are many number of tools available to the market in designing, distributing, communicating and ultimately selling the offering to the selected target market(s), but these are generally classified under four main headings the four P's of the marketing mix:

a) Product
b) Price
c) Promotion
d) Place

The elements of the marketing mix are equally applicable to services marketing as to the marketing of physical, or tangible, goods, as can be seen if they are explained further:

a) **Product**

The 'product' element of the marketing mix refers to how offering is out together – typically this will include aspects relating to:

    QUALITY
    STYLING
    COLOR
    DESIGN
    BRAND NAME
    PACKAGING
    SIZES
    GUARANTEES AND OTHER FEATURES

Whilst it is relatively easy to see that color and size range, for example, more appropriate to the development of tangible goods, there is a good deal of overlap. Services are provided to certain quality standards, they are frequently offered with guarantees and many service organizations have developed high levels of brand – name awareness. While it may be appropriate to offer a range of sizes, many services are offered with a range of levels of service cover.

b) **Price**

'Price' in marketing mix terms, covers all aspects of pricing:

    DISCOUNT PRICING
    EXTENDED CREDIT
    LIST PRICE

PAYMENT PERIOD

In services marketing, pricing may present a more complex task to the marketer due to the highly intangible nature of services as opposed to physical goods.

However, services marketers do exercise all their options in developing pricing policies to suit market needs. Airlines and hotels, for example, offer a range of service at different price levels to attract the maximum number of potential users.

Consumers are not so readily able to interpret value – for – money with services as they are for tangible goods as intangibility of services makes it hard for consumers to determine quality, for example. The price which can be charged, therefore, must take this into account, but service providers can actually win flexibility on pricing due to this. A prestige brand image can allow premium pricing policies.

c) **Promotion**

'Promotion' refers to all the ways in which the product or service – the market offering – can be promoted to the target market and the communication methods available to marketers. These fall into four main areas:

ADVERTISING
PERSONAL SELLING

SALES PROMOTION
PUBLIC RELATION

Without promotion of some kind there can be no effective marketing at all. The market must have an awareness of, and possibly some kind of understanding of what is being offered in their purchase decision making. Excellent services are of no use at all if potential consumers know nothing about them.

Each of the categories or promotional activity – the promotional 'mix' – shown above, has how become familiar in many areas of services marketing. Virtually all service use at least one such from of promotion, but the way the promotional mix is utilized depends on certain aspects of the service offering.

Services which are highly standardized, and offered to large market segments employ mass advertising techniques:
Banks and other financial services, travel and tour operators are examples of service organizations which use extensive media advertising both nationally and internationally in some cases.

Service which offer a greater degree of customization, particularly on personal level, may be promoted using more selective means. Word – of – mouth, or personal recommendation is considered very effective, and many service providers encourage this. Personal selling can play a critical role in high involvement purchases, and this is true for services as well as products.

Low – relations exercises may be used. Professional services have long been subject to very strict regulations on advertising.

Many services rely on a combination of the different elements of the promotional mix:

Financial services are frequently advertised on a wide scale, with personal selling also playing an important role.

Sales promotion techniques, especially those of the limited period discount type, or price reductions for frequent users are used by many service providers from health clubs and local authority leisure services to airlines and tour operators.

Purchase incentives are offered by many financial services providers; bank offer 'free gift' to attract students account holders, for example, and insurance companies offer incentives such as weekend break, once a policy is in place.

d) **Place**

'Place' or distribution, is often perceived as being of far less importance in services marketing than it is in the marketing of physical goods and services. At first glance, the following lots of components, which make up the 'place' element of the marketing mix, may appear to support this idea.

    CHANNELS / COVERAGE

    GEOGRAPHICAL LOCATION

STOCKHOLDING / INVENTORY
TRANSPORT

Most of these components of distribution would appear to hold far greater relevance to the marketing of tangible goods, than to services marketing. This is not true, however, and it is worth considering each of these aspects in turn:

Channels/coverage It may seem that channels are of little importance in services marketing since one of the unique characteristics of services marketing, in the traditional view, is that the service provider is also the service seller. Many service providers do have direct channels of distribution, for example:

Retail banks on the high street.

Dentists operating from their own dental clinics.

An increasing number of services, however, do have channels of distributions, for example:

Insurance may be sold directly, or through an agent.

Tour operators mainly sell through travel agents.

Freight carriers frequently arrange their business through agent.

Hotel and theater booking agencies act as wholesalers for accommodation and tickets.

Decisions about channel quality, types of channel and coverage are therefore critical.

Geographical location For many of the reasons indicated above, whether operating through channels of distribution or directly, location is of critical importance. Retail service location requires careful location decisions to attract consumers:

Banks, estate agents and dry cleaners all need to be located conveniently for their customers, while hotels and country clubs may have to look at quite different criteria in selecting desirable location.

Stock Holding / Inventory It is frequently argued that because services are perishable in that they are simultaneously provided and consumed, no stock holding is required. However, that is only one aspect of the service – in many services marketing situations there is a need for stocks or equipment to make the service possible.

Transport Although many services are not transported in the traditional sense, transport is still an important aspect of services marketing. In tourism, it may be necessary to transport the customers to the holiday destination, and the quality of legal or accounting services.

1.3.4 SPECIAL CHARACTERISTICS OF SERVICES

Services are said to have four key characteristics, which impact on marketing programs. These are:
- a)   Intangibility
- b)   Inseparability
- c)   Heterogeneity / Variability

d) Perishability (simultaneous production / consumption)

It is helpful to consider each of these characteristics briefly:

a) **Intangibility**

Services are said to be intangible – they cannot be seen or tasted, for example. This can cause lack of confidence on the part of the consumer. As was apparent earlier, in considering pricing and services marketing, it is often difficult for the consumer to measure service value and quality. To overcome this, consumers tend to look for evidence of quality and other attributes, for example in the doctor and surroundings of the beauty salon, or from the qualifications and professional standing of the consultant.

b) **Inseparability**

Services are produced and consumed at the same time, unlike goods which may be manufactured, then stored for later distribution. This means that the service provider becomes an integral part of the service itself. The waitress in the restaurant, or the cashier in the bank, is an inseparable part of the service offering. The client also practices to some extent in the service, and can effect the outcome of the service. People can be part of the service itself, and this can be an advantage for services marketers.

c) **Heterogeneity / Variability**

Because a service is produced and consumed simultaneously, and because individual people make up part of the service offering, it can be argued that a service is always unique; it only exists once, and is never exactly repeated. This can give rise to concern about service quality and uniformity issues. Personnel training and careful monitoring of customer satisfaction and feedback can help to maintain high standards.

d) **Perishability**

Services are perishable; they cannot be stored. Therefore an empty set on a plane, for example, is a lost opportunity forever. Restaurants are now charging for reservations which are not kept, charges may be made for missed appointment at the dental clinic. Perishability does not pose too much of a problem when demand for a service is steady, but in times of unusually high or low demand service organizations can have severe difficulties.

Following Table I – 4 shows the implication of service characteristics and ways of overcoming them

Table I-4

Implication of Service Characteristics and Ways of Overcoming Them

Service characteristics	Implication	Means of overcoming characteristics
1. Intangibility	Sampling difficult. difficult to judge quality and value in advance. Not possible to patent or have copyright. Relatively difficult to promote.	Focus on benefits. Use brand names. Use personalities to personalize service. Develop reputation. Increase tangibility (e.g. its physical representation).
2. Inseparability	Requires presence of performer/producer. Direct sale. Limited scale of operations. Geographically limited market.	Learn to work in larger groups. Work faster. Train more service performers.
3. Heterogeneity	Difficult to standardize quality..	Careful selection and training of personnel. Define behaviour norms. Reduce role of human element. Mechanize and automate maximum possible operation.
4. Perishability	Cannot be stored Problem of demand fluctuation.	Better match between supply and demand by price reductions in low demand season.
5. Ownership	Customer has access to but not ownership of facility or activity.	Stress advantage of non-ownership such as easier payment scheme.

Source: Adapted from Donald Cowell, "The Marketing of Services", Heinemann, Lonodn.

1.3.5 THE NATURE OF THE SERVICE PRODUCT

Both physical goods and services provide benefits and satisfactions – both goods and services are 'product' or offerings. Following are the breakdown of service offerings:

Utilities : gas, power, water

Transportation and communication

Recreation and leisure

Insurance & banking and finance

Business, professional and scientific

For most of these categories it is easy to think of 'product' associated with them; insurance policies, heating and light, package holidays and so on. This has implications for service marketing management.

As in traditional marketing concerned with tangible products, the services marketing manager needs to look closely at marketing strategy, including such aspects as:

- A Unique Selling Proposition (USP) – sometimes which makes out the service offering from its competition.
- Positioning, and differentiation of the service offering.
- The notion of the product concept, and the augmented product, which can be applied to services.
- New service development – service organizations need to be more and more innovative in today's competitive marketplace, and in the face of heightened consumer sophistication.

All of these management issues are common to both services marketing and the marketing of tangible goods.

1.3.6 AREAS RESPONSIBLE FOR PROBLEMS AND KEY ISSUES IN SERVICES MARKETING MANAGEMENT

There are number of areas of marketing management which do have special significance for services marketing. It is worth commenting on those aspects which are important to developing an awareness of problems and key issues in services marketing.

a) **Productivity and Quality**

In striving to gain and maintain competitive advantage, both productivity and quality are of key importance. However, the nature of services implies that it is difficult to avoid a trade – off situation, when improvements in service productivity can lead to sacrifices in the level of quality. This is most sensitive in services marketing where people are the service delivers.

b) **Service quality is measured on two levels:**

- Technical quality – the overall efficiency with which a bank handles its customer accounts in terms of promote statements, rates of interest offered and so on.
- Functional – quality the way the service is actually delivered; this includes personal courtesy, the service environment in terms of comfort and décor, the consumer's own role (are there long queues, are pens and forms provided to make the actual transactions simpler?).

The importance which is attached to functional and technical quality depends on the type of service, and the benefit sought by the consumer. High involvement purchases, which are typically expensive and infrequent, will also be evaluated with different set of criteria in the customer's mind to low involvement, inexpensive purchases.

Consumers evaluate service in two ways:
- Experience
- Credence

Experience is used in service situations where consumers can measure service value in terms of their own experience and expectations. This may be the case in evaluating personal services such as hairdressing or gardening. In case where the individual has little or no experience of the service offered, and has no personal knowledge in the area, they will make evaluations based on credence.

This can be virtually translated into an assessment of the service provider's credibility. Consumer behavior, and the buying decision processes, must therefore be comprehensively researched and understood by the service providers in order to manage productivity and quality levels.

Marketing Strategy

In developing marketing strategy there are essentially two tasks:

i) The selection of target markets
ii) The formulation of an appropriate marketing mix to serve those target markets.

However, before the marketing manager can consider target markets, the starting point must be marketing audit. As these terms suggests, this is an audit of the organization's marketing activities, with particular focus on the analysis of opportunities available to the organization. The management task can really be seen to fall into four main areas:

i) Marketing research
ii) Marketing planning
iii) Implementation
iv) Control

The market can generally be divided into the consumer sector and organizational users. Within each of these sectors there are likely to be a number of segments which need to be researched and evaluated before decisions can be made about selecting target segments. When attractive segments have been identified, the services marketing manager must develop an appropriate marketing mix for each segment selected, with each of the elements of the mix being finely tuned to best meet the needs of individual segments.

The role of people in the services marketing situation, and in particular, the idea of inseparability and the interactive nature of service provision, have been emphasized continuously. Internal marketing is the name given to the concept which embraces commitment to employees, and this has a very important role to play in services marketing.

Internal marketing means treating the internal customers – the employees – with the same care and attention to detail as the external customers. Thus, internal marketing programs incorporate staff development, training, communication and a total quality approach. Internal marketing relates to the importance of people in service marketing.

These aspects are especially relevant to services marketing, so this has led to the development of some additional elements which extend the services marketing mix from four P's to seven P's. These additional elements are:

- PEOPLE, where the emphasis is developing the role that people play in service deliver
- PHYSICAL EVIDENCE, which includes facilitating goods (for example, cars or tools for hire), and surroundings, décor and comfort.
- PROCESS, which is concerned with the functional aspects such as service deliver, queuing systems, timeliness and quality of delivery.

1.3.7 CLASSIFICATION OF SERVICES

Following are the methods of classification of services.

a) **End-user**

Services can be classified into the following categories:

- Consumer: leisure, hairdressing, personal finance, package holiday.
- Business to business: advertising agencies, printing, accountancy, consultancy.
- Industrial: plan maintenance and repair, work wear and hygiene, installation, project management.

b) **Service tangibility**

The degree of tangibility of a service can be used to classify services:

- Highly tangible: car rental, vending machines, telecommunications.
- Service linked to tangible goods: domestic appliance repair, car service.
- Highly intangible: psychotherapy, consultancy, legal services.

c) **People – based services**

Services can be broken down into labour –intensive (people –based) and equipment – based service. This can also be represented by the degree of contact.

- People – based services – high contact: education, dental care, restaurants, medical services.
- Equipment – based –low contact automatic car wash, launderette, vending machine, cinema.

d) **Expertise**

The expertise and skills of the service provider can be broken down into the following categories:
- Professional: medical services, legal, accountancy, tutoring.
- Non-professional: babysitting, caretaking, casual labour.

c) **Profit orientation**

The overall business orientation is a recognized means of classification:

- Non-for-profit: The Scouts Association, charities, public sector leisure facilities.
- Commercial: banks, airlines, tour operators, hotel and catering services.

1.4 NATURE & SCOPE OF THE STUDY

A survey was undertaken to delve into the marketing practices of the financial service organizations and for the purpose of the study, the financial service organizations situated in the State of Gujarat were chosen. The study is a combination of exploratory, descriptive and casual research design. The data was collected from primary sources with the help of a structured questionnaire as well as from secondary sources available within and outside the financial service organizations.

In this study an attempt is made to ascertain the extent of association between input and output, the variable chosen for input are marketing practices and output is growth rate. Ideally, better marketing practices should lead to higher growth rate (which is the goal of financial service organizations). As the scale of operations of various financial service organizations differs, growth parameters i.e. advance growth rate, investments growth rate, deposits growth rate, commissions/fees growth rate have been used as output variable.

1.5 LIMITATIONS OF THE STUDY

The study was subject to certain limitations:

(i) Data on expenditure aspects could not be collected fully. As the financial service organizations were unwilling to divulge information pertaining to expenditure aspects.

(ii) The marketing practices of the financial service organizations concerning 'channel decisions' could not be analyzed in this study, as very few organizations (only 10 from the sample of 52 units) indicated that their they use 'channel' for generating business. It was felt that the results of these 10 respondents when analyzed might not conform to the realities of the situation.

(iii) The study examines the relationship between growth rate and marketing practices. However, there may be several other factors than marketing practices, which influence growth rate. (Other factors may be said to include role of Govt., market situation, rate of inflation etc.)

(iv) Due to constraints of time and finance, the study could not be broad based is confirmed to financial organizations situated in State of Gujarat.

1.6 **ORGANIZATION OF THE STUDY – CHAPTERIZATION**

Chapter I is an introductory chapter, which brings out the importance of marketing in economic development. The developments of marketing theory, the marketing environment, the development of the marketing concept, marketing mix and characteristics service products are also highlighted. The nature and scope of the study, as also the limitations of the study are brought out.

Chapter II highlights findings of a few studies. A case for a study on the marketing practices of the financial organizations is made out.

Chapter III is wholly devoted to the theoretical frame work of financial services, viz. special characteristics, competitive environment, financial services marketing mix, types of financial services etc. It also covers the role of regulatory authority in marketing of financial services. It also covers the rationale for a study on the marketing practices of financial service organizations.

Chapter IV describes the plan and procedure of the study in detail. This includes sample selection, development of the questionnaire, research objectives (hypothesis) and the statistical techniques used in analyzing data.

Chapter V is the first of the two chapters were the data collected was analyzed. Here, the level of performance of the different groups with respect to each of the marketing variables is discussed. The different groups are also compared and differentiated in terms of their marketing practices.

Chapter VI also deals with analysis and interpretation of data. The results accrued from the application of the step – wise regression technique are discussed the criterion variable being growth rate and predictor variable, the different marketing practices.

Chapter VII presents a summary of the study and highlights it major findings. The implications of the study are also discussed alongside.

Besides, there are appendices giving the questionnaire, the scoring key and some other related particulars.

REFERENCES

1. Business World, January 1998.

2. FICCI report on Development of Indian Economy, 1997.

3. 7th five year plan Book, Government of India

4. Kacker, Madhav., Relevance of Marketing to Planned Economic growth in Marketing and Economic Development edited by Madhav Kacker, New Delhi: Deep & Deep Publications, 1982.

5. Kaynak Erdener., Marketing in the Third world, New York: Praeges, 1982.

6. Ibid.

7. Drucker, Peter F., 'Marketing and Economic Development' Journal of Marketing Vol. 22, January 1958.

8. Hirsch, Leon V., 'The Contribution of a National Market and its Economics Development' A generally neglected area'. Proceedings of the Fall conference of the American Marketing Association, Fall, 1965.

9. Ibid.

10. Ibid.

11   Rostow, Walt W. "The Concept of a National Market and its Economics Growth Implications", proceedings of Fall conference, Chicago: American Marketing Association, 1965.

12   Knecht, John., 'Marketing Communication and Economic Development' in Marketing and Economic Development edited by Madhav Kacker, New Delhi: Deep and Deep Publications, 1982.

13   Copulsky, William, "Forecasting sales in under developed countries", in marketing and Economic Development edited by Madhav Kacker, New Delhi: Deep and Deep Publications, 1982.

14   Borden, Neil H., "Role of Advertising in the various stages of Corporate and Economic Growth", in Marketing and Economic Development edited by Madhav Kacker, New Delhi: Deep and Deep Publicaitons, 1982.

15   Kacker, Madhav P., "Distribution in a Developing Economy – some emerging trends and Implications for strategy", in Marketing and Economic Development edited by Madhav Kacker, New Delhi: Deep and Deep Publications, 1982.

16   Rao, Tanniru R., "Developing Countries : Role of Marketing" in Marketing and Economic Development edited by Madhav Kacker, New Delhi : Deep and Deep Publications, 1982.

17 Rostow, Walt W.: op.cit. (1965)

18 Hirsch, Leon V.: op. cit. (1965)

19 Kotler Phillip, "Marketing Management – Analysis, Planning, Implementation and Control, Prentice Hall of India Pvt. Ltd., New Delhi, (1998)

20 Stanton W. J., "Fundamentals of Marketing", McGraw Hill, New York, 1994.

CHAPTER – II
LITERATURE REVIEW AND A RATIONALE OF THE STUDY

CHAPTER – II

LITERATURE REVIEW AND A RATIONALE OF THE STUDY

2.1 INTRODUCTION

This chapter in brief provides the major findings of relevant important studies. The findings of these studies do suggest some definite basis on which further studies in the filed can be carried out. They are of considerable significance in the context of present study in as much as they provide excellent guidelines as well as important view points that are to be considered in the present investigation.

The present investigation is mainly concerned with marketing of financial services. Hence in this chapter an attempt is made to make a broad survey of the studies in the field of marketing of services.

John A. Martilla and John C. James[1] carried out study on "Importance - Performance Analysis". In his analysis he has studied the hypothesis that services can be usefully rated according to their customer importance and company performance. He studied how customers rated 14 service attributes on importance and performance importance was rated on a four-point scale of "extremely important", "important", "slightly important" and "not important". Service provider's performance was rated on a four – point scale of "excellent", "good", "fair", and "poor".

The ratings of the 14 service elements were displayed in the figure and were divided in to four sections. Quadrant A showed important service elements that were not being performed as desired levels. It reveled that the service provider should concentrate on improving the performance on service elements of this quadrant. Quadrant B showed important service elements where the service provider performed well. It reveled that the service provider should maintain the high performance. Quadrant C showed minor elements, since they were not very important the service provider should not pay more attention. Quadrant D showed that the service elements of this quadrant were being performed in an excellent manner. The author made an attempt to measure service attributes according to their importance and performance and inform marketers where to focus their efforts in marketing of services.

John Goodman[2], made an attempt to study "Complaint Handling and Service Recovery of US customers". His studies of customer dissatisfaction show that US customers are dissatisfied with their purchases about 25% of the time. How often do they complain? The surprising finding is that only about 5% complain. The other 95% either feel that it is not worth the effort to complain, or that they don't know how or to whom to complain.

```
                        Extremely
                        important
    ┌───────────────────────┬───────────────────────┐
    │ A. Concentrate here   │ B. Keep up the good work │
    │                       │                       │
    │              1        │      3                │
    │           2           │  4                    │
    │                       │    5   6              │
    │                       │  7                    │
    │                       │      8                │
    │                       │  10                   │
Fair│                       │                       │Excellent
perf│         9             │                       │performance
    ├───────────────────────┼───────────────────────┤
    │                       │                       │
    │                       │                       │
    │     11     12         │                       │
    │                       │                       │
    │         13            │                       │
    │                       │      14               │
    │                       │                       │
    │ C. Low priority       │ D. Possible overkill  │
    └───────────────────────┴───────────────────────┘
                        Slightly
                        important
```

Importance Performance Analysis Matrix

Of the 5% of customers, who complain, only about 50% report a satisfactory problem resolution. Yet the need to resolve a customer problem in a satisfactory manner is critical. Whereas, on average, a satisfied customer tells three people about a good product experience, a dissatisfied customer gripes to 11 people. If each of them tells still other people, the number of people exposed to bad word-of-mouth may grow exponentially.

Often the customers who are most upset are the company's best customers. Another finding is that customers whose complaints are satisfactorily resolved often become more company – loyal than customers who were never dissatisfied. About 34% of customers who register major complaints will buy again from the company if their complaint is resolved, and this rises to 52% for minor complaints. If the complaint is resolve quickly, between 52% (major complaints) and 95% (minor complaints) will buy again from the company.

The Straits Times[3] carried out a survey on "Service Almost as Important as Price to Shoppers". In his study, shopper's reaction to poor service were found to be as follows:

- 70% Will not complain but will shop elsewhere.
- 39% Will not complain because it is too troublesome.
- 24% Will tell others not to shop there because of poor services.
- 17% Will write to complain about the standard of service.
- 09% Will chide the salesperson for poor service.

09%   Will ask for a refund for poor service.

Therefore, companies need to develop a service recovery problem. The first requirement is that companies make it easy for dissatisfied customer to complain. This can be accomplished by providing customer satisfaction forms and prominently featuring a "hot line". The second requirement is that the company's employees who receive complaints are well trained and empowered to resolve customers problems speedily and satisfactorily. Studies show that the faster the company response to the complaint, the higher the amends offered, and the better the attitude, the higher the customer's satisfaction with the company. The third requirement is to go beyond satisfying particular customers and discovering and correcting the root causes of frequent problems. By studying the pattern of complaints, the company can correct system failures, which are typically the source of these problems.

Rajeev K. Seth [4] carried out study on "Marketing of Banking Services", in his study he dealt with the typical marketing – related issues facing bankers at the policy making as well as operational grass – root levels. He presented a set of practical ideas and strategies for managing them.

Dibakar Panigrahy[5] carried out study on "Marketing of Plastic Money" where he carried out study conducted a survey among the credit card holders of State Bank of India to know of their awareness, ideas, opinions, satisfaction and preference for different types services regarding the credit card.

V. K. Varma[6] carried out a study on "Costing and Pricing Concept and Philosophy". He divided his study into two sections, Section – I – discusses the introduction a costing exercise in Indian commercial banks and Section – II – examines the philosophies and methods used in establishing prices of bank services.

Dr. M. L. Agrawal[7] carried out study on "Branding and Advertising of Financial Services", in his study he highlighted that various concepts of marketing can be directly applied to financial products to gain a competitive edge in the market place. Since, more often than not, investment in financial products is a one-time decision and a customer's need for reliable and valid information is very high, the focus of the entire marketing effort must not deviate from providing these basic information to the investor.

Following list gives the information pertaining to various related studies / research.

Table II-1
List of related studies / research

1	"Learning to love service economy", Irving D. Canton, Harvard Business Review, May-June, 1984.
2	"How to transform your product business into a service", AMACOM, New York, 1992.
3	"Local companies should tried for top class services", The Straits Times, (Singapore), Aug. 31, 1994.
4	"Creativity of the marketing of services" The Singapore Marketer, Nov. 1993.
5	"Strategies for change in the service sector", Michael J. Dowling, California Management Review, 1994.
6	"Serving the Aftermarket in Japan & The United States", Paul A. Herbig, Industrial marketing management, Nov. 1993
7	"A Conceptual Model of Service Quality and its Implications for Future Research", A. Parasuraman, Journal of Marketing, 1985.
8	"Service America", Karl Albrecht and Ron Zemke, Homewoeed, 1985.
9	"Marketing Services", Free Press, New York, 1991.
10	"Making complaint a management tool", Ronald T. Rust, & Mark Wells, Marketing management vol. 1, No. 3, 1992.
11	"Mickey Mouse Marketing", N. W. Pope, American Banker, July 1979.
12	"Customer Service: a tool for growing increased profits", Ross M Scovotti.
13	"Production line approach to service", Theodore Levitt.
14	"Marketing Intangible Products and Products Intangible", Theodore Levitt.
15	"Services Marketing is different", business, May – June 1980.
16	"Sophisticated ATMs make their debut at Japanese Banks", The straits Times, September 1994
17	"Service positioning through structural change", Journal of Marketing January 1987.
18	"Quality Control in a service Business", Harvard Business Rivew, Aug. 1975
19	"Big Ideas in Services Marketing" Leonard Berry.
20	"How Consumer Evaluation Processes differ between Goods and Services", Valarie A. Zeithaml.
21	"Look to Consumers to Increase Productivity", C. H. Lovelock.
22	"Learning from the Best for Unexcelled Customer Service", Nissan / Infiniti.
23	"How service needs influence product strategy", M. M. Lele.
24	"Service Companies Focus or Falter", Davidow, Harvard Business Review, Aug. 1989.

2.2 A RATIONALE FOR THE STUDY ON MARKETING OF FINANCIAL SERVICES

A fresh wave of economic liberalization and globalization has been sweeping most of the world since the 1980s, and India from 1990 onwards. Consequently the financial services scenario also has been undergoing a transformation, especially with regard to competition, technological advancement and innovation. Due to the competition from within and without, and the relentless improvement in the field of technology as applied to financial services, financial service organizations have been compelled to constantly innovate new products, new delivery techniques and convincingly attract customers. In addition, they have to make concerted efforts to retain them. To do this, they require sharp marketing skills.

Marketing is a well-researched subject. A large number of authoritative treatises are already available. Even the characteristic features of marketing in Indian context have been extensively analyzed.

A recent FICCI paper avers that the service sector can contribute more than 50 per cent to the national GDP by AD 2000 provided it grows at a rate of 5.3 per cent annually. It this works out, the projected growth in this sector is going to surpass the growth in the agricultural and industrial sectors. It is also noted that dissatisfaction with services rendered (be it banking, insurance, railways, health, tourism, postal services or whatever) is high. This may even be termed a period of service crisis. How to exploit growing opportunities in the services sector and heighten satisfaction with service delivery is an extremely typical issue for in-depth analysis. Financial services, as a crucial segment of the services sector, are today face-to-face with the issue. In a scenario like this, the discipline of financial services marketing is going to acquire critical importance in the foreseeable future, if it has not already.

Though product and services marketing are similar in many ways, there are some very crucial points of difference between them. For example, the intangible nature of service products and the strong presence of the human factor in services marketing. The need to view financial service marketing from the unique standpoint of services marketing is, therefore, obvious and strong.

Indian financial service is fundamentally different from financial services elsewhere. Features like low degree of technological sophistication, a highly unionized workforce and a cumbersome legal system mark it.

The inference is clear. Indian financial service marketing must develop its own body of concepts and principles revolving around distinctive characteristics of services marketing and tempered with the imperatives of the Indian situation. It must wriggle out of the stranglehold of product marketing influence. The long-term objective would be the development of a comprehensive theory of financial services marketing in the Indian Context, This study is an effort towards this objective. It endeavors to highlight the area of financial service marketing on the basis of peculiar features attendant to financial service marketing in India rather than a classical product marketing situation.

REFERENCES

1. John A. Martilla and John C. James, "Importance Performance Analysis", Journal of Marketing, January 1997

2. John Goodman, Technical Assistance Research Programs (TARP), "US office of Consumer affairs study on complaint handling in America", 1986.

3. The Straits Times (Singapore), "Service Almost as Important as Price to Shoppers", January 16 1993.

4. Rajeev K. Seth, State Bank of India. "Marketing of Banking Services", 1997.

5. Dibakar Panigrahy, "Marketing of Plastic Money", 1999.

6. V. K. Varma, Senior Manager, Planning, Bank of Baroda, "Costing & Pricing in Banks: Concept & Philosophy, 17th Bank Economists' Conference, Sept. 1994.

7. Dr. M. L. Agrawal, XLRI, Jamshedpur, "Branding and Advertising of Financial Services".

CHAPTER – III
FINANCIAL SERVICES MARKETING

CHAPTER – III

FINANCIAL SERVICES MARKETING

3.1 INTRODUCTION

Marketing of financial services begins with the mightily problem in that the service designer to promote more or less a uniformed product, which unlike most packaged goods have intrinsic differences. For instance a certain group of people will insist that no other noodles taste like Maggie. But money is money, no matter whether it came from Canara Bank, Unit Trust of India or Life Insurance Corporation.

3.2 FINANCIAL SERVICES IN THE INDIAN CONTEXT

The main explanation put forward to explain Indian financial market today is what has now got termed as " the great consumer boom". In the seventies, the Indian economy was characterized by industrial recession. The middle class thrust then was on accumulating substantial savings. Whatever conspicuous demand existed (for items such as Tvs, tape recorders, kitchen gadgets, cosmetics etc.) was partly met by the inadequate domestic production and balance by way of imported goods brought into the country through appropriate and inappropriate channels.

By mid-80s the country saw a bargaining middle-class population, estimated anywhere between 100-200 million, who wanted an outlet for their savings. The catalyst, of course, was the process of economic liberalization.

The chart below illustrates the metamorphosis.

Around 60's	Today
"Debt" a dirty word	"Debt"-A comfortable proposition
Limited number of financial products	Innumerable financial products
Vehicale for mass promotion non-existent	Today the TV reaches 42% of India's population.

Regardless of limited funds on hand the Indian consumer today does not mind borrowing. Today, broadly he borrows for

a) House Purchase
b) Vehicle Purchase
c) Consumer Durable Purchase
d) Purchase against Credit cards.

What the attitudes of this new generation show is the movement into the cult of the individual. We are in the environment of personal expression. Successful brands being the ones, which sell themselves by, allowing consumer to feel it is their choice-e.g. Citibank Diners Club Credit Card," the Reward for Success" campaign.

In a research done by a company in U.K. on consumer attitudes towards financial products, it was discovered that 5 distinct purchasing desires could be identified against the two dimensions, viz. 'the importance of money' and 'confidence'.

Financial Attitude Group	Attitude displayed
Connoisseur	Have interest & confidence in the financial product; are objective & go straight to the company offering the product.
Pragmatists	View financial products attaching significant importance but not so important in & of itself. Are confident about their judgement of financial products. Simple Sales proposition would do for them.
Carefree Optimists	For them, money is a means of and for glamour. No desire to seek out financial products available to them. tendency to spend all their money leaving no scope for investments
Traditionalists	They comprise the bulk of the community for whom the obvious choices are bank accounts, public provident fund, National Saving etc.
Anxious	Money may be important but its significance is indicated by the absence of it.

3.3 SPECIAL CHARACTERISTICS OF FINANCIAL SERVICES

Services tend to share four important characteristics which distinguish them from physical products and impact on marketing programs, namely:

Intangibility

Inseparability

Heterogeneity/variability

Perishability

Financial services share these characteristics to a degree but also exhibit certain differences. Some of these similarities and differences are as under

a) Intangibility

Financial services and generally intangible, but the service providers go to considerable lengths to ' tangibilise' the service for customers. A bank passbook, regular bank statement 'gold' credit cards and insurance policies are all examples of the way in which financial services are presented to consumers. They can enhance the image of the service product, brand name and value serve to reassure the consumer and help the organization's positioning.

b) Inseparability

The degree of inseparability depends on the type of service and the actual supplier. Whilst the service will frequently be inseparable from the service provider, such as the quality of service received by a customer visiting their bank to pay some bills, the situation is frequently less clear. Many everyday transactions are carried out now via automated services- the automated teller machines (ATMs) which are now so familiar. Because access to these systems has broadened to allow use of any particular machine by customers of other institutions, the customer will often not be dealing directly with their own provider.

Additionally, many financial services are sold by brokers and agents of various kinds and this has led to difficulties and dissatisfaction when consumers have been sold unsuitable products or been wrongly advised. Pensions providers, for example, have been left to resolve the problems caused by thousands of people being encouraged to leave company schemes and buy personal pension plans by commission-hungry agents with no formal standing in the company. Other services are frequently handled by agents overseas such as credit card agencies and other currency/traveler's cheque encashment. The good name of the actual service provider, for example the credit or charge card company, will be wholly contingent upon the efficiency and reliability of the services.

c) **Heterogeneity/variability**

In this case, the complexity of the service transaction process will determine the extent of variability and this can differ to a large extent between institutions and even within one institution. The greater the degree of automation within any transaction process, the greater the degree of standardization. Thus, simple transactions may be carried out via ATM and completely standardized or via a branch counter where they might be fairly standardized but subject to some variation in quality.

Total standardization is not necessarily desirable from the consumer's point of view. A friendly greeting or being addressed by name can enhance service delivery and while an ATM cannot arrange an emergency overdraft facility when funds are low, branch staff can look at the standing of individual customers and make arrangements where appropriate, satisfying the customer and profiting from charges applied to the account. Some customers may want transactions to be handled as speedily and efficiently as possible while others may prefer a caring approach and a friendly chat. Customer care is a key for organizations whether engaging with customers in a simple 'free' transaction such as paying a bill or a long-term commitment such as a mortgage or pension. Tailoring the approach to the needs of the individual customer as far as possible may be the best policy.

d) **Perishability**

Again, the degree of perishability depends on the type of service. If a cheque needs to be cleared by a certain date and the system causes a delay then the benefits to the consumer are lost so the service could be said to be perishable. By and large, however, money and financial services are enduring in nature. If a bank's reserves are not fully utilized profitably through lending or investment they will still retain their worth and may be utilized again at a later date. A bank branch which does not have any customers at all on a particular day may actually gain rather than lose profit as staff may be able to use the peace and quiet to catch up on other work.

Similarly, customers perceive many financial products to be enduring or long-term commitments. An insurance policy becomes perishable the minute it expires, but for the whole of its active duration it represents an ongoing service. Production and consumption is frequently not simultaneous with financial services. Whilst a customer ordering a meal in a restaurant does so on the understanding that their needs will be satisfied the same evening, a customer signing for a savings plan may expect benefits in five or ten years, or even longer. There may be no immediate benefit- on the contrary having to make regular payments may easily be seen as a disadvantage or a cause of worry. Even financial services which offer a benefit such as a loan or mortgage which enables the customer to purchase something which they otherwise could not afford are not usually produced and consumed simultaneously, although very fast or 'instant' decisions on loan facilities within certain limits are increasingly offered as a benefit by finance companies.

A key task in financial services marketing is to create awareness of long-term benefits and helping customers to recognize the need for financial services such as pensions which they may not see themselves needing for many years, or needs which they may not want even to consider at all such as life insurance. Financial service providers also need to reduce cognitive dissonance in consumers who might back out of a commitment due to second thoughts. Regulations decree nowadays that most financial services are sold on the basis that customers have a short ' cooling off' period, in case the customer changes their mind or to offer them protection if heavy-handed sales pressure has been used. Everything which can be done to tangibilise the services by offering clear and attractive documentation, for example, and offering reassurance and confidence to the consumer should be looked at by the service provider.

e)   **Other characteristics**

There are other characteristics which apply to many types of financial services and which must be taken into consideration by marketers. These vary between type of service and type of service provider but the following examples illustrate key ideas;

High involvement purchases/complex products Many financial services are high involvement purchases. This will mean that the customer will shop around for the best advice or the best offer and will generally take a long time to plan the purchase, for example with a mortgage or a pension. Information will be sought about competing brands and products, usually from a variety of sources including advertising, the press, informal advice from colleagues or family, perhaps, and formal advice from the bank manager or a financial consultant.

The process can be linked to buying a car or any other major purchase, except that the customer often perceives greater risk as financial services are frequently highly complex and it is difficult for the layperson to assess their value/potential. Someone buying a car is usually happy to rely on the supplier's guarantee that any faults will be put right but a customer looking for a good investment has no such guarantee-often a warning instead that investment products may go down as well as up in value.

High levels of brand loyalty Customers tend to stay with financial service providers and use them to satisfy their different needs at different stages of their life. Banks recognize this well and are keen to provide student overdrafts in the hope of retaining a professional salaried account holder for many years. Many people choose the same bank as their parents because the parents open an account for them. Children and teenagers are a key target market for banks because of the possibilities of future business. Insurance companies emphasis in their advertising that they offer services of meet a whole lifetime of needs from a first-time mortgage, life insurance and household insurance for family protection, savings and pensions for old age and even funeral costs cover. Customer retention is the aim for financial service providers. Customers will, and increasingly, change providers if they are very dissatisfied, however, or if they perceive better value elsewhere, thus increasing the competitive pressure between institutions.

Financial services also tend to be join purchases, very often, with decisions made by more than one person. The nature of many products mean that repeat purchase is very low or infrequent so the service provider needs to maintain contact with the customer over time whenever possible through annual statements, sales follow-ups and so on. Service providers need to keen abreast of significant changes in their customers circumstances as far as possible so that they can offer new services as required and safeguard both their own and the customer's interests in case of financial difficulty.

Many areas identified above are not unique to financial services but must be taken into consideration when planning effective marketing programmes. Other similar characteristics include the following :

- The importance of advertising in creating strong brand image and positioning .
- Distinct market segments and the use of target marketing, especially in growing markets (for example career women, the over 55's).

- Increasing price sensitivity and heavy price competition (for example car and home insurance, bank and credit card charges).
- Growth in the importance of customer care in service differentiation.

3.4 THE MARKETING AND COMPETITIVE ENVIRONMENT

Environmental analysis and monitoring is of critical importance in any industry especially in the dynamic financial services industry with its proliferation of products and services and changing industry structure. External environmental analysis usually involves assessing influences on the organization's business activity under the following main headings:

Political/legal
Economic
Socio-cultural
Technological

Some key influences in each of these categories and the competitive environment will be reviewed here:

Political/legal Some major political and legal developments have been reviewed in the preceding section which have highlighted the radical changes which have been brought about by these influences. Other influences which can have an impact on financial services and consumer confidence include the following:

- Government attitude towards home ownership
- State provision of pensions

- Government encouragement of savings and investment (via tax benefits, for example)
- Regulatory control and protection (to prevent the collapse of financial institutions and protect investors' money).

Economic Economic factors are key variables which will impact on activity in the financial services sectors. The level of consumer activity is governed almost entirely by income levels and personal wealth. As income levels grow, more discretionary income is available to spend on financial services. Consumer confidence in the economy and in job security also has a major impact; if lean of expenditure. Consumers may also seek easy access saving and be unwilling to tie up their money for longer periods with potentially more attractive investments.

The main economic factors, which should be monitored with regard to financial services marketing, are as follows:
- Personal and household disposable income
- Discretionary income levels
- Employment levels
- The rate of inflation
- Income tax levels and taxation structures
- savings and investment levels and trends
- Stock market performance
- Consumer spending
- Consumer credit

Socio-cultural Many demographic factors have an important bearing on financial services markets. Certain factors have been particularly noticeable in recent year such as the growth of inherited wealth through property ownership and changing attitudes towards consumer credit and debt. Key influences include:

- Changing employment patterns
- Numbers of working women
- The aging population
- Number of first-time house buyers
- Changes in the number of households
- Marriage/divorce/birth rates
- Consumption trends

Technological Technology has had a major impact in many industries including financial services and banking in particular. ATM services which not only provide cash but allow for bill payments, deposits and instant statements are widely used. EFTPOS (electronic funds transfer at point of sale), where cards such as Standard and Chartered, American Express, are debited automatically when payment is made for goods and services without the need for cheques, is a clear example. From the customer's viewpoint, technology has played a major role in the development not of the financial product itself but of the process whereby the service is delivered. Automated queuing systems have made visits to the bank easier and more convenient. Telephone banking and insurance services such as First Direct and Direct

Line are examples of telecommunications technology being used to innovate in place of a traditional branch-based service process.

Technology has also played a major role within organizations, bringing about far greater efficiency through computerized records and transaction systems and also in business development, through the setting up of detailed customer databases for effective segmentation and targeting.

The main technological developments fall within these categories, therefore:
- Process developments
- Information storage and handling
- Database systems

Product technology is of relatively minor importance within the financial services marketplace as product innovations are usually in the form of a change in the terms of services offered or slightly different services at lower charges or higher rates of interest. It is easy for competitors to follow suit or make other changes and, once the decision has been made promotion and advertising the new or revised service will help to make it successful rather than any king of technological refinements. Some physical developments relating to technology in the production of credit cards have taken place such as the imprinting of a hologram on cards to help prevent forgery.

The competitive environment The financial services industry has undergone major changes, as discussed earlier. During the 1980s the industry expanded considerably and the number of financial products available proliferated. The trend since the early 1990s, however, is towards more streamlined business structures through rationalization to produce greater efficiency and higher profitability in a market suffering from the setbacks of the recession.

3.5   THE FINANCIAL SERVICES MARKETING MIX

The challenges facing the financial services industry mean that greater emphasis than ever before must be placed on developing and implementing successful marketing programs to create and foster a customer orientation. True differentiation of financial products is virtually impossible to achieve because they are intrinsically the same, offering similar benefits and services to consumers. The degree of substitutability between brands is correspondingly very high at the outset (for example, at the supplier or product selection stage). Once a financial product has been sold, however, the customer is frequently tied in over a long period and may even face penalties if they wish to change supplier (as in the case of fixed rate mortgages) or if they wish to discontinue the service (terminating endowment or insurance agreements before the full term has expired for example).

The key objectives for financial services providers are:
- attracting customers in the first place
- retaining customers through high levels of client satisfaction and by providing a portfolio of financial services to meet their changing needs over time.

Some key issues, which must be taken into consideration in designing the most effective financial services marketing mix, are as follows:

a) Product

As mentioned previously, there is little or no room for innovation in product design due to the ease by which competitors can make similar offerings, for example by altering charges or interest rates to meet those of competitors. Additionally, many financial services are affected by other restrictions, such as government directives relating to income tax and investments or constraints on the amounts which can be invested. Differentiation, therefore, can best be achieved through the other elements of the marketing mix. Current accounts are dominated by banks, although the building societies' share of this market in which they could not compete until recently is growing. They hold the majority of mortgage accounts, however, but this stronghold is increasingly under pressure from banks.

b) Price

The price in financial services terms relates to the cost involved to the customer in, say bank charges or credit card interest rates. These prices seem to evoke low levels of customer sensitivity as many customers enjoy 'free' banking, by maintaining their current accounts in credit, for example, or paying their credit card balances off each month. The introduction of new charges, however, such as the annual credit card fee had a noticeable effect initially, however, and sparked off competitive reaction from lenders prepared to offer cards with no annual charge.

Price also relates to the value of the product to the customer and, as such, can be highly sensitive. This can be in terms of interest rates charged on a mortgage, where reductions in interest for first time buyers or preferential rates for existing customers of other services (for example current account holders) are standard promotional tools in the industry, representing a form of discounting .the rates of return offered to investors is another element of the price and different products within the range are frequently priced at differential rates, to attract long-term savers or large lump sum investors, for example. Pricing can therefore be used to differentiate the offering and is likely to be used by customers in selecting in selecting a service.

c) **Promotion**

Major advertising campaigns are undertaken continuously by banks and other major financial institutions such as insurance companies. The main purpose of the advertising is to strengthen awareness of the brand and company image and to inform the market about the services available . The trend has also been towards developing more below -the -line promotional activities using highly sophisticated database to target direct mail campaigns at distinct market segments and using publicity, sponsorship and other promotional means. Successful advertising has been used personal selling over the telephone once the initial inquiry has been made and staff skills and customer care have been developed to enable a strong personal selling strategy to work.

Another area where personal selling is a strong tool is in the area of insurance products and the emergence of 'bancassurance'- the product offered through links between banks and insurers, commonly with banks as the controlling partner. The insurance organization's expertise in personal selling and the strong customer loyalty and extensive customer base of the banks make for synergy in business development. The importance of personal selling is now widely recognized and many institutions offer home visits by financial advisers.

d)   Place

Place or location has always been regarded as critical in retail financial services where high street positions are maintained by most of the large institutions. For transaction services where regular and frequent branch contact is required this can be important. First Direct, however, the telephone banking service, has proved that a bank without branches is possible though its customers still need access to convenient ATM outlets. Some consumers prefer personal, face -to-face contact within a branch and may be more likely to use a local branch or building society.Direct Line and other telephone insurance services are also moving away from the traditional large networks of branches and brokers or agents. Changes in distribution sysytems, technology and consumer demands are all key influences on the evolution of the 'place' component of the marketing mix.

e)   **People**

Customer care is at the forefront of both quality and differentiation in the financial services industry. Staff need to be highly trained not only in customer care but in how to respond to the rapidly changing market environment . Personnel can be used to develop competitive advantage in the market place and to build and maintain relationships with customers.

f)   **Process**

This is the main area where technological advances have led to major change. Improvements in the process stem not only from the automation of many transactions and data handling within organizations but also from process re-engineering to reduce delays in processing mortgage applications, for example, or the installation of automated queuing systems to cut down on waiting time. Country wide finance, a finance company specializing in consumer lending, offer existing and previous customers same-day acceptance of loan applications and will also arrange for courier delivery of a personal cheque for the loan amount to the customer's home if required.

g)   **Physical evidence**

The environment in banks is changing, moving away from austerity and formality to a more friendly approach reflected in more attractive branch layouts and decor. Other physical evidence plays an important part in financial transactions such as the documentation which must be presented by salespeople to prove that they are authorized to offer investment advice. This creates confidence and helps to build the relationship between customer and provider. Physical evidence is also widely used to tangibilise the service. attractive brochures and policy documents, presented in glossy folders, cheque book and credit card holders, 'gold' credit cards, children's collectable' money boxes are all examples of physical evidence being used in this way.

3.6 FINANCIAL PRODUCTS (SERVICES) - THE OPTIONS AVAILABLE

In order to appreciate better the range of financial products available to us in the country we shall briefly discuss about their " providers" and that how financial services have come to blossom.

Since bank nationalization in July 1969, banking and finance industry constituents have been broadly identified into 7 categories.

- State Bank of India and its associate banks such as State Bank of Patiala, State Bank of Hyderabad etc.
- Nationalized banks (i.e. Government of India undertaking) such as Syndicate bank, Bank of India, Canara Bank, Punjab & Sind Bank etc.
- Private sector banks such as Bank of Madura, Vysya Bank, Federal Bank etc.
- Foreign banks such as American Express Bank, ANZ Grindlays Bank, Bank of America etc.

- Insurance companies such as Life Insurance Corporation of India, General Insurance Corporation etc.
- Unit Trust of India
- Non-banking finance companies such as First Leasing, Sundaram Finance etc.

Till early eighties, no one in the highly regulated banking/finance industry showed any inclination to innovate or market new financial products; given their respective roles as bankers or finance companies all offered absolutely the same product.

Product development or innovation of financial products interestingly requires very little or no additional investment. But the downside is that no brand can boast of a Unique safeguard to some extent here is the very branding of the product.

Some Typical Financial Products (Fund Based Services)

1. **Savings & Recurring Account :** These are products available only with banks, providing relatively low yield but offer advantage of instant liquidity.

2. **Current Account :** Again, available only with banks but can be operated only by corporate entities. These is zero-yield from this product. It exists only to facilitate day-to-day company transactions and availing of credit facilities from the bank, if any. It also serves as a reference point to check on creditworthiness.

3. **Fixed Deposits :** This product is made available by banks, finance companies and certain companies. Currently, the status is that the banks offer the lowest yield on deposits. Companies pay more and the highest is offered by finance companies.

4. **Retail Loan Products:** This covers the grant of auto loan, housing loan, consumer durable loan etc. Here making the consumer finance scheme more attractive from the point of its affordability is what sells.

    Today, possession of a well-known brand of car has a reason to satisfy the status and recognition needs of the human self thus heeling him to reach the fourth step of esteem needs in Maslow's hierarchy. This facility is available both from banks as well as finance companies, the effective rate of interest charged being comparably lower in the case of banks vis a vis finance companies.

5. **Commercial Loans:** This could broadly be split into long-term borrowings (beyond a period of one year) and short-term (less than a period of one year) borrowings.

    Generally long terms loans are provided by financial institutions such as Industrial Finance corporation of India (IFCI), Industrial Development Bank of India. Short-term loans, also known as working capital are made available by all commercial banks.

    Non-banking finance companies assist corporate entities by arranging bulk amounts as deposits from third party companies, at rates of interest higher than bank's lending rate and, for shorter periods, say, 90days;180days & one year etc.

6 **Leasing & Hire Purchase:** This facility is made available, both to individuals and firms, by only finance companies. Both leasing and hire-purchase as a method of financing are essentially a provision of credit to the prospective user who does not have the immediate purchasing power to buy these goods but will have the capacity to make periodic payments for the use of such goods for specific period.

There is difference between the two terms. Leasing can be defined as a method of financing equipment/vehicles wherein the prospective 'user' known as "lessee" in consideration of making periodic payments is allowed the 'use' of equipment/vehicle during the period of lease while the legal ownership in the equipment/vehicle vests in the hand of the finance company, otherwise known as the lessor.

Under Hire-Purchase agreement, the finance company lets the goods on hire to the user for a specified period of time. However here the title of ownership lies with the user from day one.

7 **Credit Cards :** Several banks, both Indian and foreign, have moved into the credit card business. Also known as " plastic money", it offers the individual an opportunity to buy rail/air tickets, make purchases from shops, have meals & stay at hotels when they need it. And pay at leisure.

All the products discussed so far being fund based entitle banks & finance companies to earn by way of interest spreads and, optionally, nominal service charges.

8   **Venture Capital**: The term 'venture capital' comprises of two words viz. 'venture' and 'capital'. The dictionary meaning of 'venture' is a course of proceeding associated with risk, the out come of which is uncertain and 'capital' means resources to start the enterprise. In a narrower sense venture capital is understood as the capital which is available for financing new venture. Broadly, it can be interpreted as the investment of long-term equity finance where the venture capitalist earns his return from capital gain.

9   **Mutual Funds** :Mutual finds is the other area of financial services which has grown rapidly in India over the last ten years. Today they are playing significant role in mobilizing individual savings and providing stability to the Indian capital market. Mutual fund, a financial innovation, provides for a novel way of mobilizing savings from small investors and allowing them to participate in the equity and other securities of the industrial organizations with less risk.

Other Financial Products (Fee Based Services)

1   **Underwriting :** It is the act or process by an underwriting company, - banks, financial institutions, Merchant Banks. It devolves upon the

underwriters to dispose off the securities to the investing public at a price sufficiently attractive to ensure their sale and yet yield the underwriters a profit.

In addition to this, straight underwriting of a public offering, involving a firm commitment, there is this standby type of underwriting wherein the purchase group makes a firm commitment to take any balance of shares unsubscribe in a company offering subscription to investors.

2   **Broking:** It is an intermediary service of bringing together buyers and sellers of the same security or commodity, for a commission or brokerage. A broker is a specialist and accordingly well versed in the technique of his or her particular market, knowing the sources of supply and demand and being an expert on prices and price trends. The stock exchange broker is a member of the stock exchange and as such brand by the law of agency and the very rules of the stock exchange. If SEBI defines a sub-broker as a person not being a member of the stock exchange who acts on behalf of a stock broker as an agent or otherwise assisting the investors in dealing with stock broker. Stock brokers should posses the certificate granted by SEBI, to buy, sell, and deal in securities.

There are brokers who also underwrite issues. There broker – underwriters are akin to retailers. Investors get application forms and brochures etc. from these brokers.

3   **Custodial Services :** This is a modern facility offered by banks, trust companies to their customers. Custodianship accounts are also known as safe keeping, agency and financial secretary accounts.

   A custodial service involves keeping the property intact; collecting income-interest, dividends, rents etc. and disbursing them in accordance with instructions: redeeming bonds called at or before maturity and disbursing proceeds according to instructions; receiving rights which may accrue on stocks, and transmitting instructions for purchase and sale of securities through a broker.

   The range of custodial services offered in India include:
   - Clearance and settlement processing
   - Registration and transfer processing
   - Assets administration
   - Valuation reporting
   - Collection of dividends
   - Subscribing to rights etc. on behalf of clients.

4   **Credit rating:** Credit rating is symbolized rating mechanism which allots symbols which corresponds to the credit quality of the issuer of securities with reference to a particular instrument. It indicates the representative character of the particular security and it does not gave any recommendations to sell or hold that security.

The rating service extends from debt (Bond) security, commercial paper rating borrower/customer rating and sovereign/country rating.

There are predominantly three credit rating agencies operating in India viz, Credit Rating and Information Services of India Limited (CRISIL),Investment Information and Credit Rating Agency (ICRA) and Credit Analysis and Research Limited (CARE).

These companies are similar in providing the type of service. CRISIL mainly rates bonds, ICRA rates the debt instruments like long-term short-term and medium-term instruments, CARE rates the debt instruments such as debentures, fixed deposits, certificate of deposits, commercial paper and structured obligations.

The parameters taken as a base by these agencies are business risk, financial risk, credit quality, and management styles and practices.

A new form of rating system is coming into practice in the area of customer/borrower rating. This looks into the repayment abilities of the borrower. The agency formed for this venture is Onida Individual Credit Rating Agency of India Limited (ONICRA) in a technical collaboration with James Martain and Company, US, the parameters on which the rating is based are bank balances net-worth, earnings and repayment capacity of the borrower.

Moody's rating assess the country risk for international investments. The parameters taken into account for a country rating are economic and political stability, current account deficit, fiscal deficit to GDP, foreign exchange reserves balance of payments picture and the country's debt servicing capacity. The users of this service are institutional investors, collaborators, banks etc. with the boom in the credit business a lot of competitive activities and synergies are being planned by existing credit rating agencies of India.

5. **Merchant banking:** In the present day capital market scenario the merchant banks play as an encouraging and supporting force to the entrepreneurs, corporate sectors and the investors. The recent modifications of the India Capital market environment have emerged the various institutions have appeared in the financial spectacle and merchant bankers have joined to expand the range of financial services. Moreover, the activities of these Merchant bankers have developed considerably both horizontal and vertically, to cope with the changing environment so that these financial institutions can be constituted as a subsidiary of the parent bodies. Merchant Banks also called 'Investment Banks' is most significant institutions in the financial markets of the developed countries. They help in promoting and sustaining capital markets and money markets, and they provide a variety of financial services to the corporate sector.

6. **Loan syndication:** Loan syndication refers to the services rendered by the Financial service expert or firm in procurement of term loans

and working capital loans from financial institutions, banks and other financing and investment firms for his/its client.

7. **Share registration services:** In a company, the secretary or other official of the company will normally deal with the company share registration work. With the increase in public issues and number of investors, a specialized service called 'share registration services' has emerged as one of the important facets of financial services sector.

8. **Debenture Trusteeship:** When a company seeks to issue debentures or debenture stock, or even unsecured loan stock, it is customary to appoint a trustee to protect the interests of the debenture holders or stockholders. The issuer is normally constituted under a trust deed entered into between the company and the trustee. The powers and duties of the trustee will be set out in the deed.

9. **Insurance:** The Insurance Services eliminates the uncertain risk of loss for the individual through the combination of a large number of similarly exposed individuals who contribute to a common fund premium payments sufficient to make good the loss caused to any one individual.

Insurance cover divides the risk over a large number of persons. The divisions of adversity decreases in intensity and division of happiness makes more people happy. Insurance is a quality of money. Those who seek it endeavor to avert disaster from them by shifting possible losses on the shoulders of others that are willing for pecuniary consideration to take risk thereof. The primary function of general insurance is thus the elimination of uncertain risk of loss for the individual.

Insurance of Property:

Burglary Insurance

Cash Insurance

Engineering Insurance

Fire Insurance

Motor Insurance

Insurance of Liability:

Employee's Liability

Product Liability

Public Liability

Insurance of Persons:

Bhavishya Arogya

Group Mediclaim

Group Personal Accident

Overseas Mediclaim

Developing Financial Products:

1 **Factoring :** We can define factoring as the sale of book debts by a firm to a financial intermediary called the factor on the understanding that the factor will pay for the debts as and when they are collected or on a guaranteed payment date. Usually, the factor maker makes part

payment immediately after the debts are purchased thereby providing immediate liquidity to the client.

1. Client concludes a credit sale with the customer.
2. Client sells the customer's account to the factor and notifies the customer.
3. Factor makes part payment (advance) against the account purchased after adjusting for commission and interest on the advance.
4. Factor maintains the customer's account and follows up for payment.
5. Customer remits the amount due to the factor.
6. Factor makes the final payment to the client when the account is collected or on a guaranteed payment date.

Factoring being a fund-based activity cannot be made viable unless sources of funds are available to the factoring organizations at lower costs. This is especially true in case of full and international factoring.

Hence they should have facilities of refinance, raising of deposits and credit insurance etc. for the type of activity from the respective sources.

2 **Forfaiting:** In practice forfaiting is a flexible instrument, which can be tailored to meet the exporter's need.

The operation of the deal is simple; The transaction is first vetted by the forraiter, to arrive at a price. Once the price agreed upon, forfaiting is similar to discounting export bills locally – that is after shipment, the exporter presents the documents to the buyer's banker for acceptance. These accepted bills of exchange are sent to the fortfailer who then remits the discounted amount to the EXIM bank of India. EXIM in turn transfers the amount to the exporter's bank. The discount fee is paid up front as the operation is without recourse to the seller. The entire process takes 10 – 20 days. Which is equivalent to the time it takes to process the sight bill.

The merit of forfaiting is that, the exporter does not exhaust his post-shipment credit limits. This is because forfaiting turns a usuance export into cash sale.

The merit is true that most Indian exports have little problems in getting such limits from banks in case of export bills discounted, forfaiting in certain instances presents a cheaper alternative to the credit taken under the Pre-shipment Credits in Foreign Currency (PCFC) scheme.

3   **Depository services:** It is a system whereby the transfer and settlement of scripts take place not through transfer deeds and physical delivery of scripts which are traditional, but through the modern system of effecting transfer of ownership of securities by means of book entry on the ledgers of the Depository without the

physical movement of scripts. The new system would eliminate paper work, facilitate electronic book entry of the reduction in settlement periods and ultimately contribute to the liquidity of investment in provide depository services must register with SEBI. The depositor services will be available in respect of securities as may be specified by SEBI.

4 **Commercial Paper:** Commercial Paper (CP) is defined as short-term money market instrument, issued by way of promissory notes for a fixed maturity. It will be totally unsecured and will have a maturity period ranging from 90 days to 180 days. A CP differs from other money market instruments like banker's acceptance, which are obligations of both the drawer and the accepting bank. It could be compared with Company Fixed Deposits, through it differs from them as regards to the method of issue and the structuring of interest element. As CPs do not carry any security backing the RBI has allowed only sound companies to issue them initially. CPs will meet the short-term investments for parking temporary surpluses by corporate bodies as well as investments institutions.

5 **Treasury Bills:** Treasury Bills are short-term finance bills issued by the government usually at a discount. There are 91 days bills and 364 days bills, which are neither purchased nor discounted by the RBI. There are ordinary bills and ad-hoc bills too. The ordinary treasury bills are issued by the government to supplement its short-term needs while, the ad-hoc bills are created in favour or RBI to replenish the

cash balances of the government. Currently as the 364 days bills have a higher yields rate, they are more in demand than the 91-day bills. In May 1995 RBI has offered to convert 364 day T-bills in 5 years dated stock.

6. **Derivatives:** A Derivatives, such as option or features, are financial contracts which derive their value off a spot price time – series, which is called "the underlying". The world over, derivatives are a key part of the financial system. The most important contract types are futures and options, and the most important underlying markets are equity, treasury bills, commodities, foreign exchange and real estate. In a forward contract, two parties agree to do a trade at some future date, at a stated price and quantity. No money changes hands at the time the deal is signed.

Forward markets worldwide are afflicted by several problems: (a) Lack of centralization of trading (b) illiquidity, and (c) counterparty risk. Futures markets were designed to solve all the three problems (a, b and c listed above of forward markets in terms of basic economics. However, contracts are standardized and trading is centralized, so that future markets are highly liquid. There is no conunterparty risk (thanks to the institution of a clearinghouse, which becomes counterparty to both sides of each transaction and guarantees the trade). In futures markets, unlike, in forward markets, increasing the time to expiration does not increase the counterparty risk.

3.7 TECHNOLOGY POWER FOR FINANCIAL PRODUCTS

The growth of banking concept has been dramatic in recent times. While banks have been instrumental for various technological innovations, they have also been adapting the breakthrough to further their service by adding newer dimensions.

Apart from the extensive use of computers for accounting purposes and communications network of the general order, banks have introduced innovative concepts like Magnetic Ink Character Recognition (MICR) cheques, Bankers Automated Clearing Services (BACS), Clearing House Automated Payment Systems (CHAPS), Cash Dispensers (CDs), Automated Teller Machines (ATMs)are towards instant operational convince, including cash withdrawals. Point-of-Sale (POS) terminals facilitate instant retail banking transactions. Laser Cards have enhanced the utility of credit cards. The formations of Society for Worldwide inter Financial Telecommunications (SWIFT) coordinates international banking transactions through Satellite communications.

3.8 FINANCIAL SERVICES REGULATION AND LEGISLATION: IMPACT ON FINANCIAL SERVICES

All functions and responsibilities of financial service organizations (both Indian and foreign) are governed by the regulations stipulated by the Reserve Bank of India (RBI). For banks the two critical elements of Cash Reserve Ratio and Statutory Liquidity Ratio are fixed by RBI.

From time to time strictures are issued for matter such as revision of interest rates; change of policy ; foreign exchange regulations.

The Financial Services Regulations by SEBI & RBI are largely brought about to regulate the financial service organizations and protect the consumers. Financial Organizations including insurance companies have to abide by the regulations set down.

RBI has appointed various committees to carry out reforms in financial sector and have proper functioning and monitoring of financial service organizations as well as to protect the interest of consumers who avail services form financial service organizations.

All marketing efforts are financial service organizations have to be carried out within the boundaries of the recommendations of various committees. It may interest to take note of, while studying the marketing practices of financial service organizations, various recommendations made by various committees. Major recommendations of following committees are annexed with the study (as Appendix – II) to have an insight on marketing of financial service organizations.

1. Chakravarty Committee, 1985 (Committee to review the working of the monetary system)
2. Vaghul Committee, 1987 (Working group on the money market)
3. Narasimhan Committee, 1991 (Committee on the financial system)
4. Basu Committee, 1992 (Task force on money market mutual funds)

5. A. C. Shah Committee, 1992 (Working group on non-banking financial companies)
6. J. V. Shetty Committee, 1993 (Committee on consortium lending)
7. R. Jilani Committee, 1993 (Working group on cash credit system)
8. D. R. Mehta Committee, 1994 (Committee to review IRDP)
9. W. S. Saraf Committee, 1994 (Committee on technological issue)
10. O. P. Sodhani Committee, 1995 (Expert group of foreign exchange markets)

The role played by SEBI can also not be ignored while studying marketing of financial services. The Securities and Exchange Board Act of 1992 provides for the establishment of a Board to protect the interest of investors in securities and to promote the development and regulations of securities market. Various guidelines given by SEBI, for example, Guidelines for Debentures, Guidelines for Right Issues, Guidelines for Preferential Allotment, Guidelines (Norms) about Publicity and Issue Advertisement etc. are to be considered while studying / designing marketing strategies of financial service organizations.

CHAPTER – IV
METHODOLOGY

CHAPTER - IV

METHODOLOGY

4.1 INTRODUCTION

This chapter describes how the research proposal came to be formulated and how the research was carried out.

A review of some studies on Marketing of Services and a case for a study on the marketing practices of financial services organizations has already been given in chapter II, hence the same is not being repeated.

(a) Statement of Problem :

As the study is concerned with marketing aspects only, the problem that is taken up for investigation is to find out how systematic and scientific are marketing practices of the financial service organizations.

(b) Research Objectives :

The objectives of the study are:

i) to ascertain, the level of performance of the financial services organizations on the different marketing practices;

ii) to ascertain, the existence of relationship and the extent of relationship between the performance variable, (growth rate), and predictor variables, (the marketing practices), both for the entire sample and for sub-samples. The marketing practices include are:

- Competitive and demand practices (CDP),
- Product/ Service practices (PDP),
- New product/ Service practices (NPP),
- Pricing Practices (PRP),
- Promotion practices (PMP);

iii) to differentiate the various sub-groups in respect of their marketing practices. The sub-groups that are mutually exclusive are,

- "Risk taker" group – "Safe Player" group,
- "Professionally Managed" group–"Traditionally managed" group,
- "Fund Based Services" group– "Fee Based/Advisory Services" group,
- "Private Organizations" group – "Nationalized Organizations" group.
- "Consumer Finance" group – "Industrial Finance" group

(C) Focus of research

The focus of research in the present study is concerned with relationship among the characteristics of the objects, (here the objects are the financial service organizations and characteristics are the different variables under study).

The research design, for acquiring the information needed is inclusive of exploratory, descriptive and casual studies. An 'experience survey' was undertaken by the investigator in an attempt to obtain information on the strengths and weaknesses of financial service organizations with special reference to the marketing aspects.

Further, three financial service organizations situated in Baroda were chosen at random for the purpose of pilot study. The managers / senior officers were interviewed (informally) regarding the various issues, problems and functioning of their organizations. In this way, the investigator gained insight into the actual working of the financial service organizations. The extent of co-operation that could be expected from financial services organizations and also as to which are the 'sensitive' areas for the financial service organizations.

4.2 SAMPLING

(a) **Sample Frame**

The list of organizations providing services in Gujarat was prepared but for the purpose of study, only financial service organizations are of relevance. Hence, a study population was derived from this list, which brought out 522 organizations providing financial services.

Thus the sampling frame consisted of 522 financial service organizations included in the study population. These units were then classified on the basis of the two broad categories of services they render namely viz. Fund/ Asset based services and Fees based / Advisory services.

(b) **Sample Size :**

It was decided that 10% of the study population would be drawn as the sample size. This works out to 52 financial service organizations, which was considered to be an expedient size from all practical aspects.

(c) **Sampling Technique**

Having decided on the sample size, the next aspect to be considered is the method of drawing the sample. As indicated earlier the 522 financial service organizations of the study population do provide different financial service groups. Therefore, it was decided to go in for 'Stratified Random Sampling'.

(d) Sample Selection

The sampling units included in the study population were grouped into different strata and then each of organizations of each strata was numbered serially, and, 'Table of Random Numbers' was referred to select the sample.

<u>The extent</u> of the sample was confined to the State of Gujarat

<u>The time</u> when the sample was drawn is January 1997.

<u>The elements</u> in the sample were to comprise either the fund based financial service organizations of fee based / advisory service organizations.

4.3 <u>INSTRUMENTATION – QUESTIONNAIRE</u>

To carry out the survey, a questionnaire had to be developed. This was necessitated since the means of obtaining information from respondents was through 'Structured – Direct Interviews'.

While framing the questionnaire the research objectives were assimilated and the information required to be collected were listed.

As the respondents formed a heterogeneous group, and as only on questionnaire was developed, care was taken to see that it would cater to all elements in the sample, and also, comprehensible by the least able respondent.

The questionnaire was divided into 6 sections. Sections one included questions of a very general nature, which would help in the classification of respondent organizations. Section two to section six contained questions on the various marketing practices of the financial services organizations. These are described a little later in the chapter.

Having decided on the various questions to be asked, the next issue was regarding the 'response format' to the questions. In the questionnaire, two types of formats were used, namely, dichotomous questions and multiple-choice questions.

Before the questionnaire is pressed into the field, it needs to be pre-tested and revised if necessary. This is required in order to search out areas for improvement.

Pre-testing of the questionnaire was done in two stages. In the first stage the 'Delphi Method' was used. Three experts in the field were chosen and they were individually requested to estimate the questionnaire regarding its contents, comprehension and ambiguity. The remarks /comments / suggestions of the three judges were then pooled in and the questionnaire accordingly revised.

The second stage in the pre-testing of the questionnaire was done in the field itself. Three financial service organizations were chosen at random and the questionnaire was administrated to them. The feed back received in the pre-testing of the questionnaire was taken care of and, the final draft of the questionnaire was ready for field operations.

4.4 SCORING TECHNIQUE

While developing a questionnaire and important aspect to be borne in mind is, the measurement of the response / data collected. The responses that are codified should be capable of lending themselves to the type of analysis with which the data are to be treated. Keeping this in mind the following scoring technique was developed.

The questionnaire contains 6 sections. (A copy of the questionnaire enclosed as and annexure may be referred). Section '1' contains questions of a general nature and thus no scores were allotted to the same.

Section 2, 3, 4, 5 and 6 deal with the different marketing practices of the financial services organizations, and scores have been allotted to every question in each of these sections.

Three types of scoring were adopted in assigning scores to the various questions. They were, namely –
- Equal scoring,
- Unequal scoring, and
- Frequency.

The score allotted to questions, whose response format is dichotomous in nature, was 'ONE SCORE' only. That is, the respondent had to answer either 'YES' or 'NO'. Those respondents who answer in the affirmative were to be allotted one score each and in calculating the extent of the particular marketing practice only the 'FREQUENCY' had to be taken.

Yet another type of question used in the questionnaire is one in which the question has many sub-divisions and for each of these, the response format is dichotomous in nature. Hence, an affirmative response would score ONE and each sub-division is allotted a score of ONE only. Thus all sub-divisions of a single question have and 'EQUAL' scoring.

The system of 'UNEQUAL' scoring has been adopted where a questions has many sub-divisions an incorrect answer would get a nil score, a partially correct answer a lesser score than a fully correct answer.

In questions that have many sub-divisions but in response where 'only one tick' has been specified, the query carries a score of ONE only (i.e. a system of equal scoring).

For a detailed account on the scores allotted to each question, the annexure on 'scoring technique' may be referred.

A questionnaire of the kind administrated in the present study does not measure attitudes or preferences but only facts. The questionnaire in the present study seeks to ascertain the marketing practices adopted by the financial services organizations in their various marketing decisions. Thus there arose no requirement to conduct a reliability and validity test for questionnaire. Nevertheless to overcome any incongruencies, the 'Judgmental Method' of testing was once again applied. Three judges (experts in the field) were chosen and they were asked to evaluate the scores allotted to the different queries in the questionnaire. The options of the three judges was then pooled in the necessary changes made in the allotment of scores.

4.5 DATA COLLECTION

The questionnaire after having passed through all the stages enumerated above was pressed into the field. The investigator personally interviewed the respondents and collected the data.

At the time of administering the questionnaire additional information, as detailed below was collected from each respondent –

(i) Total income/revenue for three consecutive years (1994-'95, 1995-'96, 1996-'97);

(ii) Growth rate for 3 consecutive years, (1994-'95, 1995-'96, 1996-'97);

(iii) Number of employees for 3 consecutive years, (1994-'95, 1995-'96, 1996-'97);

4.6　DATA ANALYSIS

In marketing the choice of the appropriate statistical technique, the objectives of the study were given due consideration.

To fulfill objective (i) of para 4.1 b above, simple techniques such as arithmetic mean, standard deviation, co-efficient of variation and percentages were used.

In trying to fulfill objective (ii) of para 4.1 b outlined above the following aspect had to be considered i.e. the nature of assumed prior judgements on how the data matrix is to be partitioned in terms of the number of sub-sets, and also, the number of variables in each of these partitioned sub-sets the criterion versus predictor variables. Taking all these aspects into account the statistical technique chosen for the fulfillment of the objective is the 'step-wise multiple regression technique'. This would help in bringing out which of the predictor variable are of importance and their order of importance / contribution to the criterion variable.

The third objective outlined in para 4.1 b above involves the differentiation of the sub-groups in terms of marketing practices. One way of accomplishing the same is through the use of discriminate analysis, which helps in determining weather differences in average score profiles for two or more groups are statistically significant. This can be done by undertaking group classifications. Thus it is possible to discriminate between two groups (as in the present study) on the basis of a few variables (in the present study it would be marketing practices).

4.7 CLASSIFICATION OF RESPONDENTS ORGANIZATIONS

For the purpose of analysis the respondent organizations were divided into groups on the basis of six different criteria, each of them is examined below.

(i) "Risk Taker" group (RTG) – "Safe Player" group (SPG)

A close look at the functioning of the Financial Service Organizations discloses the operational patterns of the financial service providers. There are some financial service organizations that want to play safe and minimize their loss (if any).

Such financial service organizations undertake servicing activity only when they have firm clients to serve. This is to say that they are operational only when the organizations have firm clients to serve. Such financial service organizations are termed as 'Safe Player Group' in the study.

In contrast to the group described above there is another set of financial service organizations that are term as the 'Risk Taker Group'. The organizations in this group are in operation right through the year. They set for themselves a particular level of performance, which they feel they can achieve without much difficulty. They continue servicing and at the same time are looking for different target groups/customers to whom they can serve.

The percentage of financial service organizations coming in each of these categories is given in the Table IV-1.

Table IV-1
Composition of "Risk Taker" Group and "Safe Player" Group in the sample.

Description	No. of Organizations	% to total
1. "Risk Taker" group	34	65.38
2. "Safe Player" group	18	34.62
Total...	52	100.00

(ii) "Professionally Managed" group (PROF.MG.)- "Traditionally Managed" Group (TRAD.MG.)

This dichotomous classification is based on the 'management approach of organizations'. The criterion used here is the approach involved in the management of the organizations.

In the professionally managed organization, it is found that activities are performed professionally and competent persons are assigned activities. Under this type of organization, there is always greater chance for the organization functioning and performing better as resources and talents are pooled in.

In contrast to the group described above, in the "Traditionally Managed" group, right type of personnel are not engaged to carry out various activities of financial service organizations.

The composition of the "Professionally Managed" group and "Traditionally Managed" group is given in the Table IV-2. The reason behind this classification is to ascertain which type of organization is performing better by way of growth rate.

Table IV-2

Composition of Professionally Managed Group and Traditionally Managed Group in the sample.

Description	No. of Units	% to total
1. Professionally Managed Group	35	67.31
2. Traditionally Managed Group	17	32.69
Total...	52	100.00

(iii) "Fund Based Services" Group (FBSG) – "Fee Based/Advisory Services" Group (ABSG)

This dichotomous classification is based on the basis of financial services rendered by financial service organizations. Financial services fall broadly into two groups: Fund/Asset Based and Fee /Advisory. Fund based services include higher purchase finance less finance, insurance services, venture capital financing, factoring, housing loan, term loan, cash credit, etc. while fee based / advisory services include merchant banking, capital issue management, stock broking, credit rating, letter of credit, bank guarantee, merger and acquisition etc.

As to how organizations came under each of these categories is given in Table IV-3.

Table IV-3
Composition of "Fund Based Services" Group (FBSG) – "Fee Based/Advisory Services" Group (ABSG) in the sample.

Description	No. of Org.	% to total
1. Fund based services groups	23	44.23
2. Fee Based/Advisory Services groups	29	55.77
Total	52	100.00

(iv) **Private Organizations Group (POG) – Nationalized Organizations Group (NOG)**

Under this dichotomous classification financial service organizations are classified as private organizations i.e. private banks, private mutual funds, and nationalized organizations i.e. public sector banks, all India Financial institution, State level Finance institutions etc.

The size of each of these groups is given in Table No. IV-4.

Table IV-4
Composition of Private Organizations Group and Nationalized Organizations Group in the sample.

Description	No. of organizations	% to total
1. Private Organizations	11	21.15
2. Nationalized Organizations	41	78.85
Total...	52	100.00

(v) **Consumer Finance Group – Industrial Finance Group**

This is the last of the dichotomous group used in this study. Here the bifurcation is based on the basis of nature of finance and market segments for financial service organizations. Consumer finance organizations are those who purely deal in providing finance to end-users i.e. consumers. Such finance includes housing loan, vehicle loan, and other consumer durable loan. Industrial finance group is those who provide finance to business houses. Such finance includes term loan, cash credit, bills discounting etc.

The composition of the consumer finance organizations and industrial finance organizations in the sample is given to Table IV-5.

Table IV-5
Composition of Consumer Finance Organizations and Industrial Finance Organizations in the sample.

Description	No. of Organizations	% to total
1. Consumer Finance Organizations	08	15.38
2. Industrial Finance Organizations	44	84.62
Total...	52	100.00

Before concluding this chapter it is of relevance to look into the different marketing variables used to the present study.

4.8 VARIABLES IN THE PRESENT STUDY

The different aspects covered each of the variables are described below:

a) **Variable 1**

The first variable stands for growth rate, i.e. the overall growth rate in terms of deposits/funds mobilized and revenue/income generated in a year.

b) **Variable 2**

The second variable stands for marketing concept adoption in competitive and Demand practices. This is covered in section II of the questionnaire and concerns the following aspects:
- Knowledge of target market
- Information on competitors and their strategies;
- Estimation of total demand and market share etc.

c) **Variable 3**

This variable denotes marketing concept adoption in the sphere of product/service practices. It has been dealt with in section III of the questionnaire and includes aspects such as,
- Customer's preferences / requirements in the particular product/service;
- Estimation of growth rate (i.e. growth rate forecast)
- Practice of sales analysis;
- Knowledge of product/service life cycle and the ensuing product/service innovation;
- Constraints on the product/service etc.

d) **Variable 4**

The fourth variable is also a marketing variable and denotes marketing concept adoption in new product (service) decisions. This is covered in section IV of the questionnaire and is inclusive of-
- Introduction of new products (services);
- Genesis of new products (services);

- Costing of new products (services);
- Production (servicing) capacity for new products (service) etc.

e) **Variable 5**

Variable 5 denotes marketing concept adoption in pricing practices and section V of the questionnaire includes aspects such as –
- Objectives in pricing;
- Number of parameters considered in pricing
- Limitation in price fixation;
- Break-even analysis and its applications.

f) **Variable 6**

This is the last of the marketing variables and stands for marketing concept adoption in promotion decisions. Section VI of the questionnaire covers this variable and the different aspects considered in this section are –
- The necessity to communicate with target market;
- Purpose of advertising
- Methods of sales promotion used;
- Publicity;
- Responses sought through communication etc.

The data thus collected was processed on the computer,

CHAPTER - V
ANALYSIS AND INTERPRETATION OF DATA: COMPARISON AND DIFFERENTIATION OF GROUPS

CHAPTER - V

ANALYSIS AND INTERPRETATION OF DATA: COMPARISON AND DIFFERENTIATION OF GROUPS

5.1 INTRODUCTION

This is the first of the two chapters in which the data collected are analyzed, interpreted and discussed.

In the present chapter, the different groups are compared and differentiated with respect of each of the marketing variables. In section I, the level of performance of the groups in each marketing practice is highlighted. Also, the variability in the practice of each of marketing decisions for each of the groups is discussed. The statistical techniques for analyzing the data utilized here are, arithmetic mean, standard deviation, co-efficient of variation and percentages.

In section II of the present chapter, each dichotomous classification is taken up for discussion at a time, and the groups are differentiated on the basis of marketing practices. The grouped t test is applied to test the difference between the two means. At first the F test is applied for testing the quality of variance, next either the pooled variance estimate t test or the separate variance estimate t test is applied (depending on the F value). Thus the two groups are discriminated on the basis of various marketing practices.

Section – I

5.2 PERFORMANCE OF THE SAMPLE ON DIFFERENT MARKETING PRACTICES

Before going into the group – wise discussion, the performance of the sample as a whole on the various marketing practices to be stated.

This facilities better comparison on the performance level of the various sub-groups in respect of their marketing practices.

Table V-1 gives the mean, standard deviation and co-efficient of variation for the sample as a whole.

Table – V-1
Performance of the entire sample on different marketing practices

Variable	Entire Sample (n = 52)		
	X	σ	V
2 CDP	10.75	5.56	51.74
3 PDP	11.17	4.31	38.58
4 NPP	9.81	6.73	68.65
5 PRP	9.25	4.05	43.76
6 PMP	12.62	6.16	48.84

Note :   X denotes mean

^6 denotes standard deviation, and

V denotes co-efficient of variation

5.3 RISK TAKER GROUP (RTG) COMPARED WITH SAFE PLAYER GROUP (SPG) IN TERMS OF ADOPTION OF MARKETING PRACTICES

The first of the classifications taken up for analysis is the risk taker group and the safe player group. Table V-2 gives the following information* on the two groups.

- the mean scores on each of the marketing practices,
- the standard deviation on each of the marketing practices,
- the co-efficient of variation (V), in other word, the variability on each of the marketing practices,

* The same information for the different group classification is found in Table V-3, V-4 and V-5.

- the mean score of the variable expressed as a percentage of maximum possible score that is allotted to each variable (for maximum scores allotted to each variable, the annexure on the scoring technique may be referred), and,
- the overall mean (i.e. the mean of the 5 marketing variables taken together).

In interpreting the data presented in Table V-2, the following may be stated. (It may also be noted here that for the sake of clarity the possible reasons for the better / poor performance of the groups is discussed under the different marketing variables i.e., 5.3 C).

a) Regarding the average scores which indicate the performance on the various marketing practices

Table V-2
Comparison of RTG-SPG groups on different Marketing Practices

Variable	RTG Group (n = 34)			SPG Group (n = 18)			X as % of maximum score	
	X	^6	V	X	^6	V	RTG	SPG
1	2	3	4	5	6	7	8	9
2 CDP	12.18	5.25	43.15	8.06	5.24	65.06	55.35	36.62
3 PDP	12.62	3.90	30.91	8.44	3.76	44.54	66.41	44.44
4 NPP	11.44	6.54	57.18	6.72	6.12	91.10	35.75	19.14
5 PRP	10.12	3.89	38.46	7.61	3.93	51.61	53.25	40.06
6 PMP	14.71	6.35	43.15	8.67	3.24	37.34	52.52	30.95
Overall Avg.	12.21	-	-	7.90	-	-	52.66	34.24

Note :-   X denotes mean,   ^6 denotes standard deviation
            V denotes co-efficient of variation.

i) the RTG group secured a higher average than the SPG group on all the marketing variables;

ii) not only are the average scores of the SPG group lower than those of the RTG group, they are lower than the performance of the entire sample (on all the marketing practices). Table V-1 may be referred for average scores on entire sample;

ii) on all the marketing practices, the average of the RTG group were higher than that of the entire sample.

b) Regarding the variability in the marketing practices, it is found that a fairly large heterogeneity exists in the practices of the two groups. It should be note here that higher the value of 'V' the greater the heterogeneity (i.e. less the homogeneity).

i) In the risk taker group greater heterogeneity (i.e. maximum availability of 58%) is found in the marketing practice of new product/service decisions, and greater homogeneity (i.e. minimum availability of 31%) is found in the practice of product/service decisions.

ii) In the safe player group, greater heterogeneity (a maximum variability of 91%) is found in the practice of new product/service practices, and, greater homogeneity (a minimum variability of 37%) is found in the practice of promotion decisions.

iii) For both RTG group and SPG group, the maximum variability is found with respect to new product/service practices.

c) Regarding the performance of the two groups – RTG and SPG – on the different marketing practices, the following observations are made.

i) **Variable 2 : Competitive and demand practices:**

The mean score of RTG group in this variable is 12.18, while that of the SPG group is 8.06. This clearly indicates the better performance of the RTG group on competitive and demand practices. In order to have an even clearer picture these average scores are converted to percentages on the maximum possible score of the variable. (Refer column 8 and 9 of Table – V-2). Here it is found that RTG group secured 55% while the SPG group secured 37% only.

In interpreting the performance of the two groups, it may be said that the performance of the RTG group is average and that of the SPG group is poor.

The possible reason for the poor performance of the SPG group can be drawn from the criterion of the group classification. The organizations of the SPG group operate only when firm clients are in hand. Such organizations are busy rushing here and there to procure business, hence they are unsystematic in gathering knowledge on competitors and their strategies.

ii)   Variable : 3 Product Practices:

The mean score of RTG group on this variable is 12.62 and that of SPG group is 8.44. These scores when converted as percentages of maximum score of the variable read as 66% and 44% respectively. Thus the performance of the RTG group may be said to be 'above average' and that of the SPG group 'low'.

From these percentages, it may summarized that the organizations of the RTG group give considerable attention to service quality, customers requirements, etc. while taking decisions on the product/service.

The possible reasons for the low performance of the Safe Player Group could be, at times, such organizations in their anxiety to procure business sometimes overlooks the fact that they may not be in a position to provide quality services.

iii)   **Variable : 4 New Product/Service Practices :**

In practices relating to new product/service decisions, the RTG group secured on average of 11.44, and, SPG group secured and averages of 6.72. These scores when converted as percentages of maximum score on the variable are 36% and 19% respectively. The performance of the RTG group may be considered to be average, while that of the SPG group is below average.

The innovation of products/services brings on the acceptance of the product life cycle. Any product/service has to go through 4 stages namely, Introduction, Growth, Maturity and Decline. Many financial service organizations find it difficult to accept the decline stage of the product life cycle.

Out of 34 organizations belonging to the RTG group only 21 (i.e. 61.76%) of them agree that every product/service has a decline stage. Yet, it is found that their practices on introduction of new product/service are average. In the safe player group 6 out of 18 member (i.e. 33.33%) accept the decline stage of the product/service. Thus it may be said that marketing practices regarding new product/service decisions are average in the financial service organizations.

The average performance on aspects concerning 'product (service) – idea – development', innovation, introduction and allied decisions on new products/services could be due to lack of priority given to these aspects. Also, the facilities for development of new products/services are inadequate in the financial service organizations.

iv) **Variable 5 : Pricing Decisions :**

The RTG group secured on average of 10.12 while that of SPG group is 7.61. These when converted as percentages to the maximum possible score on the variable read as 53% and 40% respectively. The performance of the RTG group may be said to be average and that of the SPG group low.

Many products/services are becoming price competitive in the market. As the safe player groups function only when firm clients are in hand, it is difficult for the organizations to take stand on pricing. This may lead to unscientific adoption of pricing practices.

Another possible reason why the financial organizations are unable to undertake market oriented pricing may be due to constraints imposed by cost and availability of resource requirements.

(iv) **Variable : 6 Promotion Practices**

The RTG group secured an average of 14.71 as against 8.67 in the SPG group. These when converted as percentages to maximum possible score read as 53% and 31% respectively. Thus the performance of the RTG group may be considered to be average, while that the SPG group may be said to be poor.

One of the quoted reason, is that the financial services organizations are unable to indulge in effective promotion strategies due to lack of proper management and allocation of funds. The attitude of the safe player group is conditioned and moves in the direction of securing business and they may not have any specific target market as their priority.

Having discussed the performance of the RTG and SPG groups on the different marketing practices, the discussion moves on to performance of the professionally managed group and traditionally managed groups.

5.4 PROFESSIONALLY MANAGED GROUP (PROF.MG) COMPARED WITH TRADITIONALLY MANAGED GROUP (TRAD.MG.) GROUP IN TERMS OF ADOPTION OF MARKETING PRACTICES

The performance of the professionally managed group and traditionally managed group, on the different marketing practices are given in Table V-3. The following comparisons are drawn regarding the two groups.

(a) Regarding the average scores, which indicate the performance of the PROF.MG. and TRAD.MG. group on the various marketing practices:

i) The average scores of the professionally managed group are higher than those of the traditionally managed group in practices relating to:
- Competitive and demand decisions,
- Product/service decisions and,
- Pricing decisions

ii) The mean scores of the traditionally managed group are higher than those of the professionally managed group jin practices relating to,
- new product/service decisions, and,
- promotion decisions.

Table V-3

Comparison of PROF.MG. -TRAD.MG. Groups on Different Marketing Practices

	PROF.MG. Group (n = 35)			TRAD.MG. Group (n = 17)			X as % of maximum score	
Variable	X	^6	V	X	^6	V	RTG	SPG
1	2	3	4	5	6	7	8	9
2 CDP	11.97	5.73	47.84	8.24	4.35	52.85	54.41	37.43
3 PDP	11.51	4.60	39.93	10.47	3.68	35.11	60.60	55.11
4 NPP	9.77	6.56	67.16	9.88	7.28	73.66	30.53	30.88
5 PRP	9.97	4.08	40.96	7.77	3.65	46.99	52.48	40.87
6 PMP	12.57	6.03	47.98	12.71	6.61	52.04	44.9	45.38
Overall Avg.	11.16	-	-	9.81	-	-	48.58	41.93

Note :- X denotes mean,   ^6 denotes standard deviation

V denotes co-efficient of variation.

(b) Regarding the variability in the marketing practices of the two groups:

i) In the professionally managed group, greater heterogeneity (i.e. a maximum variability of 67%) is found in marketing practices relating to new product/service decisions, and greater homogeneity (i.e. a minimum variability of 40%) is found in the practice of product/service decisions.

ii) In the traditionally managed group, greater heterogeneity (a maximum variability of 74%) is found in the practice of product/service decisions.

iii) It needs to be noted that for both groups maximum variability is found in new product/service practices and minimum variability in product/service practices.

(c) Regarding the performance of the two groups PROF.MG. and TRAD.MG. – on the different marketing practices, the following observations are made :

i) **Variable 2 : Competitive and demand Practices :**

The mean score of PROF.MG. group on this variable is 11.97, while that of the TRAD.MG. group is 8.24. These averages when expressed as percentages to maximum possible score of the variable read as 54% and 37% respectively. Thus it may be stated that the performance of the PROF.MG. group is average, while that of the TRAD.MG. group is poor.

The probable reason why the organizations of the TRAD.MG. group are unable to ascertain their competitive position in the market may be due to paucity and lack of time.

The professionally managed group, inspite of having an added advantage over the TRAD.MG. group, their performance on competitive and demand practices is average only. Probably the gains that may be realized in gathering information of competitors and their strategies, as also computing demand and market share is not known to them, or if they do, they don't know how to go about it or don't indulge in this practice due to other constraints.

ii) **Variable 3 : Product Practices:**

The mean score of the PROF.MG. group on this variable is 11.51 and that of TRAD.MG. group is 8.24. These scores when expressed as percentages of maximum possible score of the variable read as 61% and 55% respectively. The performance on this variable is better than it is in the earlier variable. This is to say that organizations of both groups are giving greater priority to marketing practices relating to product/service decisions. It may be recalled here that the variability figures for both groups are very close (PROF.MG. – 40%, and TRAD.MG. 35%).

iii) **Variable 4 : New Product/service Practices:**

In practices relating to new product/service decision, the PROF.MG. group secured an average of 9.77, and TRAD.MG. group secured an average of 9.88. These scores when expressed as percentages to the maximum possible score read as 31% and 31% respectively. It is very surprising to note that the performances of both groups are practically the same, The performance of both groups may be considered to be poor. It is also found that both groups have greater heterogeneity in the practice of new product/service decisions. New product/service practices seem to be a 'week area' for the financial service organizations. Probably one reason for it being so could be that the financial service organizations are not properly oriented on the importance, and introduction of new products/service.

iv) Variable 5 : Pricing Practices :

The PROF.MG. group secured an average of 9.97 and TRAD.MG. group secured an average of 7.77 on the marketing variable, pricing practices. These scores expressed as percentage to the maximum possible score of the variable read as 52% and 41% respectively.

The performance of the PROF.MG. group may be taken as average, while that of TRAD.MG. group may be said to low. The average secured by the TRAD.MG. group is lower than that of the average of the entire sample (Table V-1). One tends to feel that those financial service organizations who preferred to go in for full cost pricing are always anxious about growth rate, that they do not want to take a chance by going in for any other system of pricing. Yet, another trend among the financial service organizations is to follow the competitor. Sometimes this is done blindly without even working out the costs in their own organization.

v)   **Variable 6 : Promotion Practices :**

The PROF.MG. group secured an average score of 12.57 as against 12.71 of the TRAD.MG. group. These scores expressed as percentages of the maximum possible score read as 45% and 45% respectively. These percentages may be said to represent low performance.

During the survey, it was found that a majority of the financial service organizations depended on their limited contacts to secure business. A few enlightened financial service organizations had more segments to serve.

The next set of groups taken up for discussion is the FBSG group and ABSG group.

5.5   FUND BASED SERVICES GROUP (FBSG) COMPARED WITH FEE BASED/ADVISORY SERVICES GROUP GROUP (ABSG) IN TERMS OF ADOPTION OF MARKETING PRACTICES.

The performance of fund based services group and Fee Based/Advisory Services groups are given in Table V-4. The following comparisons are drawn regarding the two groups.

Table V-4

Comparison of FBSG – ABSG Groups on Different Marketing Practices

	FBSG Group (n = 23)			ABSG Group (n = 29)			X as % of maximum score	
Variable	X	$^\wedge 6$	V	X	$^\wedge 6$	V	RTG	SPG
1	2	3	4	5	6	7	8	9
2 CDP	9.52	5.55	58.29	11.72	5.47	46.66	43.28	53.29
3 PDP	10.61	4.36	41.26	11.62	4.28	36.83	55.84	61.16
4 NPP	9.70	4.59	47.21	9.90	8.13	82.15	30.12	30.93
5 PRP	8.91	4.07	45.63	9.52	4.09	42.92	46.91	50.09
6 PMP	11.74	6.17	52.53	13.31	6.18	46.41	41.93	47.54
Overall Avg.	10.10	-	-	11.21	-	-	43.62	48.60

(a) Regarding the average scores which indicate the performance on the various marketing practices, the following may be stated :

　　i) The ABSG group secured a higher average than the FBSG group on all the marketing variables.

　　ii) The average scores of FBSG group are lower than the average scores of the entire sample on all the marketing practices.

iii) The average scores of the ABSG group are higher than the average scores of the entire sample.

(b) Regarding the variability in the marketing practices of the two groups,

i) In the FBSG group, greater heterogeneity (a maximum variability of 58%) is found in the practice of competitive and demand decisions, and greater homogeneity (a minimum variability of 41%) is found in product/service practices.

ii) In the ABSG group, greater heterogeneity (a maximum variability of 82%) is found in new product/service practices, and greater homogeneity (a minimum variability of 37%) is found in product/service practices.

iii) For both FBSG and ABSG groups minimum variability is found in product/service practices.

(c) Regarding the performance of the two groups FBSG and ABSG – on the marketing practices the following observations are made.

i) **Variable 2 : Competitive and demand practices :**

The mean score of the FBSG group on competitive and demand practices is 9.52, and that of ABSG group is 11.72. These averages expressed as a percentage of maximum possible score read as 43%

and 53% respectively. The performance of the FBSG group in the variable may be said to be low, while that of the ABSG may be considered to be average.

Organizations of the FBSG group, by virtue of they being ABSG group did not have to face severe competition on a day to day basis as the ABSG group. That is to say, that FBSG group had to be on the looks out for customers but once the fund based services provided for a period ranging from one to five years, till the expiry of that period the organization may not face much marketing problems. So probably this was one reasons why performance of the FBSG group in competitive and demand practices are low.

ii)   **Variable 3 : Product Practices :**

The FBSG group secured an average of 10.61 on this variable and ABSG group secured an average of 11.62. These average scores expressed as a percentage of maximum score of the variable read as 56% and 61% respectively. There is not much difference in the performance of these two groups, also, the performance may be considered to be average.

iii)   **Variable 4 : New Product/service Practices :**

The average secured by FBSG group in new product/service practices is 9.70, while that of ABSG group is 9.90. These scores expressed as percentages to maximum score of the variable read as 30 % and 31% respectively. The performance of both these groups are poor and also their level of performance may be considered to be the same. Thus for most of the groups under the different classification have performed rather poorly on new product/service practices. This indicates the lack of orientation of the financial service organizations on this aspect.

iv)   **Variable 5 : Pricing Practices :**

The FBSG group scored an average of 8.91 and ABSG group an average of 9.52. These scores expressed as percentages of the maximum possible score on the variable are 47% and 50%. Thus, it is seen that is not much of a difference in the performance of the two groups on pricing practices.

v)   **Variable 6 : Promotion Practices :**

The mean score of the FBSG on promotion practices is 11.74 and that of ABSG group 13.31. These mean scores expressed as percentages of maximum possible score of the variable are 42% and 48% respectively. The performance of both the groups may be considered to be rather low.

It cannot be said, that FBSG group need not indulge in Promotion practices. In fact, their existence should be made known to all industrial/manufacturing organizations that require the services offered by them. Thus effective and scientific promotion strategies does have a role to play in the marketing of FBSG.

It goes without saying that ABSG would do well to adopt the marketing concept in their promotion decisions.

The last of the groups to be compared here are the private organizations group and the nationalized organizations group.

5.6 PRIVATE ORGANIZATIONS GROUP (POG) COMPARED WITH NATIONALIZED ORGANIZATIONS GROUP (NOG) IN TERMS OF ADOPTION OF MARKETING PRACTICES.

The performance of the POG group in the different marketing practices is given in Table V-4. The following comparisons are drawn from the data given in the table.

(a) Regarding the average scores of the POG and NOG groups on the different marketing variables, the following observations are made:

    (i) Except in marketing practices relating to pricing decisions, the average scores of the POG group are higher than NOG group in all other marketing variables.

    (ii) The average scores of the POG group are higher than the average scores of the entire sample

Table V-5

Comparison of POG – NOG Groups on Different Marketing Practices

	POG Group (n = 11)			NOG Group (n = 41)			X as % of maximum score	
Variable	X	^6	V	X	^6	V	POG	NOG
1	2	3	4	5	6	7	8	9
2 CDP	11.46	6.35	55.40	10.56	5.40	51.17	52.07	48.00
3 PDP	13.27	4.36	32.86	10.61	4.17	39.31	69.86	55.84
4 NPP	10.27	7.85	76.41	9.68	6.51	67.19	32.10	30.26
5 PRP	8.82	4.51	51.18	9.37	3.97	42.36	46.41	49.29
6 PMP	13.64	6.36	46.64	12.34	6.16	49.90	48.70	44.08
Overall Avg.	11.49	-	-	10.51	-	-	49.83	45.49

On all marketing variables except pricing practices.

(iii) The average scores of the NOG group are lower than that of the average scores of the entire sample on all marketing variables except in the practice of pricing decisions in which it is higher.

(b) Regarding the variability in the marketing practices of the two groups:

(i) In the POG group, greater heterogeneity (a maximum variability of 76%) is found in the practice of new product/service practices, and, greater homogeneity (a minimum variability of 33%) is to be found in the practice of product/service practices.

(ii) In the NOG group, greater heterogeneity (a maximum variability of 67%) is found in the practice of new product/service practices, and greater homogeneity (a minimum variability of 39%) is found in the practice of product/service practices.

(iii) Thus for both groups, there exists greater heterogeneity in new product/service practices and greater homogeneity in product/service practices.

(c) Regarding the performance of the two group-POG and NOG- on the different marketing practices, the following observations are made.

i) **Variable2: competitive and demand practices:**

The POG group secured an average of 11.46 and NOG group an average of 10.56. these expressed as percentages on the maximum score of the variable are 52% and 48% respectively. These may be, considered to be average/low performance. The level of performance in competitive and demand practices is not what it should be, The possible cause for such situation could be the lack of awareness among financial service organizations as to the gains that can be reaped by indulging in market oriented practices in competitive and demand decisions.

ii) Variable 3: new product practices:

The mean score of POG group on this variable is 13.27 and that of NOG group is 10.61. These mean scores expressed as percentages of maximum possible scores of the variable are 70% and 56% respectively. The mean score of the POG group may consider being good. This means that in financial services organizations which are POG, adequate care is taken by them to adhere to the marketing concept in their product/service practices. The performance of NOG on product/service practices may be said to be average.

iii) Variable 4: new product practices:

The mean score of the POG group on this variable is 10.27 and that of the NOG group is 9.68. These scores expressed as percentages to maximum score of the variable read as 32% and 30% respectively. The level of performance of both groups is more or less identical and at the same time may be considered to be poor. It is found that financial service organizations are lacking in the adoption of the marketing concept with respect to innovation and introduction of new products.

iv) **Variable 5: pricing practices:**

The mean score of the POG group on pricing practices is 8.82 and that of NOG group is 9.37. These mean scores expressed as percentages of maximum possible score on the variable are 46% and 49% respectively. There is not much difference in the marketing practices of the two group with respect their pricing practices, which may also be considered to be low.

v) **Variable 6: promotion decisions:**

The mean score of the POG group is 13.64 and that of the NOG group is 12.34. These scores expressed as percentages of the maximum possible score of the variable are 48% and 44% respectively. The level of performance of both groups is low.

The above discussion was on the comparison of the various groups in respect of their marketing practices. An attempt is made to bring out the salient features of the comparisons in the following pragraphs.

5.7 CONCLUDING REMARKS IN SECTION I

The performance of the financial service organizations on the different marketing practices is summarized in the following paragraphs.

(i) The performance of the financial service organizations on competitive and demand practices may be said to be average.

The financial service organizations can improve upon their competitive and demand practices by taking into account certain aspects, such as,

- knowledge of the competitors is a MUST,
- the financial services organizations must endeavor to create new customers i.e. searching new market segments.
- they must be able to recognize, who, where and why of their customers.
- Competitive strategies may be used to penetrate substitute's gaps or penetrate directly the competitors position(s),
- Also, they must anticipate the extent of the market, so that they may not have to incur unnecessary cost.

(ii) The performance of the small financial service organizations on product/service practices ranges between average and good. This is the only variable where by and large most of the financial service organizations have better performance (in comparison to other marketing practices). It goes without saying that every financial service organizations must know the strengths and weakness of their product/service and must endeavor to match their product/service with the market.

(iii) The performance of the financial service organizations on new product practices may be said to be poor. A few indicators that may be borne in mind while making product/service choice are:
- absolute market share,
- market concentration,
- trends in market size,
- trends in market share,
- trend in the price of the product,
- competitive trends,
- productivity (sales per employee),
- trend in material cost,

(iv) The performance of the financial service organizations on pricing practices may be said to be low.

Often the so-called best pricing, from the view point of maximizing profit may not be the best selling price for the product/service. Where to fix higher prices or lower prices depends on the pricing criteria, to cite a few examples,
- when a firm goes in for little promotion the product/service may be low priced;
- when coverage is intensive, the product/service may be low priced;
- when turnover is fast, then the product/service may be low priced, and when it is slow it may be high priced;

- when the market is mature, the product/service may be low priced, and when new/declining it may be high priced, etc.

(v) The performance of the small financial service organizations on promotion practices may be considered to be low.

Promotion may be used to stimulate non-users, light users, and increase frequency of usage of services.

Regarding the performance in the different groups the following is stated:

(vi) The RTG group secured an overall average of 53% in marketing practices, while the SPG group secured 34%. the difference in the level of performance is 19%. Therefore, it may be said that the marketing practices of the RTG group are definitely better than those of the SPG group.

(vii) The PROF.MG. group, secured and overall average of 49% in marketing practices and TRAD.MG. group secured an average of 42% the difference between the two means is 7%. Although the mean of PROF.MG. group is higher than that of the TRAD.MG. group, the difference may be considered to be marginal.

(viii) The FBSG group secured an overall average of 44% in marketing practices and ABSG group an average of 49%. The mean of the ABSG group is higher than that of the FBSG group by 5%. The difference in the performance level of both groups may be said be nominal.

(ix) The POG group secured an overall average of 50% in all marketing practices and that of the NOG group is 45%. The difference in the performance level is 5%, and this may be considered to be nominal.

SECTION – II

5.8 INTRODUCTION

Discriminate analysis may be applied in testing whether significant differences exit among the average score profiles of two or more a priori defined groups. In the present study, the two groups in each classification are tested to see if significant differences exist in their various marketing practices. The different predictor variables used in the analysis are the same as those under step-wise regression analysis undertaken in the next chapter. The different predictor variables are the various marketing practices (CDP,PDP,NPP,PRP and PMP). Variable 1, namely growth rate, which is treated as criterion variable under regression analysis, is treated as predictor variable under regression analysis is treated as predictor variable in the present analysis. The first of the groups taken up for discussion are the RTG and SPG groups.

5.9 THE RISK TAKER AND SAFE PLAYER GROUPS DIFFERENTIATED ON VARIOUS MARKETING PRACTICES

The statistical technique and procedure for differentiating two groups has already been described under para 5.1 in section I above. The results of the tests are given in Table v-6, and the following information pertaining to RTG and SPG group is found in the table.

- : the average growth rate of both the groups,
- : the mean scores on each of the marketing practices,
- : the value of t,
- : the value of P, and
- : the significance at the respective confidence level.* (The confidence limits are restricted to .05 and .01 levels only).

The interpreting the data presented in Table v-6, the following observations are made.

(a) Significant variables :

The t value is found to be significant in all the marketing variables, namely,

- competitive and demand practices,
- product/ service practices,
- new product/ service practices,

- pricing practices, and
- promotion practices.

Thus the marketing practices of the RTG and SPG group are different from each other.

Table V-6
Differentiation of the RTG –SPG groups

Variable	Mean Value		T Value	P Value	Significance
	RTG (n =34)	SPG (n =18)			
1 (Growth rate)	13.89	7.99	1.80	.078	Not Significant
Marketing Practices					
2 CDP	12.18	8.06	2.69	.010	Significant P <.01
3 PDP	12.62	8.44	3.72	.001	Significant P <.01
4 NPP	11.44	6.72	2.53	.015	Significant P < .05
5 PRP	10.12	7.61	2.20	.032	Significant P <.05
6 PMP	14.71	8.67	4.54	.001	Significant P <.001

(b) variables –not significant

The only variable whose t has proved to be insignificant is growth rate. The mean value of growth rate for the RTG group is 13.89, while that of the SPG group is 7.99. The difference between the two means is 5.90, yet the 't' result has proved that the two groups do not differ with respect to growth rate. The probable reason why this could be so, is that inspite of having a low performance on the different marketing practices, the financial service organizations of the SPG group are successful in securing and completing the activities of servicing the firm client in hand.

(c) Marketing variables

As all the marketing variables have turned out to be significant, each of them are taken up for discussion at a time and the differences in the practices of the two groups are brought out.

i) **Variable 2: Competitive and demand practices:**

The RTG and SPG groups differ in their competitive and demand practices at .01 level of significance, the difference in the average scores of the two groups is 18% (refer Table v-2, 55% minus 37%), with the RTG group performing better than the SPG group.

A few of the marketing practices which come under the purview of competitive and demand decisions are described with reference to the two groups.

Computing and gathering information on competitors and competitor's strategies is of vital importance to the financial service organizations. If the financial service organizations are operating in the specific market, then they bought to know who else is rendering similar services in the same market. If the financial services organizations is operating in the general market, then it is imperative that they know who they have to contend with. From the survey it was found that,

- : 50% (17) organizations of the RTG group, and,
- : 22% (4) organizations of the SPG group, definitely know who are their competitors.

Information gathered on competitors can relate to several aspects. First, regarding present activities of the competitors, the information is available with,

- : 24% (8) organizations of the RTG group, and,
- : 28% (5) organizations of the SPG group,

Second, information on market share of each of the competitors is gathered by,

- : 35% (12) organizations of the RTG group, and,
- : 22% (4) organizations of the SPG group

Third, information on the promotional activities of the competitors is gathered by,

: 47% (16) organizations of the RTG group, and,
: 22% (4) organizations of the SPG group.

Fourth, information on the quality of the competitor's products/ services is gathered by,

: 79% (27) organizations of the RTG group, and
: 56% (10) organizations of the SPG group.

Certain clarifications need to be made here, regarding the figures stated above. The percentages of the RTG and SPG group, on, 'who know their competitors' may not tally with other percentages regarding 'information on competitors' this is because under 'knowing their competitors' only those organizations who had a complete list of their competitors were included. Other organizations, who had information on one or a few of their competitors were not included in these figures. This accounts for the higher percentages (in some cases) while discussing 'information on competitors'.

At this stage one may question that if the financial service organizations have no much knowledge about his competitors, then why should they have any problem? The reason for this may be found in the erratic/unscientific/improper way of collecting this information. Or, the financial service organizations may not be able to use this information effectively to their advantage.

Two other aspects described here pertain to estimation of demand. It is necessary for the financial service organizations to estimate total demand and their market share, so that their services can be streamlined such that they do not have to face low growth rate, From the survey, it was found that,

- 76% (26) organizations of RTG group, and
- 44% (8) organizations of SPG group, try to

estimate the total demand for the product(s)/services they render. Also, approximation of their market share was undertaken by,

- 56% (19) organizations of RTG group, and
- 28% (5) organizations of SPG group.

The clarifications offered on the gathering the information on competitors, in the aforegoing paragraphs is valid here also.

ii) **Variable 3 : Product/ service Practices**

The RTG and SPG groups differ in their product/ service practices at .01 level of significance. The difference in the mean scores of the two groups is 22% (Table V-2), with the RTG group performing better than SPG group.

Practices relating to product/service decisions are described below. The first aspect taken up is, the 'stages of the product – lifecycle'. The concept of the product – lifecycle is important to the financial service organizations because they have to be ready with the either product/service alternations or new product/services so that the same may be introduced when their product/service reaches the decline stage in the cycle. The problem arises because many small financial service organizations do no accept all four stages of the product/service, namely, introduction, growth, maturity and decline. From the survey, it was found that, only,

- 62% (21) organizations of RTG groups, and,
- 33% (6) organizations of SPG group accept all the 4 stages in the product life cycle.

A certain amount of business analysis is a must for every firm. In the present survey, it was found that,

- 71% (24) organizations of RTG group, and,
- 61% (11) organizations of SPG group,

calculate the 'sales'(growth rate) generated by each and every product/service they render at the end of each year. It was also found that,

- 68% (23) organizations of RTG group, and,
- 56% (10) organizations of SPG group,

calculate the 'profit' generated by each product/service at the end of each accounting year.

iii) Variable 4 : New product/service practices

The RTG and SPG groups differ in their new product/service practices at .05 level of significance. The difference in the mean scores of the two groups is 17% (Table V-2) with the RTG group performing better than the SPG group. But it may be recalled here, that the performance of RTG group was considered to be poor (section – I). Although during the survey, organizations of both groups have indicated indulging in certain practices regarding new product/service decisions, yet, their overall performance on the variable has been poor.

A financial service organization needs to be prepared with new product/service(s), in the event of any of the existing product/service(s) not doing well for any reason whatsoever. Regarding the preparedness of the financial service organizations, it was found that

- 74% (25) organizations belonging to RTG group, and,
- 44% (8) organizations belonging to the SPG group had expressed they had alternate plans for adding / deleting a product/service, if such an eventually should arise.

The financial service organizations that had approached formal research organizations or scientists to secure new product/service are to be extent of

- 21% (7) in the RTG group, and,
- 6% (1) in the SPG group.

Financial service organizations that carry out in house some type of research activity are to the extent of,
- 32% (11) in the RTG group, and
- 39% (7) in the SPG group.

It needs to be noted here that, research activity in the financial service organizations is not along the lines found in large companies.

Once the product/services are developed, an important decision that needs to be taken is the pricing of the product/service.

iv) Variable 5 : Pricing practices

The RTG and SPG group differing in their pricing practices at, .05 level of significance. The difference in the mean scores of the two groups is 13% (Table V-2), with RTG group performing better than SPG group.

In the survey two types of costing were included. It was found that the organizations that priced their product/services on the basis of marginal costing were,
- 18% (6) from the RTG group, and
- 17% (3) from the SPG group.

Organizations who utilized the full cost method of pricing were,
- 76% (26) from the RTG group, and
- 67% (12) from the SPG group.

From the above figures it is evident that a greater percentage of financial services organizations preferred the method of full costing to marginal costing, while fixing the prices on their new product/services.

Most financial service organizations consider that recovery of costs and making a profit is of prime importance, which need to be taken care of, while fixing price for their product/services. Two other aspects which are of equal importance in price fixation are 'demand intensity' and 'consumer philosophy'. The result of the survey indicate that,
- 56% (19) organizations of the RTG group, and,
- 50% (9) organizations of the SPG group do take into consideration the demand intensity of the product/service during price fixation. The survey also brings out that,
- 47% (16) organizations of the RTG group, and,
- 56% (10) organizations of the SPG group take consumer philosophy into consideration during price fixation.

Often an organization is unable to fix the price it desires due to many factors that cause restraint. A few of these were taken up in the survey, and the results of the same are as follows. Competitors and

their strategies can be an important constraint in price fixation. Of the organizations who agree to the same,
- 71% (24) belong to RTG group, and
- 61% (11) belong to the SPG group.

It was found that,
- 59% (20) organizations of the RTG group, and
- 72% (13) organizations of the SPG gorup felt that

a considerable amount of constraints in price fixation was caused by suppliers of needed inputs.

Government regulations may in some cases protect the consumers and as such are a constraint in the price fixation. Financial service organizations that experience this constraints were :
- 53% (18) form the RTG group, and,
- 50% (9) from the SPG group.

The concept of 'break-even' has many utilities, such as determining the probable unit cost at varying levels of production; comparing the probable operating profits of different organizations a various levels of operation; it helps in comparing net sales, expenses and operating profits with a budget; it measures the effect of varying levels of sales secured at various levels of selling and manufacturing cost, etc. Of the financial service organizations that are aware of the concept of break-even.

- 79% (27) belongs to the RTG group, and,
- 61% (11) belongs to the SPG group.

v) **Variable 6 : Promotion practices :**

The RTG group and SPG groups differ in their promotion practices at .001 level of significance. The difference in the mean scores of the two groups is 22% (Table v-2) with the RTG group performing better than the SPG group. The level of significance indicates that the two groups differ absolutely and widely in their marketing practices relating to promotion decisions.

This result could rightly be so, because the RTG group has to appeal to the different market segments, while the target market for the SPG group could be confined to certain targets only. Organizations of the RTG group have to concentrate on various market segments. But for the SPG group, the task is more simplified. If the SPG organizations are operating in the specific market, then their target customers could be of one particular segment only.

Regarding promotion strategies, the importance of communication is to be discussed. Communications perform many functions, such as giving information on product/service existence, descriptions of the product features, boosting confidence level of the different market segments, establishing of firm's / brand image, communicating satisfying offers of buyers etc. only a few financial service organizations accept all these functions are performed by communication. Of these,

- 35% (12) belongs to the RTG group, and
- 11% (2) belong to the SPG group.

The communication mix is inclusive of advertising, personal selling, sales promotion and publicity. From the survey, it was found that,

- 35% (12) organizations of RTG gorup, and ,
- Nil % (0) of the SPG group are aware that,

These four aspects together represent communication.

Having dealt with the differences in the marketing practices of the RTG and SPG groups, the discussion moves on professionally and traditionally managed groups.

5.10 THE PROFESSIONALLY MANAGED AND TRADITIONALLY MANAGED GROUPS DIFFERENTIATED ON VARIOUS MARKETING PRACTICES

The relevant data pertaining, to the PROF.MG. and TRAD.MG. groups can be found in the Table V-7 in interpreting the data presented in the Table the following observations are made.

a) **Significant Variables:**

i) The first variable namely, growth rate is found to be significant at .05 level of confidence. The mean growth rate of PROF.MG. group is 14.27 and that of TRAD.MG. group is 6.86. Thus the growth rate of the PROF.MG. group are higher than that of TRAD.MG. group.

Table V-7
Differentiation of PROF.MG. – TRAD.MG. groups

Variable	Mean Value PROF.MG. (n =35)	Mean Value TRAD.MG. (n =17)	T Value	P Value	Significance
1 (Growth rate)	14.27	6.86	2.43	.019	Significant $P < .05$
Marketing Practices					
2 CDP	11.97	8.24	2.37	.022	Significant $P < .05$
3 PDP	11.51	10.47	0.82	.418	Not Significant
4 NPP	9.78	9.88	0.06	.956	Not Significant
5 PRP	9.97	7.77	1.89	.065	Not Significant
6 PMP	12.57	12.71	0.07	.942	Not Significant

This means to say that the two groups significantly differ with respect to growth rate, with the PROF.MG. group performing much better than the TRAD.MG. group.

    ii)   The only marketing variable whose t value is found to be significant relates to marketing practices in the sphere of competitive and demands decisions.

b)   Variables – not significant :

Four marketing variables are not found to be significant. The first relates to product/service practices. The PROF.MG. group secured a higher average than the TRAD.MG. group by 6% (Table V-3). Yet, since the t value is insignificant the performance level of both groups with respect to product/service practices may be considered to be the same.

The second marketing variable whose t value is found insignificant relates to new product/service practices. Here it is found that both groups secure an average of 31% (Table V-3) which may also be considered to be poor.

The third marketing variable whose t value is found to be insignificant relates to pricing practices here the average of the PROF.MG. group is higher than that of the TRAD.MG. group by 11% (Table – V-3), yet the level of performance in pricing practices for both groups may be considered to be the same.

The fourth marketing variable whose t value is found to be insignificant relates to promotion practices. Also, the mean scores expressed as percentage read as 45% for both groups (Table V-3)

c) **Marketing Variables :**

As indicated earlier, the only marketing practices that differentiate the two groups refer to competitive and demand practices. The t value is found to be significant at .05 level of confidence also the mean of the PROF.MG. group is higher than that of the TRAD.MG. group by 17% (Table V-3). A few of the aspects on competitive and demand practices are taken up for discussion and are related to the professionally and traditionally managed groups.

Every organization ought to know its target market. That the target market comprises actual and potential users is known only to

- 43% (15) organizations of the PROF.MG. group, and,
- 18% (3) organizations of the TRAD.MG. group.

Competition has become an important influence that the financial service organizations need to contend with. Thus every financial service organizations needs to gather information on its competitors

and their strategies. The information gathered under competitors is discussed under four aspects. Form the survey, it is found that,
- 29% (10) belong to the PROF.MG. group, and,
- 18% (3) belong to the TRAD.MG. group gather information on the 'present production/service' of their competitors. Apart from this the financial service organizations need to ascertain the market share of each of their competitors. This is done by
- 37% (13) organizations belong to the PROF.MG. group, and
- 18% (3) organizations belong to the TRAD.MG. group.

Further financial service organizations have to find out the promotional activities of their competitors, so as to out-maneuver them. Information relating to promotional activities of the competitors is generated by,
- 46% (16) organizations belong to the PROF.MG. group, and,
- 24% (4) organizations belong to the TRAD.MG. group.

Yet another aspect of importance pertains to the quality of the product/services rendered by the competitors, so that an organization may judge the weakness or strength of its own product/services. It is found that,
- 74% (26) organizations of the PROF.MG. group, and,
- 65% (11) organizations of the TRAD.MG. group.

Took note of the quality of the product/service rendered by their competitors.

Weather organization operates in the local market of outside it, it should have an idea of the total demand for similar product/services in the particular market. This exercise was undertaken by,
- 71% (25) organizations belonging to the PROF.MG. group, and
- 59% (10) organizations belonging to the TRAD.MG. group.

After estimating the total demand, it is necessary for the organization to find out how much of this forms its share. From the survey, it is found that,
- 57% (20) organizations of the PROF.MG. group, and,
- 24% (4) organizations of the TRAD.MG. group.

Try to estimate their market share.

Although the PROF.MG. and TRAD.MG. groups differ significantly with respect to on marketing variable only, i.e., competitive and demand practices, yet they seem to differ significantly with respect to growth rate. Therefore, an attempt is made to ascertain the growth performance in both of these groups.

Table V-8 describes the growth rate in both the PROF.MG. & TRAD.MG. groups.

Table V-8 :
Growth Rate in Professionally and Traditionally Managed Groups.

	PROF.MG. group (n=35)		TRAD.MG. group (n=17)	
Growth Rate (%)	Frequency	%	Frequency	%
0-5	9	25.71	10	58.82
5-10	11	31.43	3	17.65
10-15	5	14.29	3	17.65
15-20	4	11.43	1	2.86
20-25	1	2.86	-	-
25-30	3	8.57	-	-
-	-	-	-	-
50 and above	2	5.71	-	-
	35	100.00	17	100.00

The above table clearly brings out that the performance of PROF.MG. group is better – only 26% of their organizations have growth rate below 5% whereas 59% of organizations belonging to TRAD.MG. group have sales below 5%.

5.11 FUND BASED SERVICES GROUP AND FEE BASED/ADVISORY SERVICES GROUP DIFFERENTIATED ON VARIOUS MARKETING PRACTICES

The relevant data petering to the FBSG and ABSG groups can be found in Table V-9. In interpreting the data presented in the table, the following observations are made.

(i) The mean value of growth rate in ABSG group is higher than that of FBSG group, but since the t value is not found to be significant, this difference in mean values is not taken into consideration. Therefore, it may be said, that there is no difference in the growth rate of both groups.

(ii) As regards marketing variables, from the Table, it is found that the average scores of the ABSG group are higher than those of the FBSG group, yet not a single t is found to be significant. This means to say that, there is no difference in the level of practices of the two groups as regards the various marketing decisions.

The performance of the two groups on the different marketing practices and allied aspects have already been dealt with under section I, hence the same is not repeated here.

Table V-9
Differentiation of FBSG – ABSG groups

Variable	Mean Value		t Value	P Value	Significance
	FBSG (n=35)	ABSG (n=17)			
Growth Rate	8.38	14.60	1.60	.117	Not significant
Marketing Practices					
2 CDP	9.52	11.72	1.43	.158	Not significant
3 PDP	10.61	11.62	0.84	.406	Not significant
4 NPP	9.70	9.90	0.11	.911	Not significant
5 PRP	8.91	9.52	0.53	.598	Not significant
6 PMP	11.74	13.31	0.91	.366	Not significant

5.12 PRIVATE ORGANIZATIONS AND NATIONALIZED ORGANIZATIONS GROUPS DIFFERENTIATE ON VARIOUS MARKETING PRACTICES

The last classification taken up for analysis here is on capital intensity. An attempt is made to differentiate the POG and NOG groups in terms of marketing practices. The relevant data are presented in Table V-10. In interpreting the data presented in the table, the following observations are made.

i) The mean value of growth rate for the POG group is more than twice that of the NOG group, but since the value of t is not significant, the level of growth rate for both groups may be considered to be the same.

ii) In pricing practices, the NOG group has secured a higher average than the POG group. But in all other marketing practices the mean scores of the POG group are higher than those of the NOG group. Yet, since the t value is not significant on all the five marketing variables, these two groups cannot be differentiated on the basis of their marketing practices.

Table V-10

Differentiation of POG – NOG groups

Variable	Mean Value		t Value	P Value	Significance
	POG (n=11)	NOG (n=41)			
Growth Rate	21.27	9.32	1.46	.175	Not significance
Marketing Practices					
2 CDP	11.46	10.56	0.47	.641	Not significant
3 PDP	13.27	10.61	1.86	.068	Not significant
4 NPP	10.27	9.68	0.26	.799	Not significant
5 PRP	8.82	9.37	0.40	.694	Not significant
6 PMP	13.64	12.34	0.62	.541	Not significant

5.13 CONCLUDING REMARKS

The entire discussions in section I and section II of this chapter is concluded here.

i) The maximum adoption of the marketing concept is found in product/service practices. This is followed by competitive and demands practices. In respect of other practices, the adoption of the marketing concept has been either low or poor.

ii) The RTG was on the top in so far as the adoption of the marketing concept was concerned. All other groups were either low or poor in this respect.

iii) Of the four classification in this study the groups in each of the two classifications, namely, FBSG – ABSG and POG-NOG, do not differ in terms of adoption of the marketing concept in marketing practices.

In the marketing remaining two classifications, it is found that differences are significant in respect of adoption of the marketing concept in marketing practices. The RTG-SPG groups may be differentiated in the practice of competitive and demand decisions, product/service decisions, new product/service decisions, pricing decisions and promotion decisions. The PROF.MG.-TRAD.MG. group may be differentiated on the basis of their growth rate, and competitive and demand practices.

iv) The exercise on differentiation of groups has brought to the light two aspects that are or importance to financial services organizations namely,

- Risk Takers Organization, & Safe Players Organizations.
- Professionally & Traditionally Managed Organizations.

Regarding the first, risk takers is found conductive to better adoption of the marketing concept in marketing decisions. The second aspect indicates that professionally managed organization is preferable, as it is conductive to higher growth rate.

In the next chapter, the technique of step-wise regression is used to ascertain the association between growth rate and marketing practices.

CHAPTER VI

ANALYSIS AND INTERPRETATION OF DATA: ASSOCIATION BETWEEN GROWTH RATES AND MARKETING PRACTICES

CHAPTER VI

ANALYSIS AND INTERPRETATION OF DATA: ASSOCIATION BETWEEN GROWTH RATES AND MARKETING PRACTICES

6.1 INTRODUCTION

In the present chapter that analysis and interpretation of data are undertaken with the help of regression technique. An attempt is made to explain the variance of growth rate in relation to the marketing practices. That is, measure the overall strength of association between growth rate and the full set of marketing practices. As the analysis of regression is undertaken stepwise, the contribution of each of the marketing variables to total explained variation in growth rate is described.

The approach used here is, to first of all ascertain the presence of relationship between the criterion (growth rate) and predictor variables (marketing practices), and then proceed towards prediction. The former is established by correlation and the latter by regression.

Before going on to describe and interpret the data, the symbols indicating the different variables need to be clarified to avoid any confusion. In the present chapter, the following are used:

Y : Criterion variable: Variable 1: Growth rate.

X_1 : independent variable: Variable 2: marketing concept adoption in competitive and demand practices (CDP)

X_2 : independent variable: Variable 3: marketing concept adoption in product/service practices (PDP).

X_3 : independent variable: Variable 4: marketing concept adoption in new product/service practices (NPP).

X_4 : independent variable: Variable 5: marketing concept adoption in pricing practices (PRP).

X_5 : independent variable: Variable 6: marketing concept adoption in promotion practices (PMP)

a : Constant (intercept)

b_1 : regression co-efficient or beta weight for the first predictor variable X_1

b_5 : regression co-efficient or beta weight for the fifth predictor variable X_5.

The alpha reading in the regression equation is merely a constant, which determines the general level of the line. The b co-efficient gives the slope of the regression line and denotes a ratio. It tells how many units Y increases with every increase of one unit in X. It needs to be note here that the value of multiple R has been examined for its significance. This is done with the help of F-ratio test.

While interpreting the results, the levels of confidence arbitrarily fixed by the investigator are .01 and .05 levels of significance, and all the results are adjusted to the relevant degrees of freedom.

The analysis and interpretation of data is described in two sections. In the first section the regression technique is applied to the data pertaining to the entire sample and the significant predictor variables are drawn out. In the present study marketing variables CDP and PMP have been found to be significant and contributing to explaining the variation in growth rate. Therefore in the next section i.e. section two, each of the groups is taken up for analysis at a time and regression technique applied, to find out, to what extent these variables, i.e. CDP and PMP, contribute in explaining the variation in growth rate.

SECTION – I

6.2 STEPWISE REGRESSION APPLIED ON ENTIRE SAMPLE

(a) Correlation of all variables

As a first step correlation between all the 6 variables are worked out. (refer Table –VI-1).

Table VI-1
Correlation Matrix of all the six variables (n=52)

	Var.1	Var.2	Var.3	Var.4	Var.5
Var.2	.531*				
Var.3	.385*	.560*			
Var.4	.236*	.341**	.555*		
Var.5	.301*	.348**	.342**	.175*	
Var.6	.420*	.507*	.554*	.466*	.472*

* Significant at .01 level.
** Significant at .05 level.

Correlation expresses the degree of relationship or association between two variables. Sacncheti and Kapoor have provided the student with broad categories for interpreting the results of correlation, the details of which are to be found in Table VI-2.

Table VI-2
Interpretation of correlation results

	Direction	
Degree	Positive	Negative
Perfect	+1	-1
Very High	+.75 to +1	-75 to -1
High	+.50 to +.75	-.50 to -.75
Low	+.25 to +.50	-.25 to -.50
Very Low	0 to +.25	0 to -.25
Absent	0	0

Of the many categories described in Table VI-2, for the purpose of the present study, the category, which indicates a high degree of correlation, is chosen. Accordingly in Table VI-1, there are five readings which lie between +.50 to +.75. These correlations are:

Growth rates is correlated highly with marketing concept adoption in competitive and demand practices only. The correlation of .531 indicates that the growth rate increases as the organization goes in for greater scientific decisions in competitive and demand practices.

Two variables are highly correlated with competitive and demand practices, they are product/service practices (.560), and, promotion practices (.507). But, the relationship between CDP and PMP is less (marginally) than the relationship between CDP and PDP.

The marketing practices related to product/service decisions are highly associated with new product/service practices and promotion practices, the strength of the former relationship is .555, while that of the latter is .554. From these figures one may say, that, the relationship of PDP with NPP is more or less the same as that of PDP and PMP.

(b) Regression of Variable : 1 (Growth rate) on Variable : 2 (CDP)

The first predictor variable turns out to be variable 2, namely, marketing concept adoption in competitive and demand practices. The result of the regression are give in Table VI-3.

Table VI-3
Contribution of predictor variable 2 (CDP)

Variable	Multiple (R)	F Value	Significance
CDP (X_1)	.531	19.58	$P<.01$

Regression of variable 1 (growth rate) on variable 2 (CDP) yields a multiple R of .531. In order to find out the significance of multiple R the F – ratio test is applied and the value of F is found to be 19.58 which is significant at .01

level. The result may be interpreted by squaring multiple R and then expressing it as a percentage.

$$\text{i.e. Multiple R} = .531$$
$$R^2 = .282$$
$$R^2 \times 100 = 28.2\%$$

Thus, it may be stated that 28.2% of variation in variable 1 (growth rate) is explained by predictor Variable 2, namely, marketing concept adoption in competitive and demand practices.

The alpha reading and the beta weight are required to express the result in the form of a regression equation. The relevant details for regression line of Y on X is found in Table VI-4.

Table VI-4

Regression of Variable 1 (Growth rate) on Variable 2 (CDP)

Variable	Multiple (R)	Alpha Value	Beta Value
CDP (X_1)	0.531	-2.918	1.356

Hence the regression line of Y on X may be written as,

$$Y = a + b_1 X_1$$

Substituting,

$$Y = -2.918 + 1.356 \times X_1 \ldots \ldots (1)$$

(c) Regression of Variable 1 (Growth rate) on variable 2 (CDP) and 6 PMP

Regression analysis is continued and the next variable found significant is stepwise regression is PMP. This means to say that, after CDP, it is PMP that contributes most towards the explanation of variation in growth rate. (Refer Table VI-5).

Table VI-5
Contribution of Variables 2 (CDP) and 6 (PMP)

Variable	Multiple (R)	F Value	Significance
CDP and PMP (X_1 and X_5)	.546	11.12	P<.01

From the above Table, it is found that Multiple R reads as .546, and the F test proves it to be significant at .01 level. As the square of multiple R is .298, it may be stated that 29.8% of variation in criterion variable 1 (growth rate) is explained by predictor variables CDP and PMP.

By adding variable PMP the contribution has moved from 28.2 to 29.8%. That is, an addition of 1.6% made by variable PMP.

The regression line incorporating both of these variables (i.e. CDP and PMP) may be written after ascertaining the alpha and beta values which are given in Table VI-6.

Table VI-6
Regression of Variable 1 (Growth rate) on Variable 2 and 6 (CDP and PMP)

Variable	Beta Value	Alpha Value	Multiple (R)
CDP (X_1)	1.092		
		-6.004	.546
PMP (X_5)	0.469		

Thus, the regression of Y on X is written as :

$$Y = a + b_1 X_1 + b_5 X_5$$

Substituting,

$$Y = -6.004 + 1.092 X_1 + 0.469 X_5 \quad .....(2)$$

(d) Regression of Variable 1 (Growth rate) on Variable 5, 3 & 4 (PRP, PDP & NPP)

The next variable that came up in the stepwise regression is marketing concept adoption in pricing practices. The multiple R after adding Variable PRP reads as .562 and when adjusted to the relevant degrees of freedom reads as .537. The adjusted multiple R of .537 (after adding variable PRP) is noted to be lower than the multiple R of .546 contributed by inclusion of variables CDP and PMP (put together). Thus, it may be concluded, that, inclusion of predictor variable PRP does not contribute towards explaining the variation in criterion variable growth rate. Likewise, it is found that other predictor marketing variables PDP and NPP did not contribute towards explaining the criterion variable growth rate. As additional predictor variables are added R^2 cannot decrease but usually diminishing returns set in, so that, in most applications it is rare to find much increase in R^2 beyond the first several predictor variables. (In this case only two variables). The regression equation therefore ends with the addition of variable 6 (PMP).

(e) Interpretation of Regression results for the entire sample

The purpose of regression equation is to make prediction on a new sample of observations from the findings on a previous sample of observations. Therefore from the regression equation (2) one may say that for every unit increase in marketing practices relating to competitive and demand decision growth rate go up by 1.1 units and for every unit increase in promotion practices, growth rate goes up by half a unit (.5). The multiple R of .540

indicates that 29.8% variation in growth rate can be explained by competitive and demand practices and promotion practices.

It will be of relevance to discuss at this juncture, as to what are the different aspects that are covered under variable CDP and PMP that make it so significant.

6.3 DISCUSSION ON VARIABLE TWO (CDP)

As variable 2, marketing concept adoption in competitive and demand practices, is found to be a significant contributive factor to growth rates, a discussion on the several aspects involved in this variable is enter herein. The salient results of field survey pertaining to CDP will be discussed here.

A distinguishing characteristic of the financial service organization, is their responsibility for interpreting conditions in the marketplace. Critical to the success of most marketing program is a careful analysis of demand. There are two broad classes of services that have distinct demand characteristics – firstly, consumer finance and secondly, industrial finance. Consumer finances are rendered to households or individuals, while industrial finances are given to business firms. Industrial finance includes term loan, cash credit etc. Their demand is influenced significantly by factors such as economic outlook, technological changes etc.

It is found that 8 (15.4%) of the 52 units are involved in the services of consumer finance, while 44 (84.6%) units are involved in the services of industrial finance.

There are two basic problems faced by servicing firms in analyzing demand. Firstly, identifying and locating the buyer or market and secondly the services they will be required.

From the survey it is found that not all the financial service organizations know their target market. The revelations are as under, (Table VI-7).

Table VI-7

Identification of the target market

Particulars	Consumer finance group (n = 8)	Industrial finance group (n = 44)
Target market identified	3 (37.5%)	15 (34.1%)

Figures in parenthesis indicate percentages to group totals.

The classification used in describing the various results of the field survey here are the two main groups – consumer finance group & industrial finance group.

From a sample of 8 involved in the consumer finance group only 3, i.e. 38% have been able to identify their target market. Among the industrial finance only 15 (34%) organizations have been able to identify their target market.

The next aspect that is being discussed is market demand. The survey tried to ascertain as to how many organizations indulge in the practices of estimating and forecasting total market demand. The relevant details are shown in Table VI-8.

Table VI-8

Estimate and forecast of total market demand and market share.

Particulars	Consumer finance group (n = 8)	Industrial finance group (n = 44)
1. Practice regarding estimate and forecast of total market demand	4 (50%)	18 (40.9%)
2. Practice regarding estimate and forecast of total market share	2 (25%)	11 (25%)

Figures in parenthesis indicate percentage to group totals.

It is found that 50% of financial service organizations of consumer finance group and 41% of organizations of industrial finance group follow the marketing practice of estimation of the present market demand and forecast the probable total market demand three years hence. It must be noted that, it is not possible to make generalizations on this practice, as each product/service is highly individualistic when it comes to demand analysis.

Often a firm's sales does not reveal how well the company is doing relative to its competitors, as, increase in a firm's sales could be due to economic conditions or improved performance in sales itself. For this reason the organization needs to keep track of its market share. If the firm's market share goes up, the firm is gaining on its competitors, if it goes down, the firm is losing relative to its competitors. The extent of this practice among the organizations is given in Table VI-8.

From Table VI-8 it is found that the percentage of financial service organizations who practice estimation and forecast of market share in both consumer finance group and industrial finance group is identical, that is, 25%.

There are yet two additional forces that are of concern to the management in the matter of problems associated with demand analysis. They are, firstly, the interpretation of individual buyer behavior, and, secondly, the assessment of competitive behavior. A few aspects of the letter have been included in the present survey.

A firm's marketing system is surrounded and affected by a host of competitors. These competitors have to be identified, monitored and outmaneuvered to gain and maintain consumer loyalty. The aspects included in the questionnaire are : the financial services organization has to keep track of the

- present production/services of competitors,
- Market share of each competitor,
- Promotional activities undertaken by each of the competitors,
- The quality of the product/service maintained by each competitor.

Table VI-9 indicates to what extent the financial service organizations are really competitive.

Table VI-9

Information on Competitors

Particulars	Consumer finance group (n = 8)	Industrial finance group (n = 44)
Information Compiled on Competitors	4 (50%)	5 (11.36%)

Figure in parenthesis indicates percentage to group totals.

The financial service organizations involved in the consumer finance group seem to be more aware of the importance of compiling information on competitors since nearly 50% follow this marketing practice as against only 11% in the industrial finance group.

The above are some of the major aspects dealt with in study, under the variable, marketing concept adoption in competitive and demand practices (variable 2).

The discussion that follows relates the marketing concept adoption in promotion practices (variable 6).

6.4 DISCUSSION ON VARIABLE : 6 (PMP)

Promotion stands for the various activities the firm undertakes to communicate its product/service's merits and to persuade target customers to buy them, i.e. it encompasses all forms of communication that a firm uses in promoting its product/service. The primary function of promotion is to move buyers along a continuum of product/service knowledge to product/service purchase.

From the present survey a few of the result are discussed here. The first aspect covered in the discussion is the importance of communications. In the financial service organizations the capability to spend on the 'promotion' tool is limited but all the same it is very important for the financial services organizations to realize the need for communication, so that they may use their limited resources in the best possible promotion strategies. Communication performs the function of –

- giving information about the existence of the product/service,

- describing product/service features and how these would benefit the buyers,
- gaining confidence of the different market segments,
- establishing a reputation for the firm regarding its trust-worthiness and progressiveness,
- building confidence in its customers, etc.

The results of the survey indicate, as to how many of the financial service organizations, realize the purpose served by communication (refer Table VI-10). Promotion is an essential tool in realizing better sales, which eventually lead to the goal of higher profits.

Why does a firm need to communicate with its target market? This is understood by only 13% of consumer finance group and 30% of industrial finance goods.

Table VI-10
Promotional Aspects

Particulars	Consumer finance group (n = 8)	Industrial finance group (n = 44)
1. Need for communication	1 (12.5%)	13 (29.5%)
2. Recognition of the Utility of advertising	1 (12.5%)	5 (11.4%)
3. Evaluated the response on promotion expenditure	4 (50%)	29 (65.9%)

Figures in parenthesis indicate percentages to group totals.

There is a lot of misconception among the organizations and often the word communication denotes 'advertising' and advertising stands for communication through the print media only (i.e. news papers and magazines). Thus the financial service organizations are unable to deploy their resources in the appropriate strategies.

Advertising in one of the elements of the communication mix and it serves many purposes such as building up a brand image, creating an image for the firm, apart, from other aspects such as, giving information about the product/service and its features. The utility of this tool is recognized by only a small section of the financial service organizations. Table VI-10 tells us as to what is the position in financial service organizations.

The table reveals that only 13% of CFG of and 11% of IFG are capable of appreciating the utility of the promotion tool – advertising.

The aim of communication is to move the buyer along the continuum of product/service knowledge to product/service purchase. Yet in this study each response in the continuum is treated separately, to find out if there are any specific problem areas. The results are tabulated in Table VI-11.

Table VI-11
Response sought through communication

Response sought	Consumer finance group (n = 8)	Industrial finance group (n = 44)
Exposure	6 (75%)	15 (34.1%)
Attention	5 (62.5%)	27 (61.4%)
Comprehension	5 (62.5%)	15 (34.1%)
Favorable Attitude	5 (62.5%)	26 (59.1%)
Weaken doubts of customers	3 (37.5%)	21 (47.7%)

Figures in parenthesis indicate percentage to group total.

It is found that wide disparity in responses sought exists between the two groups in the two stages, namely, 'exposure' and 'attention'.

(a) The organizations (75%) of consumer finance group are looking for more exposure for their product/service while it is not the case among industrial finance group (34%).

(b) A greater percentage (63%) of consumer finance group were bothered about explaining their product/service and have the buyers comprehend their product/service, while the percentage among the industrial finance group is only 34%.

Evaluation of any strategy is essential in order to obtain a feed back on the effectiveness of the same. Thus, it is desirable that organizations evaluate the response got by way of increased sales (or otherwise) on their promotion expenditure. As to how many the financial services organizations follow this marketing practice is given in Table VI-10.

It is revelation worthy of future investigation, as it is found that nearly 64% (i.e. 33/52x 100) organizations have reported that carry out an exercise to find out the effect of promotion expenditure got by way of increased growth rate. From the industrial finance group as much as 66% take the trouble to find out the extra sales they made by spending on a particular promotion strategy as against 50% among consumer finance group.

Nevertheless during personal interviews the investigator found that financial services organizations do find an effective way of spending their promotion budgets (example, like advertising in industrial directories, industrial manuals and periodicals etc.) The discussion moves to significance of the very same contributive prediction variable 2 and 6 among the different groups of classification.

SECTION – II

6.5 REGRESSION ANALYSIS – CONTRIBUTION OF SIGNIFICANT VARIABLES 2 AND 4 IN THE DIFFERENT GROUPS OF CLASSIFICATION.

(a) Introduction

Compare and contrast tend to bring out better results and for the purpose of the same the sample is divided into different groups on the basis of 4 types of classification. These have already been discussed in the chapter on methodology but for the present the groups are repeated to facilitate recall –

- risk taker group
- safe player group
- professionally managed group
- traditionally managed group
- fund based services group
- Fee Based/Advisory Services" group,
- private organizations group
- nationalized organizations group.

In the preceding sub-section 6.2 (c) it is found that the most contributive marketing variable in explaining the variation in growth rate are variable CDP and PMP. It is the endeavor or the investigator to find out if these two variables have the same significance when applied to the different groups. In other words, the contribution of variables 2 (CDP) and 6 (PMP) to each group of classification is being examined.

The discussion will follow the patterns of first giving sample correlation between the criterion variable and predictor variables in the respective group and then describing the extent to which predictor variables 2 and 6 (together) contribute to criterion variables Growth rate.

(b) Risk Taker Group (RTG)

The simple correlation between growth rates (var. 1) and marketing practices (variable 2, 3, 4, 5 and 6) are presented in Table VI-12.

Table VI-12

Simple Correlation in the Risk Taker Group (n = 34)

Variable	Correlation	Significance
1 x 2	.5251	$P < .01$
1 x 3	.3735	$P < .05$
1 x 4	.2174	Not Significant
1 x 5	.2702	Not Significant
1 x 6	.4089	$P < .01$

Looking at the above table and referring to Table VI-12 in the interpretation of correlation results, it may be said that a high positive correlation of .2551 exists between growth rate (variable 1) and marketing concept adopting in competitive and demand practices. For the results in regression, Table VI-13 may be referred.

The multiple R of .510 brought out by the regression analysis is found to be significant at .01 level. Thus, the variation in growth rate is explained to the extent of 26% (R^2 x 100) by Table VI-13.

Table VI-13
Regression of Variable 1 on Variable 2 and 6 in the Risk taker group.

Variable	Beta Value	Alpha Value	Multiple R	F Value	P Value
PMP (X_5)	.511				
		-9.993	.510	6.792	.004
CDP (X_1)	1.345				

Marketing concept adoption in competitive and demand practices and promotion practices.

The regression line of Y on X for the risk taker group is written as

$$Y = a + b_1 x_1 + b_5 x_5$$

Substituting,

$$Y = -9.993 + 1.345 x_1 + .511 x_5 \quad \ldots(3)$$

The beta co-efficient of CDP and PMP taken from regression equation 3 brings out the following with respect to RTG group. Thus it may be said that for every unit increase in CDP, growth rate increases by 1.3 units and for every unit increase in PMP, growth rate increases by half a unit.

(c) **Safe player group (SPG)**

An attempt at simple correlation between growth rate and marketing practices is made to see if any relationship exists between the two (refer Table VI-14)

Table VI-14

Simple Correlation in the Safe player group (SPG)

Variable	Correlation	Significance
1 x 2	.5302	P < .05
1 x 3	.2413	Not Significant
1 x 4	- .0523	Not Significant
1 x 5	.1972	Not Significant
1 x 6	.0393	Not Significant

A high positive correlation is noticed between growth rate (Variable 1) and marketing concept adoption in competitive and demand practices (variable 2), which is significant at the .05 level. The analysis now moves on to regression of variable 1 on variable 2 and 6, in the safe player group. Table VI-15 may be referred for the outcome of the same.

Table VI-15
Regression of Variable 1 on Variable 2 and 6 the safe player group.

Variable	Multiple (R)	F Value	P Value
CDP and PMP ($X_1 \times X_5$)	.434	2.962	.082

The Multiple R of .434 is found to be insignificant which means to say that marketing practices have no bearing on growth rate. These results reveal the way the organizations of safe player group function / manage their organizations.

(d) **Professionally managed group (PROF.MG.)**

For the professionally managed group also as in the earlier groups simple correlation between the criterion variable and predictor variable are calculated. These are given in Table VI-16.

Table VI-16

Simple Correlation in the Professionally managed group (n=35)

Variable	Correlation	Significance
1 x 2	.519	$P < .01$
1 x 3	.469	$P < .01$
1 x 4	.341	$P < .05$
1 x 5	.309	$P < .05$
1 x 6	.556	$P < .01$

All the correlation between growth rate and the five marketing practices are found to be significant, but only two high correlation are noticed.

Thus growth rate is highly correlated with competitive and demand practices (.519) and with promotion practices (.556). This may be interpreted as, high growth rate is accompanied by high scores in CDP and PMP. When these two variables namely, CDP and PMP are entered in the regression, they yielded a multiple R of .586 which is found to be significant at .01 level (refer Table VI-17). This is to say that 34.3% (R^2 x 100) of variation in growth rate (variable 1) is explained by marketing concept adoption in competitive and demand practices and promotion practices (Variable 2 and 6).

Table VI-17

Regression of Variable 1 on Variables 2 and 6 in the Professionally managed group.

Variable	Beta Value	Alpha Value	Multiple R	F Value	P Value
PMP (X_5)	1.071				
		-9.996	.586	9.859	.0005
CDP (X_1)	0.903				

As multiple R is found to be significant the regression equation of Variable 1 on variable 2 and 6 for the professionally managed group may be written as -

$$Y = a + b_1 x_1 + b_5 x_5$$

Substituting,

$$Y = -9.996 + .903 x_1 + 1.071 x_5 \quad \ldots(4)$$

With respect to PROF.MG. group, it may be said that for every unit increase in PMP, growth rate increases by 1.1 units and for every unit increase in CDP growth rate increases by .9 unit only. (refer regression equation 4).

(e) Traditionally managed group (TRAD.MG.)

It is of importance to find out if there is significant difference in the way from PROF.MG. & TRAD.MG. The analysis follows the same sequence as earlier. As a first step the simple correlation between sales and marketing practices are worked out. These correlations are shown in Table VI-18.

The result of this correlation exercise stands unique in the sense that not evens one correlation turned out to be significant. Nevertheless the regression analysis was applied to ascertain whether the outcome would turn out to be insignificant or not. The results obtained are

Table VI-18
Simple Correlation in the Traditionally managed group (n=17)

Variable	Correlation	Significance
1 x 2	0.398	Not Significant
1 x 3	- 0.339	Not Significant
1 x 4	- 0.298	Not Significant
1 x 5	- 0.177	Not Significant
1 x 6	- 0.030	Not Significant

Presented in Table VI-19.

Table VI-19
Regression of Variable 1 on variable 2 and 6 in the Traditionally managed group

Variable	Multiple (R)	F Value	P Value
CDP and PMP (X_1 and X_5)	.412	2.642	0.106

The regression of variable 1 on variable 2 and 6 yielded a multiple of R of .412, which is found to be insignificant at .05 level. The correlation and regression results confirm the absence of any relationship between growth rate and marketing practices. We may, therefore, conclude that perhaps professionally managed groups are better organizations.

(f) **Fund based services group (FBSG)**

- It is worthwhile to find out whether ancillary industrial units function in a like manner as Fee Based/Advisory Services" group,

- Are their marketing norms similar to those of Fee Based/Advisory Services" group,? In pursuance of the same simple correlation between growth rate and marketing practices were worked out. The results given in Table VI-20.

Table VI-20
Simple Correlation in the FBSG group (n = 23)

Variable	Correlation	Significance
1 x 2	.4869	P < .01
1 x 3	.2639	Not Significant
1 x 4	.0166	Not Significant
1 x 5	.1814	Not Significant
1 x 6	.4566	P < .05

Of the five correlation given above, only two of them are significant (1 x 2, 1 x 6) but neither of them is a high correlation. Despite the same, the regression test of variable 1 on variable 2 and 6 was worked out and the outcome is recorded in Table VI-21.

Table VI-21
Regression of Variable 1 on Variable 2 and 6 in the FBSG group.

Variable	Beta Value	Alpha Value	Multiple R	F Value	P Value
CDP (X_1)	.766				
		-6.129	.530	5.301	.014
PMP (X_5)	.614				

The multiple R of .530 is found to be significant at .05 level. Therefore, it may be stated that, variation in growth rate can be explained to the extent of 28.1% (R2 x 100) by marketing concept adoption in competitive and demand practices and promotion practices. The regression equation is written as,

$$Y = a + b_1 x_1 + b_5 x_5$$

Substituting,

$$Y = -6.129 + .766 x_1 + .614 x_5 \quad .....(5)$$

Referring to regression equation 5, the following may be said about the FBSG group. For every unit increase in CDP, growth rate would increase by .77 units and for every unit increase in PMP growth rate increases by .61 units.

- Fee Based/Advisory Services" group,

One would except a better performance in the marketing variables in Fee Based/Advisory Services group than in fund base services group. Table VI-22 indicates whether it is true.

Table VI-22
Simple Correlation in the ABSG Group (n = 29)

Variable	Correlation	Significance
1 x 2	.530	$P < .01$
1 x 3	.436	$P < .01$
1 x 4	.284	Not Significant
1 x 5	.337	$P < .05$
1 x 6	.379	$P < .05$

Although four relationships (1x2, 1x3, 1x5, 1x6) are found to be significant only one is found to be of high correlation namely 1 x 2, i.e. correlation between growth rate and marketing concept adoption in competitive and demand practices. In the FBSG group no high correlation between growth rates and marketing practices were found. Perhaps rightly there is high correlation between growth rate and competitive and demand practices in the ABSG group as they have to put up with competition. The analysis now moves to regression and results are shown in Table VI-23.

Table VI-23
Regression of variable 1 on variables 2 and 6 in ABSG Group

Variable	Beta Value	Alpha Value	Multiple R	F Value	P Value
CDP (X_1)	1.445				
		-4.101	.476	5.113	.013
PMP (X_5)	0.132				

Regression of variable 1 on variables 2 and 6 yielded a multiple R of .476 and is found to be significant at .05 level. The square of multiple R expressed as a percentage i.e. 22.7% is the extent to which variation in growth rate is explained by marketing concept adoption in competitive and demand practices and promotion practices. The regression of Y on X is written as,

$$Y = a + b_1 x_1 + b_5 x_5$$

Substituting,

$$Y = -4.101 + 1.445 x_1 + .132 x_5 \quad .....(6)$$

Referring to regression equation 6 it may be said, that for every unit increase in CDP growth rate would increases by 1.45 units and for every unit increase in PMP, growth rate increases by .13 unit.

In the fund based services group variable 2 and 6 marketing practices contributed 28.1% in explaining the variation in growth rate, while in the Fee Based/Advisory Services" group,

contribution is only 22.7%. The FBSG's groups figure is higher than that of ABSG's group figure by 5.4%. This results in contrary to normal expectations as one would expect the fee based/advisory services to have their marketing variable perform better as they have to face with a lot of competition.

(g) Private Organization Group (POG)

Most of the POG organizations follow systematic and effective marketing strategies. It is the endeavor of the investigator to investigate into the performance of marketing practices in the POG. To begin with simple correlation between criterion, variable, growth rate, and predictor variables, marketing practices, are worked out. These are presented in Table VI-24.

Table VI-24
Simple Correlation in the Private organizations Group (n=11)

Variable	Correlation	Significance
1 x 2	.824	$P < .01$
1 x 3	.517	Not Significant
1 x 4	.453	Not Significant
1 x 5	.477	Not Significant
1 x 6	.653	$P < .05$

Table VI-24 brings out two (1 x 2 and 1 x 6) significant relationships among the variables. Growth rate in highly correlated with competitive and demands practices and promotion practices. Thus high growth rate is accompanied by high marketing concept adoption in competitive practices. Also, high growth rate is accompanied by high marketing concept adoption in promotion practices. Theses two variables are entered into regression and the results obtained are presented in Table VI- 25.

Table VI – 25

Regression of variable 1 on variables 2 and 6 in the POG..

Variable	Beta Value	Alpha Value	Multiple R	F Value	P Value
CDP (X_1)	3.135				
		-21.342	.779	8.698	.010
PMP (X_5)	0.491				

From the regression table it is found that regression of growth rate on CDP and PMP gives to multiple R of .779 which is found to be significant at .01 level. It may be stated that 60.6% of variation in growth rate is explained by marketing practices described in variable CDP and PMP. Making use of alpha and beta values in the above table the regression equation of Y and X may written as,

$$Y = a + b_1 x_1 + b_5 x_5$$

Substituting,

$$Y = -21.342 + 3.135 x_1 + .491 x_5 \quad .....(7)$$

Regarding private organizations group, it may be said that for every unit increase in CDP growth rate increases by 3.14 units and every unit increase in PMP growth rate increases by half a unit. (refer regression equation 7). It is found that (referring to beta co-efficient) the ratio of growth rates to CDP has been the highest among all the groups (3.14 : 1).

From the above discussion it may be concluded that financial service organizations of POG take care to formulate effective marketing strategies in the sphere of competitive and demand practices and promotion practices which in turn bring about increased growth rate.

(h) **Nationalized Organizations Group (NOG)**

In order to establish any relationship between growth rate and marketing practices, the rest of simple of correlation was carried out. The results are expressed in Table VI-26.

Table VI-26

Simple Correlation in the Nationalized organizations Group (n=41)

Variable	Correlation	Significance
1 x 2	.4317	$P < .01$
1 x 3	.2779	$P < .05$
1 x 4	.0276	Not Significant
1 x 5	.2999	$P < .05$
1 x 6	.3645	$P < .01$

The above table reveals that 4 correlation (1x2, 1 x 3, 1x5, 1x6) are significant but none of them were high correlation. They may be described as relationships of a low degree. Thus there is no strong relationship between growth rate and marketing practices. The analytical exercise is carried further and the test of regression was applied. The results are enumerated in Table VI-27.

Table VI-27
Regression of Variable 1 on Variable 2 and 6 in NOG.

Variable	Beta Value	Alpha Value	Multiple R	F Value	P Value
CDP (X_1)	.416				
		-2.032	.429	5.499	.008
PMP (X_5)	0.235				

The results of regression indicate a multiple R of .429, which is significant at .01 level of confidence. This means to say that variable 2 and 6 as against 60.6% in the private organizations group explains 18.4% of variation in growth rate (variable 1).

The regression of Y on X can be written as

$$Y = -2.032 + .416\, x_1 + .235\, x_5 \quad .....(8)$$

Thus for a unit increase in CDP, growth rate would increase by .42 units and for every unit increase in PMP growth rate would increase by .24 units.

(i) Concluding Remarks in Section II

The maximum contribution of marketing variables CDP and PMP in explaining the variation in growth rate is found in the POG group (61%) followed by PROF.MG. group (34%). This helps us to draw a conclusion that in private organizations group and professionally managed group there is greater adherence to the marketing concept (with respect to CDP and PMP) as contribution to explaining variation in growth rate is a lot higher in these groups than other groups.

The ratio of growth rate to marketing practices in the sphere of competitive and demand decisions is best in the POG group (3.14 : 1) followed by ABSG group (1.45 : 1) and RTG group (1.34 : 1).

The ratio of sales to promotion practices are better in FBSG group (0.6 : 1) followed by RTG and POG groups (0.5 : 1).

Marketing variables CDP and PMP are not significant in SPG and TRAD.MG. groups.

CHAPTER VII
SUMMARY, IMPORTANT FINDINGS AND THEIR IMPLICATIONS

CHAPTER VII

SUMMARY, IMPORTANT FINDINGS AND THEIR IMPLICATIONS

7.1 SUMMARY OF THE STUDY:

The marketing practices of the financial services organizations is by and large an unmapped area, and the present study is an investigation on the same.

In the first chapter the role of marketing in the economic development of a country and its special relevance in financial service organizations are discussed. Besides this, the developments of marketing theory, the marketing environment, the development of the marketing concept, marketing mix and characteristics of service products are also highlighted. The nature and scope of the study, as also the limitations of the study are also brought out.

The second chapter is devoted to a review of some studies on the financial service organizations. The findings of selected studies are enumerated. The findings of all these studies indicate the presence of marketing problems. The extent of the marketing problem in the financial service organizations is brought out. Besides this, allied problems of financial service organizations are pointed out. Further, a case for a study on the marketing practices of financial service organizations is made out.

This is followed by a discussion on the population (Gujarat) from which the sample for the study was drawn.

The plan and procedure of the study are enumerated in the chapter on methodology. At first, the statement of the problem, the research objectives and focus of research are spelt out. The specific objectives of the study are:

(i) to ascertain the level of performance of the financial services organizations on the different marketing practices.

(ii) To ascertain the existence of relationship and extent of relationship between the performance variable – growth rate and predictor variables- the different marketing practices, both for the entire sample and for sub-samples and

(iii) To differentiate the various sub-groups in respect of their marketing practices.

For the purpose of the study a questionnaire on the various marketing practices was developed and a system of scoring the responses was formulated. Two other aspects are dealt with in this chapter. First, the classification of respondent organizations was done into mutually exclusive groups for the purpose of study and analysis. The dichotomous groups are, risk taker & safe player groups; professionally & traditionally managed groups; fund based services group & Fee Based/Advisory Services groups; private organizations & Nationalized organizations groups. Second, the different marketing variables on which the financial service organizations are examined to competitive and demand practices, product/service practices, new product/service practices, pricing practices, and promotion practices.

Chapter V is the first of the two chapters on analysis and interpretation of data. For comparing the different groups on their performance on the various marketing practices, simple statistical techniques such as, arithmetic mean, standard deviation and co-efficient of variation were applied.

The differentiation of the groups was undertaken by discriminating them on the various marketing practices, which involved grouped t tests, where first the F-test for quality of variances was determined.

Chapter VI attempts stepwise regression analysis. The entire sample was at first subject to regression analysis and the significant variables were drawn out. Next, regression was applied to each of the groups to ascertain the contribution of the significant marketing variables in explaining the variation in growth rate.

7.2 **FINDINGS AND THEIR IMPLICATIONS:**

Major conclusions reached in this study are presented in a tabular form and these are subsequently discussed in this chapter.

Table VII-1
Major Findings.

Particulars	Significant results / findings
Marketing practices considered as a whole	The RTG group conductive to marketing concept adoption.
Maximum adoption of marketing concept	Product/service Practices.
Minimum / least adoption of marketing concept	New product/service Practices.
Low/adoption of marketing concept	Pricing Practices
Significant in explaining growth rate	Competitive & demand practices. Promotion Practices.
Growth rate	PROF.MG. conducive to sales.
Groups	CDP & PMP good in POG SPG and TRAD.MG. poor performers. Practically no difference between (A) FBSG – ABSG groups and (B) POG – NOG groups.

Considering all the marketing practices together, from the survey it was found that the risk taker group is more conducive to marketing concept adoption in its various marketing decisions. This group secured the highest group average. These findings bring out the relevance of a financial service organizations being risk takers and also the priority that needs to be given to customers overall other functional areas.

The maximum adoption of the marketing concept was found in respect of product/service practices. Also, greater homogeneity was found in decisions regarding product/service. The average scores of the groups indicate that most of them are average or good in the marketing variable relating to product/service decisions.

The least adoption of the marketing concept is found with respect to new product/service practices. It was also found that there was greater heterogeneity among the financial services organizations in the practices relating to new product/services. This implies that the financial service organizations do not adopt appropriate practices when they think of introducing new product/service in the market. This points out to the need for systematic approach by financial service organizations. Market information centers may be set up by financial service organizations.

It has been found that marketing concept adoption in pricing practices has been relatively low. It may be said that the financial service organizations are shrewd and know their profits, but it has happened may times that out of the many services they rendered only a few may be doing very badly but overall profits are good they never get to know it. The financial service organizations need to be trained and aware of the gains that can be accrued from proper book keeping and also from adopting other measures of pricing than full cost pricing.

Marketing practices relating to competitive and demands decisions and promotion decision have come out as the only two significant variables that contribute towards explaining the variation in growth rate. This implies that every financial service organization should take care to adhere to the marketing concept when they take decisions regarding competition and demand and promotion practices. By doing this they may improve the growth rate/commission/ revenue of their organization.

The only classification where growth rates turned out to be a significant differentiating factor is professionally - traditionally managed groups. From this, it may be said that professionally managed group is conducive to higher growth rate. Also is this classification, one other marketing variable is significantly differentiated and there is competitive and demands practices.

The risk taker group and safe player group differ significantly in all their marketing decisions. This means that there is a lot of differences in the way the financial service organizations of both these groups as functioned.

The poor performers are safe player and traditionally managed group. The style of working of these organizations is not in conformity with the marketing concept.

In the private organizations group, it is found that decisions relating to competition, demand and promotion are taken in greater adherence to the marketing concept as the regression results prove that the two variables contribute a lot in explaining the variation in growth rate.

Finally, in the two classifications namely, FBSG-ABSG and POG-NOG there is almost no difference in respect of marketing practices.

7.3 SUGGESTIONS FOR IMPROVING MARKETING OF FINANCIAL SERVICES

a) **Carrying out Customer Analysis**

Financial service organizations should profile threir current customer base to identify which segments of the market they come from and identify any common characteristics and buying behavior patterns, which might help future segmentation or marketing tactics. It is also necessary to assess their customers on following aspects:

- Who are they?
- Who is involved in the purchase decision?
- What motivates their behaviour?
- Which customers are worth most?

b) **Assessing Consumer Satisfaction**

Faced with global competition financial service organizations will have to redefine approaches and attitudes towards distribution and promotion of financial services. Growths should be sought by reinforcing brand equity and developing competitive advantage through distribution equity. Reaching out effectively, efficiently and economically to an ever increasing population spread through the length and breadth of a vast geography is becoming the service marketing mantra of today. In service sector, blue prints for growth are therefore becoming synonymous with strategies for customer satisfaction. Measurement of customer satisfaction involves developing a survey design tailor-made to individual context that would encompass amongst others and following steps:

1. Determining who is the customer: Multi – individual involvement, the processes of the sale mind set of the company's operating managers have to taken into account.

2. Determining what constitutes customer satisfaction: Identify parameters through pilot studies at senior levels – the complex interaction between them – and adopt indexed data collection approach to reduce subjectivity.

3. Designing the scale on which customer satisfaction would be measured: Simple coding of customer category (Government, corporate, private) and assigning relative importance to them by considering variables such as company's market presence business compulsions, growth directions and market complexions.

4. Measuring current levels of customer satisfaction: Qualitative personal interview data from various clients' department.

5. Trend analysis and painters for management of customer satisfaction: Data statistically analyzed, benchmarking and developing top – down models (based on the correct systems) and Bottom – up models (based on improving individuals customer satisfaction).

Each financial services organization should have to find its own path, which depends upon the kinds of financial service the organization offer and their relative strength, weakness and also on different macro and micro environmental (economic – physical) factors.

c) **Offer Product Packages**

No Customer comes to a financial service organization merely for a fixed deposit or for a loan. He comes essentially to get his problems solved and his need satisfied. Customer needs are varied, complex and multi dimensional. For the satisfaction of these multi dimensional needs, financial service organizations should offer product packages rather than stand-alone products. Financial organizations have very few product packages to offer. Some such packages are being offered to corporate customers, but not many to household segment customers. Even in the case of product packages for the corporate segment, marketing of package under a single brand name and in an integrated manner is not much in evidence.

d)   **Construct Perceptual Maps**

To device effective marketing strategy the financial services organizations must use the perceptual mapping techniques:

i)   to measure similarity or dissimilarity between pairs of services
ii) to measure performances between services of two competitive organizations
iii) to have ratings of different services on various attributes

e)   **Be Innovative**

In coming years, it would become impossible to survive and prosper unless organizational skills are effectively channelised towards innovating new ideas, new services and new strategies for winning over and retaining the customer.

A typical situation in Indian financial service organizations is that one organization floats a new product idea or a new marketing strategy and in no time ten other organizations rush to follow suit. This type of "me-too" strategy would be a recipe for mediocre marketing. Successful organizations of the future should scrupulously avoid practicing this " me-too" strategy. Innovation should be their main weapon.

Before concluding this chapter it seems worthwhile to briefly identify some related aspects – areas on which research needs to be undertake.

7.4 DIRECTION FOR FURTHER RESEARCH

Based on the findings of survey, a few suggestions for further research are indicated. It may be worthwhile to undertake a study on any of the following:

(i) Marketing concept adoption in the sphere of new product/service practices has been rather poor. Therefore an intensive study on new product/service practices beginning with product/service idea generation up to say for a period of two years after its introduction in the market may be taken up.

(ii) By and large it was found that financial service organizations went in for full cost pricing. It may be worthwhile to find out if any other system of pricing is prevalent among financial service organizations, if not, why? Is it because of their lack of awareness of the subject or else what would be the reason for the same?

(iii) Investigation of the specific marketing practice of the financial service organizations regarding collection of information – data on competitors and demand analysis may be revealing.

(iv) As day by day, new financial services e.g. depository services, derivatives etc., are being invented and avenues are opening for establishing "Financial Super Market" and the India has already agreed to sign on General Agreement on Trade in Financial Services. (GATs) (list of financial services are annexed as appendix-III.) It is necessary to device marketing strategies keeping in the mind the global environment. The study in this line will be very useful to financial service organizations for marketing effectively their financial service.

BIBLIOGRAPHY

Books & Articles

A & M, 59 Case Studies, 1989-94, **"Cash and Carry"** Spectrum Communication Pvt. Ltd., New Delhi.

A Ries and J. Trout, Positioning : **'The Battle for Your Mind'**, (Warner Books, New York, 1981.)

A. Campbell and S. Yeung, **'Do You Need a Mission Statement?'**, (Economist Publications Management Guides, London, 1990).

A. Campbell, M. Devine and D. Young, **'Sense of Mission'**, (Economist Books / Hutchinson, London, 1990.)

A. F. T. Payne, **'Developing a marketing oriented organization'**, (Business Horizons, May-June 1988)

A. Weinstein, **'Marketing Segmentation'**,(Probus Publishing Company, Chicago, 1987;

Akbar, S., **"Norms to Judge Deficiency in Service"**, Indian Express, 4th January, 1996.

Almeida, M., **"The Future's in Card"**, Business India, February 13-26, 1995.

Anderson, R.L., and T.A. Bancroft, **"Statistical Theory in Research"**, New york : Mc Graw - Hill Book Company, Inc., 1952.

B. H. Booms and M. J. Bitner, **'Marketing strategies and organization structures for service firms'** (in J. H. Donnelly and W. R. George, Marketing of Services, American Marketing Association Proceedings Series, Chicago, 1981, p.48.)

B. J. La Londe and P. H. Zinszer, **'Customer Service: Meaning and measurement'**,(NCPDM, 1976.)

B. J. La Londe, M. C. Cooper and T. G. Noordewier, **'Customer Service: A management perspective'**, (Council of Logistics Management, 1988.)

B. Shapiro, '**Rejuvenating the marketing mix**', (Harvard Business Review, September – October 1985, pp. 28-33.)

Bennett, Peter D., (ed.) **"Marketing and Economic Development, Proceedings of fall Conference"**, Chicago : American marketing Association, 1965.

Bennett,Spencer, and david Bowers, **"An Introduction to Multivariate Techniques for social and hehavioural Sciences"**, London : The Macmillan Press Ltd., 1976.

Bernhardt, Kenneth L. & Thomas C. Kinnear, **"Cases in Marketing Management"**, Dallas, Texas : Business Publications, Inc., 1978.

Berry.,L. ,and Parasuraman,A. '**Marketing Services**' ,(The Free Press,Macmillan Inc. 1991)

Bhagat, R., **"A Big Boom on the Cards"**, Indian Express, Vizianagaram, 8th March, 1994.

Biglin, R.J., **"The Challanges of Professional Services Marketing"**, The Journal of Consumer Marketing, Spring, 1985.

Blank, Steven c. **"Practical Business Research Methods"**, Westport, connecticut : Avi Publishing Company, Inc., 1984.

Bloom, P.N., **"Effective Marketing for Professional Services"**, Harvard Business Review, September-October, 1984.

Business Standards, **"The Seven Ps of Service Strategy"**, 23rd August, 1994, The Strategist.

Business Word, **"Credit Card"**, December, 1993.

C. Gronroos, '**Services Management and Marketing**', (Lexington Books, Lexington, Mass., 1990.)

C. H. Lovelock, '**Classifying services to gain strategic marketing insights**', (Journal of Marketing, vol. 47, Summer 1983.)

C. H. Lovelock, '**Developing and implanting new services**'(in W. R. George and C. E. Marshall, (eds.),

C. J. Easingwood '**New product development for service companies**', (Journal of Product Innovation Management, vol. 4, 1986.

C. J. Easingwood and V. Mahajan, **'Positioning of financial services for competitive advantage'** (Journal of Product Innovation Management, vol. 6, 1989.)

C. Lovelock, '**Seeking synergy in service operations: seven things marketers need to know about service operations'**, (European Management Journal, vol. 10, no. 1, March 1992.)

Chakravarti, S., **"Credit Card Gaining Ground"**, India Today, June 15, 1994.

Chiravuri, S., **"Is there Money in the Card Business?"**, in Money Manager, Business Standard, 4th Novermber, 1993.

Choudhuri, S., : **'No need for Cash in the Wallet:'**, Brand Equity, 1995.

Collier, D. A., **'The Service/Quality Solution'**, (Irwin Professional Publishers, Distributors by IBD, New Delhi.)

Cooley, Willian W., and paul R. Lohnes, **"Multivariate Data Analysis"**, new York: John Wiley and Sons, Inc., 1971.

Cooley, William W, and Paul R. Lohnes, **"Multivariate Procedures for the Behavioral Sciences"**, New york : John Wiley & Sons, Inc., 1962.

Cowell,D. '**The Marketing of Services'** ,(Butterworth Heinemann, 1991)

Croxton ,Frederick E., and Dudley J. Cowden, **"Applied General Statistics"**, second edition, New Delhi : Prentice - Hall of India ,1964.

D. F. Channon, **'Global Banking Strategy'**, (Wiley, New York, 1988.)

D. H. Light **'A guide for new distribution channel strategies from service firms'**, (Journal of Business Strategy, vol. 7, no. 1, Summer 1986.)

D. Helman and A. Payne, **'Internal Marketing : Myth versus reality'**, (Cranfield School of Management Working Paper, Cranfield, SWP 5/92, 1992.)

D. W. Cowell, **'New service development'** Journal of Marketing Management, Vol. 3, no. 3, 1988.

Das, R., **"Card Facts"**, The Economics Times, 14th August, 1993.

Davis, Kenneth R. **"Marketing Management"**, second edition, New York : The Ronald Press Company, 1966.

Deb, S. & Awasthi, M., **"Credit Well Deserved"**, A & M, August, 1991.

Dibb, Simkin, Pride and Ferrell **'Marketing'**, (European Edition, Houghton Miffin, 1991)

Drucker, Peter F., **"Marketing and Economic Development"**, Journal of Marketing, Vol.-22, January 1958.

Emory, C. William. **"Business Research Methods"**, Illinois : Richard D. Irwin, Inc. 1976.

Enis, Ben M. **"Depending the concept of Marketing"**, Journal of Marketing, Vol. 37, October 1973.

Ezekiel, Mordecai, and Karl A. Fox, **"Methods of Correlation and Regression Analysis"**, Third edition, New York : John Wiley & Sons, Inc., 1963.

F. A. Johne and P. M. Pavlidis, **'Product development success in banking : a review of the literature'**, City University Business School, Working Paper no. 118, May 1991.)

F. F. Reichheld and W. E. Sasser Jr., **'Zero defections: quality comes to service'**, (Harvard Business Review, September-October 1990, pp. 105-11.)

F. R. David, **'How companies define their mission'**,(Long Range Planning, vol. 22, no. 1, 1989, pp. 90-7.)

Foxall, G.(Ed.) **'Marketing in the Service Industries'**, Frank Cass and Co., U K, 1984)

G. D. Upah, **"Emerging Perspectives on Services Marketing"**, American Marketing Association, Chicago, 1983,)

G. L. Shostack, **'Planning the service encounter'**, (in J. A. Czepiel, (ed.) The Service Encounter, Lexington Books, Lexington, Mass., 1985.)

G. L. Shostack, **'Service positioning through structural change'**, (Journal of Marketing vol. 51, January 1987, pp. 34 – 43.)

G. M. Moebs and E. Moebs, **"Pricing Financial Services"**, Dow Jones – Irwin, Homewood, Illinois, 1986.)

Garrett, Henry E. and R.s. Woodworth. **"Statistics in Psychology and Education"**, Bombay : Vakils, Feffer and Simons Ltd., 1966.

Gelb, B.D., **"How Marketers of Intangibles can Raise the Odds for Consumer Satisfaction"**, The Journal of Consumer Marketing, Spring, 1985.

Green, Paul E. and Donald S. Tull. **"Research for Marketing Decisions"**, Second edition, New Delhi : Prentice Hall of India Private Limited ,1973.

Grether, E. T. and Robert J. Holloway, **"Impact of Govt. upon the Market System"**, Vol.-31, April 1967.

Guilford, J.P., **"Fundamental Statistics in Psychology and Education"**, Fourth Edition (International student edition) Tokyo : McGraw - Hill Book Company, 1956.

Gupta, M.L. **"Business Statistics"**, First edition, Baroda : Acharya Book Depo, 1981.

Gupta, S.L., '**Marketing Sense**', (S & S Publications, Delhi.)

Hise, Richard T., "Have Manufacturing firms adopted the Marketing Concept", Journal of Marketing, Vol.-29, July 1965.

I. D. Canton, '**How manufacturers can move into the service business**', (Journal of Business Strategy, July – August 1988, pp. 40-4.)

Indian Express, **"Cancard International Launched"**, 7th April, 1995.

J. B. Quinn, T. L. Doorley and P. C. Paquette, '**Beyond products: services based strategy**', (Harvard Business Review, March – April 1990, pp. 58-67.)

J. Bowen, '**Development of a taxonomy of services to gain strategic marketing insights**', (Journal of the Academy of Marketing Sciences, vol. 18, no. 1, 1990, pp 43-9.)

J. Dearden, '**Cost accounting comes to services industries**' Harvard Business Review, vol. 56, September – October 1978.

J. K. Brown, '**Corporate soul searching : the power of mission statements**', (Across the Board, March 1984, pp. 44-52.)

J. L. Heskett, W. E. Sasser and C. W. L. Hart, '**Service Breakthroughs**', (The Free Press, New York, 1990, p. 89.)

J. P. Gunman, '**The price bundling of services: a normative framework**', (Journal of Marketing, vol. 51, April 1987.

J. Rathmell, '**Marketing in the Service Sector**', (Winthrop Publications, Cambridge, Mass., 1974, pp. 92-103.)

J. W. Keon, '**Product positioning : trinodal mappings of brand images, ad images, and consumer preference**', (Journal of Marketing Research, vol. 20, November 1983, pp. 380-92.)

Jayashankar, M., " **Making up for Lost Time**", A & M, 15th February, 1995.

Joel, "**Pricing policies for new products**", Harvard Business Review, Nov-Dec. 1976.

Joseph F., and Conrad Berenson, "Techniques in Marketing Research", Harvard Business Review, Sept.-Oct. 1969.

K. Albrecht, '**At America's Service**', (Dow Jones –Irwin, Homewood, Illinois, 1988, pp. 26-7.)

Kacker, Madhav, (ed.) "**Marketing and Economic Development**", New Delhi : Deep and Deep Publications, 1982

Kamath, V., "**The Infotech Edge**", Business World, 3-16 November, 1993.

Kapoor, J., "**At Your Services**", Credit Cards, A & M, October, 1993.

Kapoor, M. C., and J. D. Singh, "**Marketing Planning Practices in Indian Companies – A Pilot Study**", Indian Management, April 1975.

Kapoor, M. C., and S. Kumar, "**Price Management in Indian Companies : An Empirical Study**", Indian Management, Oct. 1978.

Kapoor, P., "**Government Zeroes in on Credit Cards to Detect Tax Evasion**", The Economics Times, 13th December.

Kaynak, Erdener, "**Marketing in the Third World**", New York: Praeger, 1982.

Kerlinger, Fred N. and Elazer J. Pedhazur, **"Multiple Regression in Behavioral Research"**, New York : Holt, Rinehart and Winston Inc., 1973.

Kinnear, Thomas C. and James R. Taylor, **"Marketing Research, an Applied Approach second edition"**, International Student edition, Singapore : McGraw - Hill Book Co., 1983.

Kohli, V., **"Case Study on Citibank Card"**, A & M, December, 1993.

Kother, Phiilip and Sidney J. Levy **"Broadening the concept of Marketing"** Journal of Marketing, Vol.-33, January 1969.

Kotler, Philip. **"Marketing Decision Making : A model-Building Approach"**, New York: Holt, Rinehard & Winston, Inc., 1971.

Kotler, Philip. **"Marketing Management analysis, Planning and control"**, fifth edition, New Delhi : Prentice-Hall of India Private Ltd., 1986

Kotler, Philip, **"Principles of Marketing"**, second edition, New Delhi : Prentice Hall, 1984.

L. A. Schlesinger and J. L. Heskett, **'Breaking the cycle of failure in services'**, (Sloan Management Review, vol. 32, no. 3, Spring 1991)

L. Berry, **'Relationship Marketing'**, (in L. Berry, G. L. Shostack American Marketing Association, Chicago, 1983,)

L. L. Berry and A. Parasuramen, **'Marketing Services: Competing though quality'**, (The Free Press, New York, 1991)

L. L. Berry, A. Parasuraman and V. A. Zeithamal, **'The service – quality puzzle'**, (Business Horizons, September-October 1988)

L. L. Byars and T. C. Neil, **'Organizational Philosophy and mission statements'**, (Planning Review, (July – August 1987)

Latif, T.A.A. **"The Practice of Marketing"**, second edition, New Delhi : S Chand & Company Ltd., 1981.

Lawton, Leigth, and A. Parasuraman, **"The Impact of the Marketing concept on New Product Planning"**, Journal of Marketing, Vol.44, Winter, 1980.

Levin, Richard I. **"Statistics for Management"**, Third edition, New Delhi: Prentice - Hall of India Private Limited, 1986.

Levitt, T. **"Marketing Intangible Products and product Intangibles"**, Harvard Business Review, May-June, 1981.

Levitt, Theodor, **"Exploit the Product Life Cycle"**, Harvar Business Review, Nov. – Dec. 1965.

Lewis, M. Lovelock C.H , **'Services Marketing,'**(Prentice Hall Int, 1991)

Lewis, M., **'The Money Culture'**, Penguin Business Distributors, IBD, New Delhi, 1993.

Life cycle segmentation, (Compendium, vol. 4, no. 3, 1983,)

Luck,David J. & Hugh G. Wales & Donald Taylor and Ronald S. Rubin, **"Marketing Research"**, Sixth edition, New Delhi: Prentice-Hall of India Private Ltd., 1982.

M. Christopher and M. McDonald, **'Marketing: An introduction'**, (Pan Books, London, 1991.)

M. Christopher, **'The Customer Service Planner'**, (Butterworth – Heinemann, Oxford, 1992, Chapter 3.)

M. Christopher, A. F. T. Payne and D. Ballantyne, **'Relationship Marketing : Bringing quality, customer service and marketing together'**, (Butterworth – Heinemann, Oxford, 1991.)

M. E. Porter, **'Competitive Advantage'**,(The Free Press, New York, 1985.)

M. Frohman and P. Pascarella, **'How to write a purpose statement'** (Industry Week, 23 March 1987.)

MaCann, John M., **"Marketing Segmentation Response to the Marketing Decision Variables"**, Journal of Marketing Research, Nov. 1974.

Marting,Elisebeth,Ed, **"New Products, New Profits, Company Experiences in New Product Planning"**, First Indian Reprint, Bombay : D.B. Taraporrevala Sons & Co Pvt. Ltd.,1970

Massy, William F., **"Forecasting the Demand for New Convenience Product"**, Journal of Marketing Research, Nov. 1969.

Mathur, B.L., **"Managing Credit Card"**, The Journal of Management Science, Volume 1, No. 1, January, 1996.

McGoldrick, P.J. and Greenland, S.J. **'Retailing of Financial Services'**, (McGraw-Hill, 1994)

Mehta, Sanjay **"New Invention for Proper Packaging"**, Focus on Makarpura Industrial Estate. The Times of India, A special supplement, 28th August 1984.

Metha, Subhash C. Indian **"Consumers : Studies and Cases for Marketing Decision"**, New Delhi : Tata Mcgrew _ hill 1972.

Morrison, Donald G., **"On the Interpretation of Disciminant Analysis"**, Journal of Marketing Research May 1969.

N. Piercy and N. Morgn, **'Internal marketing: marketing happen'**, (Marketing Intelligence and Planning, vol. 8, no. 1, 1990)

Neelmegham, s., **"Marketing in India, Cases and Readings"**, New Delhi : Vikas Publishing House P.Ltd., 1988.

Newman, Joseph W., **"Put Research into Marketing Decisions"**, Harvard Business Review Mar-Apr. 1962.

Nitya, K. & Phandnis, C., **"War on Cards"**, The Hindu, March 17th, 1994.

Nunnally, Jum C., **"Psychometric theory"**, second edition, New Delhi : Tata Mc Graw -Hill Publishing company Ltd., 1981.

P. Gilmour, **'Customer segmentation : differentiating by market segment'**, (International Journal of Physical Distribution, vol. 7 no. 3, 1977)

P. Kotler, **'From sales obsession to marketing effectiveness'**, (Harvard Business Review, November-December 1977)

P. Kotler, **'Managing, Service Business and Ancillary Services'** in 7th Edition, 1991, Prentice Hall of India Pvt. Ltd.

P. Kotler, **'Marketing Management : Analysis, planning and control'**, (Prentice Hall, Englewood, Cliffs, 7th edn, 1991.)

P. Thompson, G. De Souza and B. T. Gale, **'The Strategic Management of Service Quality'**, (Pimsletter No. 33, The Strategic Planning Institute, 1985.)

Palda, Kristian S. **"Pricing Decisions and Marketing Policy"**, New Delhi :Prentice-Hall of India Private Ltd.,1976

Palmer,A. '**Principles of Services Marketing**' ,(McGraw-Hill, 1994)

Parjitt, J. H., and B. J. K. Collins, **"The use of consumer Panels for Brand Share Prediction"**, Journal of Marketing Research, May 1968.

Pattanaik, H., **"Report on State Bank Cheque Card"** in the District on Ganjam.

Payne,A. '**The Essence of Services Marketing**', (Prentice Hall International, 1993)

Prasad B. R. S., **"Mega Marketing"**, Indian Management" Fab. 1988.

Quraishi, Z. M., **"Nature and Concept of Regression Analysis and Prediction"**, Quest in Education, Vol.XVI, No. 3, July 1979.

R. B. Chase and R. H. Hayes '**Beefing up operations in service firms**', (Sloan Management Review, Fall 1991,

R. D. Buzzell and B. T. Gale, '**The PIMS Principals: Linking strategy to performance**',(The Free Press, New York, 1987.)

R. J. Allio and J. M. Patten, '**The market share/excellence equation**', (Planning Review, September/October 1991)

Ramdas, D., **"When Travel is on the Cards"**, The Economics Times, 2nd October, 1994.

Ramnath, P., **"Credit Cards: Spurt in Farex Earnings"**, Business India, April 26 May 9, 1993.

Rao, G.V., **"Training for Improving Customer Services"**, The Hindu, 30th January, 1992.

Rao, H. K., **"Entrepreneurship Training"**, Economic Times, 10th Oct. 1983.

Resnik, Alan J., and Peter B. B. Turney, and J. Barry Moson, **"Marketers turn to 'counter-segmentation'"**, Harvard Business Review, Sept.-Oct. 1979.

Reuter,. J.C. **"Time to Say Good Bye Credit Card, Hello Smart Card?"** The Economics Times, 21st December, 1993.

Rishi, S., **"Competitive Edge"**, A & M, February, 1994.

S. King, **'Brand building in the 1990s'**, (Journal of Marketing Management vol.7, 1991)

S. Majaro, **'Marketing in Perspective'**,(George Allen and Unwin, London, 1982.)

S. Vandermerwe and J. Rada, **'Servitization of business : adding value by adding service'**, (European Management Journal, vol. 6 no. 4, 1988)

Sancheti, D.D.and Kapoor, V.K.Statistics, **"Theory, Methods and Applications"**, second edition, Delhi : Sultan chand & sons, 1980.

Sarwate,Dilip M. **"Indian Cases in Marketing Management"**, second edition, Pune : Abhijit Publishers, 1981.

Satish, V.M., **"Electronics Cash Smart Cards to be Launched"**, Indian Express, July 20, 1995.

Sethi, Narendra K., **"Marketing Management and the Planning Process"**, Indian Management, July 1980.

Shankar, R., **'Services Marketing'**- (The Indian Experience (Ed.), Manas Publications, Delhi,1993.)

Sharma, A., **"Creating a New Credit Culture"**, The Economics Times, 17th November, 1993.

Sharma, Subhash, and Vijay Mahajan **"Early Warning Indicators of Business Failure"**, Journal of Marketing, Vol. 44, July 1980.

Sherbini, A. A., **"Marketing in the Industrialization of under – developed Countries"**, Journal of Marketing, Jan. 1965.

Shirali, A. & Herr, H., **'Cover Report on Customer Satisfaction'**, in "The Delight Doctorine", A & M, 15th September, 1994.

Shivaramu, S., **"Entrepreneurship and Enterprise growth"**, Delhi : Seema Publications,1985

Shostack, G.L., **"Designing Services that Deliver"**, Harvard Business Review, January-February, 1984.

Shuptrine, F. Kelly and Frank A. Osmanski, "**Marketing's Changing Role: Expanding or Contracting?**" Journal of Marketing, Vol.39, April 1975.

Siegel ,Sidney. "**Non Parametric Statistics for the behavioural sciences**", New York : McGraw-Hill Book Company, Inc., 1956.

Singh, S.S. "**The Purchasing Power of Plastic**", The Economic Times, 3rd October,1992.

Stanton, W.J., Etzal, M.J. and Walker, B.J., '**Fundamentals of Marketing**', (9th Edition, Mcgraw-Hill, Inc.,)

Subramaniam, S., "**Functions and Effectiveness of Product Management Institution in Indian Consumer goods industry**", Indian Dissertation Abstracts, Jan-March 1979.

Sunarrajan, Neelnegham, "**Marketing in Developing Economy with special references to Indian Man-made Textiles**", Indian Dissertation Abstracts, Special Vol. VII, 1978

T. A. Falsey, '**Corporate Philosophies and Mission Statements**' (Quorum Books, Westpoint, Connecticut, 1989)

T. C. Ragland, '**Consumer define cost, value and quality**' (Marketing News, 25, September 1989)

T. Kosnik, '**Corporate positioning : how to assess and build a company's reputation**', (Harvard Business School, Note 9-589-087, 1989.)

T. Levitt, '**Marketing myopia**', (Harvard Business Review, July – August 1960)

T. Levitt, '**The Marketing Imagination**', (The Free Press, New York, 1993.)

T. Peters, '**Strategy follows structure: developing distinctive skills**', (California Management Review, vol. 26, no. 3, 1984)

T. Peters, '**Thriving on Chaos**', (MacMillan, London, 1988.)

T. peters, and N. Austin, '**A Passion for Excellence**', (Random House, New York, 1985.)

The Economic Times, **"Cottoning on to the Customer's Quicks"**, ET Espuere, 16th July,1993.

The Economic Times, **"Hong Kong Bank, Brand Equity"**, 22nd, September, 1993.

Tolley, B. Stuart, **"Identifying users through a segmentation study"**, Journal of Marketing, April 1975.

Torkildsen,G. **'Leisure and Recreational Management'** ,E.and F.N.Spon UK, 1987)

U.N. Dept. of Economic and Social Affairs, **"Industrial Estates -Policies, Plans and Progress - a comparative analysis of International Experience"**, New York : UN, 1966.

Utterback, James M. and William J. Abernathy, **"A Dynamic Model of Process and Product Innovation"** OMEGA the Int. Journal of Management Science, Vol.3, No, 6, 1975.

V. A. Zeithaml, A Parasuraman and L. L. Berry, **'Delivering Quality Service'**, The Free Press, New York, 1990.)

V. C. Judd, **'Differentiate with the 5th P : 'People'**,(Industrial Marketing Management, vol. 16, 1987,)

Vardan, M.S.S., **"Services Sector Needs Better Management"**, The Hindu, 14th February, 1991.

Varma, H.V., **'Marketing of Services'**, Global Business Press,Delhi.

Vetha Kumar J. **"A Bank in Your Pocket"**, The Hindu, 13th November, 1993.

W. Band, **'Blueprint your organization to create satisfied customers'**, (Sales & Marketing in Canada, April 1989)

W. E. Sasser, R. P. Olsen and D. D. Wyckoff, **'Management of Service Operations'**, Allyn and Bacon, Boston, Mass., 1978.

W. R. George and H. C. Barkdale, **'Marketing activities in service businesses'**, (Journal of Marketing, October 1974)

W. R. George and L. L. Berry, **'Guidelines for the advertising of services'**, (Business Horizons, vol. 24, no. 4, July – August 1981)

W. R. George, J. P. Kelly and L. E. Marshall, **'Personal selling of services'**, AMA Proceeding Series, Chicago, 1983)

Witt,S.F. and Moutinho,L.(Eds.) **'Tourism Marketing and Management Handbook'**,(Prentice Hall International, 1987)

Y. J. Wind, **'Product Policy : Concepts, Methods and Strategy'** (Addison Wesley, Reading, Mass, 1982.)

Young, Pauline V. & Calvin F. Schmid, **"Scientific Social Surveys and Research"**, Fourth edition, new Delhi : Prentice - Hall of India Private Ltd, 1973.

Websites

sbhyd.com
sbbj.com
sbsbank.com
statebankofindia.com
obcindia.com
ucobank.com
indiaconnect.com/bom.htm
denabank.com
iob.com
syndicatebank.com
bankofindia.com
exploreindia.com/pnb
idbi.com
mandvibank.com
bankofpunjab.com
eximbankindia.com
icicibank.com
indusind.com
dcbl.com

sbtr.com
webindia.com/sbm
statebankofindore.com
corpbank.com
bankof baroda.com
punjabandsindbank.com
andhrabankindia.com
canbankindia.com
allahabadbank.com
unionbankofindia.com
indian-bank.com
rbi.org.in
timesbankindia.com
bankofmadura.com
citibank.com
globaltrustbank.com
southindiabank.com
myasa.com/jkbank
federal-bank.com

nabard.org
exportersindia.com/banks in india/index.htm
lic.com
sbimf.com
birlaglob.com
bseindia.com
indozone.com/crisil
ifci.com
accessindia.com/uti

vyasabank.com

indiaworld.co.in/home/apple
amfindia.com
nse-india.com
capitalmarket.com
icraindia.com
kotak.com

APPENDIX-I

QUESTIONNAIRE ON "MARKETING OF FINANCIAL SERVICES"

ONLY FOR RESEARCH

Umesh R. Dangarwala
Investigator

Department of Commerce including Business Administration
Faculty of Commerce,
The Maharaja Sayajirao University of Baroda,
VADODARA

GENERAL INSTRUCTIONS

THIS QUESTIONNAIRE IS TO BE FILLED ONLY BY THE MANAGER / OFFICER OF THE ORGANIZATION

Respected Sir,

This questionnaire contains six sections, Kindly answer every question in every section.

The questions are of a very simple nature requiring a minimum of your time. Separate instructions are given where required, otherwise please kindly (✓) either 'YES' or 'NO' whichever is applicable.

I assure you that the data collected in this questionnaire is purely for academic research only and the information therein will be kept strictly confidential and not divulged to anyone. I request you to please express yourself freely so as to avoid any error in analysis.

Thank you for your cooperation.

Yours sincerely,

Umesh R. Dangarwala
Investigator

Section – I

1.   (a)   Name of the Organization   :
       (b)   Address   :
       (c)   Name and designation of the respondent   :

2. In which year was your organization established?   19_____

3. Is your organization a public sector organization/ Private sector organization? _____

4. If private organization, how many directors are there in your organization? _____

5. How many of your directors are professionally qualified? (i.e. hold a MBA/CA/CFA/CS/ other related qualification) _____

ADDITIONAL INFORMATION

Kindly furnish the following data:

Particulars	1994-95	1995-96	1996-97
1. Total Revenu/Income (in Rs.)			
2. No. of qualified Employees (Nos.)			
3. Growth Rate (in %) a. in terms of deposit mobilization & b. Revenue/Income			

Section – II

7. 'Marketing Management' is said to include management of the following aspects, Do you agree?

    a) Selling and distribution   : ☐ YES ☐ NO
    b) Advertising and Promotion   : ☐ YES ☐ NO
    c) Pricing   : ☐ YES ☐ NO
    d) Product/Service   : ☐ YES ☐ NO

8. What according to you is the meaning of "Target Market"? (Kindly tick (✓) against ONE statement only)

    a) Rich People   : ☐
    b) Geographical area   : ☐
    c) Buyers having identical characteristics   : ☐
    d) Actual users   : ☐
    e) Actual and potential users   : ☐

9. For each of your services how many competitors are there (indicate numbers only)

Sr. No.	Financial Services	No. of Competitors (Gujarat)
A		
B		
C		
D		
E		

10. Regarding each of your competitors do you have the following Information?
    a) Total targeted growth rate   : ☐ YES ☐ NO
    b) Present revenue/income   : ☐ YES ☐ NO

c) Market share : ☐YES ☐NO
d) Promotional activities : ☐YES ☐NO
e) Quality of services : ☐YES ☐NO

11. Have you estimated / predicated the following data for your Services?

Particulars	Present (I)	3 years from now (II)
(a) Total demand	YES / NO	YES / NO
(b) Market share	YES / NO	YES / NO

Section – III

12. What do you think the customer is 'looking for' in your financial services?
    a) Variety : ☐YES ☐NO
    b) Brand Name : ☐YES ☐NO
    c) Promptness : ☐YES ☐NO
    d) Quality : ☐YES ☐NO
    e) Features : ☐YES ☐NO
    f) Customer advice : ☐YES ☐NO
    g) Rendering arrangements : ☐YES ☐NO

13. Have you estimated how many years your financial service would take to achieve the required level of income (growth rate) ?
    : ☐YES ☐NO

14. Do you agree that every service goes through following states?
    a) Introduction Stage : ☐YES ☐NO
    b) Growth Stage : ☐YES ☐NO
    c) Maturity Stage : ☐YES ☐NO
    d) Decline Stage : ☐YES ☐NO

15 Do you agree with the statement "There exists a
    necessity to improvise / involve the service
    continuously in order to compete successfully in
    the market?   : ☐ YES ☐ NO

16 Do you calculate the following at the end of every accounting year?
    a) Revenue/Income and growth rate generated
        by each and every financial service separately?
                                                             : ☐ YES ☐ NO
    b) Profit generated by each financial service separately?
                                                             : ☐ YES ☐ NO
    c) Market share of each financial service (product)
                                                             : ☐ YES ☐ NO

17 The necessity of review the financial services (products) in terms of
    salability and profitability arises from the changed environment
    caused by any of the following factors. Do you agree?
    a) Stiff Compensation   : ☐ YES ☐ NO
    b) Shortages   : ☐ YES ☐ NO
    c) Changes in the economy   : ☐ YES ☐ NO
    d) Changes in needs of the market   : ☐ YES ☐ NO
    e) Obsolescence   : ☐ YES ☐ NO

Section – IV

18 Do you have alternate plans for adding or deleting
    A service in the event of your service/s not doing
    Well?   : ☐ YES ☐ NO

19 Do you visualize any changes in your financial service (product) mix
    (i.e. introduction of new services and deletion of old)?
    a) Three years from now, or   : ☐ YES ☐ NO
    b) Five years from now   : ☐ YES ☐ NO

20. About the new financial service in your service (product) mix from whom did the original idea come from?
    a) Friends/Relatives : ☐ YES ☐ NO
    b) Customers : ☐ YES ☐ NO
    c) Scientists/Formal research organizations : ☐ YES ☐ NO
    d) Competitors : ☐ YES ☐ NO
    e) Company Salesman : ☐ YES ☐ NO
    f) Suppliers : ☐ YES ☐ NO
    g) Distributors / Dealers : ☐ YES ☐ NO
    h) Advertising People : ☐ YES ☐ NO
    i) Top management of your company : ☐ YES ☐ NO
    j) Your own research department : ☐ YES ☐ NO

21. How long was the inclusion of the new services debated / considered? (Kindly tick (✓) against **ONE** only)
    a) One year : ☐ YES ☐ NO
    b) Three years : ☐ YES ☐ NO
    c) Five years : ☐ YES ☐ NO
    d) Seven years : ☐ YES ☐ NO
    e) Over seven years : ☐ YES ☐ NO

22. In fixing the price for your New financial service (product), which of the following methods were used?
    a) Marginal costing : ☐ YES ☐ NO
    b) Full costing : ☐ YES ☐ NO

23. On what basis did you fix the targeted revenue/income for your new financial product?
    a) Utilization of available idle resources : ☐ YES ☐ NO
    b) Followed the competitor : ☐ YES ☐ NO
    c) Based on market survey : ☐ YES ☐ NO
    d) Just like that : ☐ YES ☐ NO

Section – V

24 While fixing the price for your service (product), what aspects are you concerned about?
    a) Recovering costs   : ☐ YES ☐ NO
    b) High profits   : ☐ YES ☐ NO
    c) Demand intensity   : ☐ YES ☐ NO
    d) Consumer psychology   : ☐ YES ☐ NO

25 Which of the following is your objective while fixing the price for your financial service(product)? (Kindly tick (✓) against ONE statement only).
    a) To maximize profit   : ☐
    b) To make high profits initially   : ☐
    c) To penetrate the market   : ☐
    d) To obtain satisfactory rate of return on Investment   : ☐
    e) To maximize current sales revenue/income   : ☐
    f) To attract customers for your complete range of financial services.   : ☐

26 According to you which of the following factors cause constraint while fixing the price? (Kindly tick (✓) as required.
    a) Distributors / Dealers   : ☐
    b) Competitors   : ☐
    c) Suppliers of service idea   : ☐
    d) Government rules and regulations   : ☐
    e) Your own company staff   : ☐

27 What do you understand by the term 'Break Even'? (Kindly tick (✓) against ONE statement only).
    a) Sales level where high profits are made   : ☐
    b) Sales level where there is no profit no loss   : ☐
    c) Sales level which is below the profit margin : ☐

28 Some of the utilities of Break Even analysis is listed below. Do you agree? Break Even point may be used.
    a) To compare net sales, expenses & operating

	Profits with a budget	: ☐ YES ☐ NO
b)	To determine the probable unit cost at Varying levels of productions	: ☐ YES ☐ NO
c)	To determine the effect of a re-organization or a change in operating policy	: ☐ YES ☐ NO
d)	To compare the probable operating profits of Different organizations at various level of Operations	: ☐ YES ☐ NO
e)	To determine the increase in net sales Required to justify a given expansion	: ☐ YES ☐ NO
f)	To balance a given reduction in selling price	: ☐ YES ☐ NO
g)	To determine the effect upon operating profits of a change in wages or in material cost	: ☐ YES ☐ NO
h)	To measure the effect of varying levels of Sales secured at various levels of selling and Manufacturing costs	: ☐ YES ☐ NO

Section – VI

29 Why do you think an organization needs to spend time and money on communicating with its target market?
Is it because the company wishes …

a)	To give information about the existence of The financial service	: ☐ YES ☐ NO
b)	To describe financial service (product) features and how These would benefit the buyers	: ☐ YES ☐ NO
c)	To gain the confidence of the different Market segments	: ☐ YES ☐ NO
d)	To establish a reputation for itself regarding Its trust worthiness and progressiveness	: ☐ YES ☐ NO
e)	To build confidence in its customers by Making satisfying offers	: ☐ YES ☐ NO

30 Which of the following would you consider as being part of the marketing communication mix?

a)	Advertising	: ☐ YES ☐ NO
b)	Personal selling	: ☐ YES ☐ NO
c)	Sales promotion	: ☐ YES ☐ NO

d) Publicity : ☐ YES ☐ NO

31 According to you which are the following purposes does advertising serve?
    a) Advertising builds up a long term image for
       The organization : ☐ YES ☐ NO
    b) Advertising builds up a brand image for
       Financial service : ☐ YES ☐ NO
    c) Advertising gives information about the
       Financial services (Product) and its features : ☐ YES ☐ NO
    d) Advertising announce the dates any
       special service : ☐ YES ☐ NO

32 Which of the following do you think are covered under sales promotion?

    a) Free sample to customers : ☐ YES ☐ NO
    b) Contests for customers : ☐ YES ☐ NO
    c) Demonstration to customers : ☐ YES ☐ NO
    d) Co-operative advertising with trade : ☐ YES ☐ NO
    e) Sales contests for dealers : ☐ YES ☐ NO
    f) Bonus for sales force : ☐ YES ☐ NO
    g) Sales contests for sales force : ☐ YES ☐ NO

33 Do you agree that "through publicity an : ☐ YES ☐ NO
    organization gains attention of the public and
    achieve high credibility".

34 According to you what does 'Publicity' mean?
    (Kindly tick (✓) against ONE statement only).
    a) Advertising in news papers and magazines : ☐ YES ☐ NO
    b) Advertising through cinema or other means : ☐ YES ☐ NO
    c) News paper (or magazine) reporters giving
       Favorable write-up on a company, its products
       Or its services : ☐ YES ☐ NO

35 When you communicate to the market through any Media what responses are you seeking from the target Market regarding your financial service (product)?

a)	Exposure	: ☐ YES ☐ NO
b)	Attention	: ☐ YES ☐ NO
c)	Comprehension	: ☐ YES ☐ NO
d)	Favorable / positive attitude	: ☐ YES ☐ NO
e)	Weaken / remove doubts of customers	: ☐ YES ☐ NO
f)	Effect purchase	: ☐ YES ☐ NO

36 Have you ever tried to evaluate, how much
Response by way of generation of revenue / income you got for the amount of money you spent on promoting your financial service?

: ☐ YES ☐ NO

ANNEXURE

SCORING TECHNIQUE

The questionnaire is not ready for field operations to; the scoring is finalized. While allotting scores care should be taken to see that undue weightage is not allotted to any particular question. This has already been discussed in the chapter on 'Methodology'.

The questionnaire is divided into 6 sections.

Section I contains questions of a general nature, and is mostly informative, providing a basis for classification of industrial units into different categories before being subject to statistical treatment.

Section II to Section VI pertain to the subject matter under study, and in assigning scores to the queries in the questionnaire, a system of,

> Equal scoring,
> Unequal scoring,
> And
> Frequency,

has been adopted. Each of these are explained below.

Under the system of 'Equal' scoring, all sub-divisions to a particular question carry equal scores, and the maximum score for that particular question would be equal to the number of its sub-divisions.

In the system of 'Unequal' scoring, different scores are allotted to the different sub-divisions of a particular question. In other words, each sub-division is allotted a score on its pre-determine importance. It may also be called weighted score.

In questions where 'Frequency' system of scoring has been adopted, an affirmative response (i.e. YES) carried a score of ONE. The allotment of scores question wise is given in the following Table – 1.

Table : 1   QUESTION WISE ALLOTMENT OF SCORES

Variable	Question Number	System of Scoring	Sub Division	Sub Division	Maximum Score
1	2	3	4	5	6
Section II Variable – 2 Competitive & Demand Practices	7	Equal	A	1	
			B	1	
			C	1	
			D	1	4
	8	Unequal	A	0	
			B	0	
			C	0	
			D	1	
			E	2	3
	9*	Unequal		2	
				1	3
	10	Equal	A	1	
			B	1	
			C	1	
			D	1	
			E	1	5
	11	Unequal	A-I	1	
			A-II	2	
			B-I	2	
			B-II	3	8
Section –III Variable –3 Product Practices	12	Equal	A	1	
			B	1	
			C	1	
			D	1	
			E	1	
			F	1	
			G	1	7
	13	Frequency		1	1

* Explained under clarifications/explanations found at the end of this table.

Variable	Question Number	System of Scoring	Sub Division	Sub Division	Maximum Score
1	2	3	4	5	6
	14*	Unequal	a+b+c	1	
			a+b+c+d	2	2
	15	Frequency		1	1
	16	Equal	A	1	
			B	1	
			C	1	3
	17	Equal	A	1	
			B	1	
			C	1	
			D	1	
			E	1	5
Section – IV Variable – 4 New Product Practices	18	Frequency		1	1
	19*	Frequency		1	1
	20	Unequal	A	1	
			B	2	
			C	3	
			D	2	
			E	2	
			F	2	
			G	2	
			H	2	
			I	2	
			J	3	21
	21	Frequency		1	1
	22	Unequal	A	2	
			B	1	2

* Refer Notes on explanations / clarifications found at the end of this table.

Variable	Question Number	System of Scoring	Sub Division	Sub Division	Maximum Score
1	2	3	4	5	6
	23	Unequal	A	2	
			B	1	
			C	3	
			D	0	6
Variable – V Variable – 5, Pricing Practices	24	Equal	A	1	
			B	1	
			C	1	
			D	1	4
	25	Frequency		1	1
	26	Equal	A	1	
			B	1	
			C	1	
			D	1	
			E	1	5
	27	Unequal	A	0	
			B	1	
			C	0	1
	28	Equal	A	1	
			B	1	
			C	1	
			D	1	
			E	1	
			F	1	
			G	1	
			H	1	8
Section – VI Variable – 6, Promotion Practices	29	Equal	A	1	
			B	1	
			C	1	
			D	1	
			E	1	5

Variable	Question Number	System of Scoring	Sub Division	Sub Division	Maximum Score
1	2	3	4	5	6
	30	Equal	A	1	
			B	1	
			C	1	
			D	1	4
	31	Equal	A	1	
			B	1	
			C	1	
			D	1	4
	32	Equal	A	1	
			B	1	
			C	1	
			D	1	
			E	1	
			F	1	
			G	1	7
	33, 34*	Unequal	A	0	
			B	0	
			C	1	1
	35	Equal	A	1	
			B	1	
			C	1	
			D	1	
			E	1	
			F	1	6
	36	Frequency		1	1
					120

* Refer Notes of explanations / clarifications found at the end of this table.

Explanation / Clarification

Some clarification/remarks with reference to particular questions are given below:

Question 9: This question is an endeavor to find out whether the respondents are in the practice of finding out which their competitors are. As such, if a respondent gave a definite figure as the number of competitors faced by him in the market, then he would get the maximum score of 3; but if the respondent gave an approximate number, then he would get 2 scores; and if the response is 'few/many/'competitors, then a score of one is allotted, and a respondent whose response is in the negative will be given 'nil' score.

Question 10: This query pertains to knowledge of 'Product Life Cycle'. It can happen that an entrepreneur is unaware of this aspect, yet he introduces new products on the basis of some thumb rules he follows. Acceptance of Product Life Cycle is a pre-requisite to innovation/introduction of new products. Each stage mentioned in the questions is a sequence of the preceding one. Hence, if a respondent affirms in sub-divisions a, b, and c, he will receive a score of one and when a respondent acknowledge all 4 stages, then he receives the maximum score of 2.

Question 19 : This question concerns introduction of new products/services and deletion of old. It has two sub-divisions and they are treated as either/or. Hence a score of one only has been allotted to this question.

Question 33, 34 : For both these questions, put together a score of one is allotted. 'Publicity' is always mixed up with 'advertising'. A respondent is allotted a score of one, only when he responds in the affirmative to question 33 and at the same time responds in the affirmative to sub-section 'c' of question 34.

All the scores indicated above in Table-1, are summed up in the following Table:2

Table : 2 Scores at a Glance

Section		Variable	Score
II	2:	Competitive & Demand Practices	22
III	3:	Product/Service Practices	19
IV	4:	New Product/Service Practices	32
V	5:	Pricing Practices	19
VI	6:	Promotion Practices	28
		Grand Total ...	120

APPENDIX – II

Major Recommendations of Selected Committees (1985-95)

I. COMMITTEE TO REVIEW THE WORKING OF THE MONETARY SYSTEM (Chakravarty Committee, April 1985)

1. The functioning of the monetary system must necessarily be in consonance with the national development strategy as articulated in the successive Five Year Plans. The monetary system should therefore, seek to perform the following tasks:
   (a) mobilize the savings of the community and enlarge the financial savings pool.
   (b) promote efficiency in the allocation of the savings of the community to relatively more productive purposes in accordance with national economic goals.
   (c) enable the resource needs of the major 'entrepreneur' in the country, viz. The government, to be met in adequate measure.
   (d) promote an efficient payments system.
2. It is essential to ensure that there is no mis-match between the responsibility of the central bank. i.e. the RBI, to supervise and control the functioning of the monetary system on the one hand, and its authority to do so on the other.
3. In order to maintain a viable balance of payments position, it is necessary to ensure that the domestic price level is not allowed to rise unduly, particularly since our major trading partners have had notable success in recent years in achieving price stability.
4. It would be desirable, in the Indian context, to assign to the monetary authority a major role in promoting price stability, and also to accord price stability a dominant position in the spectrum of objective pursued by the monetary authority.
5. The contribution of monetary policy to the control of inflationary pressures largely lies in the area of aggregate demand management and in facilitating allocation and effective utilization of credit in relatively more productive avenues.
6. The central bank also has a difficult task of determining the timing of its regulatory measures on the basis of its experience in regard to the legs involved. As the banking system has grown considerably over the years the cost of a delayed decision can be considerable. Similarly, while monetary breaks are to be applied it is necessary to start early and in a phased manner as the impact of regulatory measures cannot be allowed to be so drastic as to cause unintended hardship to specific sectors of the economy.
7. The inter-action between money, output and prices is very often summarized in the equation which takes the form of the demand function for real money balance on the postulate that the causation runs from real income to money. As the process of money creation is simultaneously a process of credit creation, it is necessary also to look upon the problem from the credit side since an output increase may require a certain amount of increase in credit.
8. The extent of increase in the price level associated with an increase in output and money will depend on the elasticity of output wit respect to credit and the elasticity of price with respect to money as well as output. Obviously these eleasticities themselves depend upon the structure of production and the flexibility of supply responses and can change with time.
9. An important area of concern to the monetary authority is the determination of the rate of growth of money supply, taking into account the inter-relationship between money, output and prices. In order to be acceptable to the monetary authority, the rate of growth in money supply should be conformity with the desired rate of growth in output and constrain the price increase to an acceptable level. From the operational point if view, without going into causation, it may be possible for the monetary authority to use such an equation to regulate the supply of money.
10. The single – most important factor influencing the conduct of monetary policy since 1970 is the phenomenal increase in reserve money. The major component of this increase was the increase in Reserve Bank credit to government on which the central bank had little control. In view of this,

the only feasible approach to the control of monetary expansion was to influence the value of the money multiplier by rising the Cash Reserve Ratio. This was done repeatedly and the rise in the average money multiplier was more or less arrested after the mod-seventies and stabilized at a level slightly below 3.0. This achievement fell far short of the requirements of the situation in several years during the period under review when a drastic reduction in the growth of M_3 was called for.

11. In India, the growth of high-powered money or reserve money has been largely the result of increase in Reserve Bank credit to government. Any measure to check reserve money growth and hence money supply woul, therefore, evidently impinge on the government's freedom to take recourse to central bank accommodation.

12. A feasible approach to evolving a policy framework for ensuring a desired rate of growth of government expenditure as well as desired rate of growth of reserve money and money supply involves a certain degree of coordination between government and the Reserve Bank in evolving and implementing agreed policies. Such coordination is essential and also feasible.

13. The objective of growth with social justice can be achieved in the context of reasonable price stability only when the compulsions of demand management are adequately reflected in the level of government's fiscal deficit financed by RBI.

14. There appears to be considerable scope for government to tap the savings of the public through an appropriate interest rate structure and offer of a wider spectrum of savings instruments with attractive features. This will have the desirable consequence of lowering the rate of expansion in reserve money and money supply associated with a given level of borrowing by the government.

15. An unambiguous, and economically meaningful measure of the monetary impact of fiscal operations is provided by the change in the Reserve Bank credit to government.

16. It is safe to assume that the public will gradually increase its subscription to government securities carrying coupon rates (explicit or implicit) which are higher than the present levels by an average of about 3 per cent per annum particularly if the securities are available more or less throughout the year.

17. Initially interest costs will increase as successive tranches of government borrowing carry the higher coupon rates but the net impact on the government budget need not be large in the long run to the extent that relatively price stability is achieved. Indeed this should be the outcome if the monetary system s suitably restructured.

18. The increased holding of Treasury Bills and government securities by the public would imply, other things being equal, a slower growth in bank deposits and correspondingly in bank credit reflecting the slower expansions of reserve money. Maintenance of desired levels of bank credit to the non – government sector can be achieved through a less – than – compensatory increase in reserve money as compared to the reduction in reserve money occasioned by the contraction in Reserve Bank credit to government (net), if the compensating reserve money expansions is in the form of RBI assistance to banks.

19. The complex nature of the administered interest rate structure has also resulted in reducing the scope for effecting counter – cyclical variations in interest rates.

20. Interest rates applicable to a substantial portion of bank's assets portfolio are either lower than or barely above its cost of funds. This is not a healthy situation.

21. The implementation of projects with poor rates of return needs to be discouraged through a policy of maintaining real rates of interest at realistic levels by eliminating or reducing the element of concessionality in the interest at realistic levels by eliminating or reducing the element of concessionally in the interest rates charged on long-term loans.

22. We, therefore, believe that while the policy of relying on monetary budgeting and credit budgeting to achieve desired sectoral credit allocation should continue, there does appear to be a strong case for greater reliance on the interest rate instrument with a view to promoting the effective use of credit and in short-term monetary management. We believe that the quantitative controls can be more effective if they are supported by a suitable interest rate policy which incorporates a subsidiary yet crucial rationing in the disbursement of credit.

23. The pre-occupation with concessional interest has, unfortunately, deflected attention away from the much more potent instrument of social justice which takes the form of adequate and timely of

credit to the neglected sectors, particularly in rural areas. We would, therefore, like to recommend strengthening of the credit delivery system with a view to provide adequate and timely credit to target groups covered under prioritysector lending, and the motivation to do so should not be allowed to be reduced through any undue emphasis placed on grant of credit at concessional interest rates, since such an emphasis could well prove to be counter-productive. As such only a very selective approach to the use of concessional interest rates seems to be warranted in contrast to the excessive reliance at present on concessional interest rates as a redistributive device.

24. A substantial volume of credit is pre-empted by government at relatively low interest rates. The complex operations of government can be made more efficient if a device like raising the cost of borrowings is more effectively and widely used.
25. Facilitating recourse to bill finance is another desirable method of promoting effective use of credit.
26. The supervision of the end-use of credit by banks is rendered more difficult by the widespread use of cash credit as a means of providing credit for working capital.
27. While the basic philosophy of the restructured system lies in affording greater flexibility to monetary and related institution at the micro level, the need to coordinate their activities in the interest of achieving national objectives of socio – economic policy remains, and the latter should be a major concern of the monetary authority. It is in this context that the need for the monetary authority to embark no monetary targeting in the formal sense acquires importance.
28. Formulation of monetary policy with M_3 as the monetary variable to be targeted becomes a feasible proposition in the restructured system envisaged by us.
29. The observed relationship between money, output and prices in India over the past two decades suggest a basis for determining range of targets for monetary growth. What we have in view is not mechanistic monetary targeting un-influenced by the impact of developments in the real sector, but what we might characterize as monetary targeting with feedback which enables changes in the targets to be made in the light of emerging trends in output and prices. The setting of the monetary target has to be in the form of a range rather than specific magnitude of monetary expansion.
30. We therefore recommend that the Reserve Bank of India adopt monetary targeting as an important monetary policy tool, subject to the cautions sounded by us and this would bind the Reserve Bank and the Government of India in a common effort to achieve desired rate of growth in money supply, as in the Indian situation control on monetary growth is impossible without the full support and understanding of the government.
31. It would be necessary to have an aggregate monetary budget annually as also for the period covered by the Five Year Plans in order that, over the medium term, reasonable coordination between production and credit plans is achieved.
32. A credit budget for the banking sector is also to be prepared as a part of the exercise on the monetary budget. The objective of the credit budget is to determine the permissible level of bank credit to the commercial sector and a broad profile of the sectoral deployment of credit.
33. Quantitative credit controls have come under severe stress in the absence of support from any price rationing mechanism.
34. The administered interest rate system has been found to be lacking the flexibility necessary for augmenting the pool of financial savings by effecting suitable changes in the deposit rates from time to time as the low profitability of banks has made banks wary of increasing the average cost of deposits.
35. A fair degree of regulation of interest rate is necessary so as to provide for an orderly mobilization of financial savings for purposes of planned economic developments as well as in the interest of viability of operations of banks of widely varying size in terms of deposits and advances and differing greatly in regard to the quality of their human resources.
36. In our view the Treasury Bills should be developed as an active monetary instrument and should constitute the ideal short-term paper in the money market. What comes in the way of such a development is its low yield.
37. Borrowing by way of Treasury Bills should not be construed as a convenient alternative to market loans of medium or long maturity. A short-term instrument cannot be used to finance essentially long-term requirements. The quantum of borrowing through the issue of Treasury Bills should

truly reflect the unanticipated variation between revenues and expenditure which need not always be large.

38. We recommend that the discount rate on Treasury Bills of 91 days should provide an yield which is marginally positive in real terms. This means that the nominal rate of discount would have to be higher than the expected change in the price level. Treasury Bills with a rate of discount of 4.60 per cent per annum need to be funded before new Treasury Bills are issued at revised rates of discount.

39. Medium and long dated government securities need to have yields which are in keeping with the expectations of the capital market in regard to the long-term movement of the price level.

40. We recommend that the yields on government securities with maturities not exceeding 15 years be so determined as to provide on an average over the entire spectrum of new issues an yield of 2 per cent per annum in real terms.

41. The concept of operational efficiency of commercial bank in India is associated with such diverse aspects of its operations as cost effectiveness, profitability, customer services, priority sector lending, mobilization of deposits and deployment of credit in the rural and backward regions and so on. Operational efficiency in banking has attained a wider connotation. Precisely for this reason, a generally acceptable definition of the concept, and selection of appropriate indicators are beset with difficulties. Nevertheless improvement in productivity in all aspects of banking operations has to be pursued by banks as an important management objective as it vitally affects the efficiency of the monetary system.

42. There is a need to introduce some element of price competition among banks. The 'controlled competition' which we have in view involves an 'administrated spread' between the interest of bank deposits with a maturity of 5 years and above, to be determined by the Reserve Bank and the basic lending rate which would serve as a floor to the non-concessional lending rates of banks.

43. Taking the present structure of interest rates and bank profitability as a guide, and also taking into account our recommendations in regard to the yield structure of government and other approved securities which are relevant in the context of the SLR investment of banks, we believe a 3 percentage point spread between the maximum rate on deposits and the basic (minimum) lending rate of bank should provide an acceptable spread to the banks.

44. It is desirable that the Reserve Bank determines the interest rate on banks deposits of one year maturity as also the maximum interest rate for deposits with a maturity of 5 years or more.

45. We recommend that the deposit rate to be offered by banks on deposits with a maturity of 5 years or more should be such as to offer the saver a minimum positive real return of 2 per cent per annum, and the deposit rate on deposits of one year maturity should be marginally positive in real terms; these deposit rates may be determined accordingly by the Reserve Bank.

46. Except for deposits with maturity of 5 years or more, the banks should be free to choose their maturity pattern of deposits.

47. The absence of a ceiling rate on bank loans and advances is a desirable feature which would promote better use of credit by borrowers on the one hand and competition among bank on the other, the latter being circumscribed by the prescribed basic (minimum) lending rate.

48. As regards bank lending to the priority sector, we recommend no more than two concessional rates, one being equivalent to the basic (minimum) lending rate, and the other somewhat below this rate.

49. Our recommendations relating to revision in the yield of Treasury Bills should provide banks with an acceptable short-term financial instrument and they need not depend entirely on the inter-bank call money market for meeting transient liquidity needs. Accordingly, the ceiling on the inter-bank call money rate would no longer serve any important purpose and we recommend that this ceiling should be removed.

50. The cash credit system, in out view, suffers from two serious drawbacks which have important implications for the working of the monetary system. Under the cash credit system the task of cash management is passed on by the borrower to the bank. Another related aspect of the cash credit system which has received somewhat less attention is the considerable benefit derived by the borrowers akin to interest income on their temporarily surplus funds. The surplus funds credited to

the cash credit account reduce interest costs at the rate charged which now stands at 17.5 per cent per annum, a level of return on surplus funds not available to other sectors of the economy.

51. It is possible that the prevalence of the cash credit system has slowed down, if not thwarted, the development of a bill market and indeed minimized the relevance of a money market to the borrowings community.

52. The development of a bill market has not been a reality despite its well-known advantages to lenders and borrowers alike and also despite the official policy actions aimed at promoting the use of bill finance. We would like to emphasis the urgency of removing the entirely avoidable procedural impediments to the use of bill finance.

53. Government should make it mandatory on the part of public sector and large private sector units to include an interest payment clause in all their purchase contracts with their material suppliers for payments delayed beyond a specified, such as 120 days, at a rate which is two percentage points higher than the basic (minimum) lending rate of the bank. Similar interest payments should also be provided for in all government purchase contracts for material supplies and purchase contracts with small scale and ancillary industries. Large units in the private sector too should naturally be required to make such a provision.

54. We recommend that cash credit limits covering supplies to government by industrial units and other suppliers may be earmarked for the purpose, and all payments by government and public sector agencies for supplies financed by these facilities should be invariably credited to the earmarked cash credit account. This arrangement would also remove one serious dislocating feature in the present system of monitoring credit limits to industry and trade.

55. We recommend that credit facilities needed to tide over temporary crises of an unforeseeable nature and due to reasons beyond the control of the borrowers should be expeditiously made by earmarking a second cash credit facility for the purpose, on lines similar to those pertaining to the cash credit facility relating to supplies to government.

56. The various credit limits sanctioned by a bank may be classified under Cash Credit I (covering supplies to government). Cash credit II (covering special circumstances or contingencies) and Normal Working limits covering the balance of the credit facilities. We recommend that the Normal Working Capital limits should be predominantly in the form of loans and bill finance limits.

57. We recommend that interest charges for assistance under Cash Credit I should be at the basic (minimum) lending rate of the bank and for Cash Credit II at the highest prevailing lending rate of the bank, the loan portion of the Normal Working Capital limits bearing an interest charge in between the two and a special lower rate of 2 percentage points below the basic (minimum) lending rate being applicable to bill finance.

58. In order that the intended benefits of instituting Cash Credit I actually accrue to the borrower it is however necessary that banks are required to amend their current practice of disregarding bills receivable or book debts which are due for more than six months in the computation of drawing power. We recommend that bills receivable and book debts should be included in the computation of drawing power of Cash Credit I so long as they are not more than 12 months old.

59. The large volume of credit being extended to the priority sector over a wide geographic area, the considerable variety of activities being financed, the large number of schemes for specific target groups, the number of agencies involved in drawing up programs to facilitate absorption of credit by the priority sector, the enormous increase in the number of loan accounts, are notable features of priority sector lending which have made the Indian banking experience in this regard quite unique.

60. A considerable amount of coordination among the development agencies at the district, block and even lower levels on the one hand and between these agencies and the banks on the other is a prerequisite for the efficient conduct of priority sector lending. This factor probably explains to a great extent the disparity in the results achieved under priority sector lending in different areas.

61. The extent overdues has been attracting critical attention in the course of evaluation of the performance of banks in the area of priority sector lending. The time has probably come to set maximum limits for overdues so that banks put in their best efforts to sty within these limits which would also serve as a caution to them not to extend credit in areas which happen to show high

62. overdues for all banks taken together. This approach would serve to elicit greater efforts from the local development agencies to improve the lending climate and the viability of priority sector projects. In this context we would like to suggest that relevant indices be developed to monitor the trends in overdues by activity and by area in respect of priority sector advances by the banking system as a whole.

62. The regulation of money supply in the developed countries is facilitated by the highly integrated money and capital markets of the developed economies. At the same time the task is rendered difficult by a high degree of integration of economic activity among these economies. In contrast several objectives need to be pursued through monetary policy in a developing economy characterized by duality in many important respects.

63. Over the years, the income velocity of M_3 has shown a steady decline. In 1950-51 the income velocity of M_3 was as high as 3.86. It came down to 3.12 in 1970-71 over a period of twenty years but exhibited a sharp decline over the next decade, its magnitude in 1980-81 being as low as 1.91 or less than one half of its level thirty year earlier. In 1983-84 the income velocity of M_3 was 1.86. This sharp drop in velocity since 1970-71 has probably been occasioned by the significant changes that have occurred in the structure of the monetary system, particularly the geographical spread of banking facilities and the relatively slower growth till recently or other financial intermediaries. It would appear that the extent of fall in velocity as a result of further expansion of banking facilities would gradually grow less and less, while the trends in the growth of other financial intermediaries may be tend to be more than offset any such fall.

64. For purpose of monetary regulation, it is important, therefore, to analyze the factors influencing change in velocity on a continuing basis as structural changes in the economy are policy-induced and could be an important source of change in velocity.

65. The major anti-inflationary factor in the long run can only be growht in output achieved through increased productivity and better technology and through an economical and effective use of credit in the economy as a whole.

66. A sustained high rate of growth in output is a strong anti-inflationary force but a policy of maintaining relatively high rates of monetary expansion on the grounds that output growth in the long run will be raised is likely to be self-defeating if price stability is endangered in the short run. A very careful balance has, therefore, to be struck in arriving at a target for monetary expansion between the compulsions of accelerating the growth rate, and the need to achieve price stability.

67. Without a detailed mod-year review it would be difficult to implement monetary regulation measures consistent with the objectives of growth, and price stability.

68. Increase in bank credit extended to industrial units should be justified by growth in sales and not merely reflect growth in inventories. Probably more attention should be given by banks to bank credit per unit of sales revenue in deciding credit requirements of their borrowers than appears to be the case at present. The use of bank credit for propping up weak and inefficient units should be reduced.

69. The availability of bank credit enables the small scale industries to continue their operations but imposes on them a burden in terms of interest cost which they find onerous. Total interest costs should be reflected in product prices, and if a part of these costs need to be absorbed by the producers at the expense of their profits, then this should be a decision to be taken by the larger producers and not forced on the small scale industries sector taking advantage of its weak bargaining power.

70. In the short run, the single most important contribution which monetary regulation measures can make towards the achievement of the goal of social justice is the maintenance of price stability.

71. A matter of concern from the point of view of monetary regulation is the high overdues which banks are contending against in the implementation of priority sector lending programs. Considering that as much as 40 per cent of total bank credit is to be allocated to priority sector advances on a sustained basis, high overdues would mean poor recycling of funds.

72. It is important also to develop an active secondary market for Treasury Bills by providing suitable support to brokers and dealers and permitting banks also to avail of their services.

73. Participation certificates provided the banks with a convenient of channel for obtaining short-term accommodation from the investment institutions who were able to provide such accommodation

during the period which intervened between their cash inflow and the disbursement of funds for capital projects. Participation certificates of this nature deserve to be encouraged. However, it might be necessary to place restrictions on the renewability of these certificates.

74. Additional institutional participants in the call money market may allowed as they do not constitute an additional source of funds to the banking system as a whole and hence do not dilute the intended effect of monetary regulation measures.

75. Development of a bill market requires an adequate supply of first class bills which alone are freely negotiable and marketable. Over the years, banks have not been encourage to co-accept bill and as a result the bill market does not have an adequate volume of first class bills. An important step that needs to be taken by the Reserve Bank is to provide the necessary guidelines to banks in regard to co-accepting of bills.

76. An active bill market will relieve pressure on banks for extending credit facilities to seller or buyers while providing banks with a financial instrument of acceptable liquidity, safety and return. The facilities of bill rediscounting may be extended by the Reserve Bank to the commercial banks according to the stance of monetary policy at any given time.

77. Evening our liquidity imbalances in the corporate sector through the development of the inter-corporate funds market would provide a means of reducing the variability in the demand for bank credit and hence providing greater maneuverability to monetary regulation measures.

78. Basically, the parallel economy represents an additional source of funds to the economic agents who fail to obtain their requirements from the normal sources, or who need the funds to support activities for which they expect no assistance from the official agencies and other sources. This represents, therefore, a dilution of the effectiveness of credit control measures, and also involves a mis-direction of resources.

79. A credit delivery system which succeeds in meeting the genuine requirements of borrowers for approved purposes in time and in adequate measure would reduce the spil-over of credit demand and make the operations of the parallel economy less relevant for the monetary system.

80. We recommend that the practice of stipulating an additional CRR requirement on incremental deposits be adopted very sparingly, for short durations, and only in special circumstances requiring drastic monetary control measures. Even if an incremental CRR is imposed, it should be converted to an average at an appropriate time.

81. Our recommendations aimed at facilitating the sale of government securities to the non-institutional public as an additional channel of market borrowing by government would lend an element of flexibility to the SLR instrument.

82. In the restructured monetary system which we have outlined, reserve money expansion is not likely to be occasioned by large increases in Reserve Bank credit to government unlike in the past. In this context the refinance instrument could be effectively use in conjuction with other measures of monetary regulation, since greater variation in the quantam of refinance would become a feasible proposition.

83. The role of open market operations as an instrument of credit control will assume importance in the restructured monetary system recommended by us. With the interest rate offered on government securities becoming truly competitive, a broad enough securities market may emerge for the Reserve Bank to use open market operations as an instrument of credit control.

84. In the restructured monetary system which we have outlined there would be scope for improving the effectiveness of Bank Rate as an instrument of monetary regulation particularly if necessary steps are taken to develop an active money market as recommended by us. Further, if bank's recourse to Reserve Bank accommodation rises as a result of our recommendations relating to regulation of reserve money expansion the Reserve Bank will be in a better position to influence bank's operations through Bank Rate policy. Again, the interest rates on Reserve Bank credit to the commercial sector could be specified only in relation to the Bank Rate.

85. The business community can and does take recourse to other sources of finance outside the organized money market and thus thwart the objectives of selective credit control. It would perhaps be inappropriate to judge the efficacy of selective credit control measures in terms of their impact on prices.

II WORKING GROUP ON THE MONEY MARKET
(Vaghul Committee, January 1987)

Call Money

1. The present interest rate ceiling on the call money fixed by the IBA should be abolished and the call money rates should be left to be determined by market forces. The call money rates should be freed only for inter-bank transactions and the ceiling rate of 10 per cent should continue to be maintained for borrowings from non-bank participants in the market, if any.
2. It would be necessary for the Reserve Bank to counsel the surplus banks to ensure that call money operations are not disruptive to the banking system and the call money rates do not rise to stratospheric levels over prolonged periods.
3. The call money market should strictly be an inter – bank market. The LIC and the UTI may be permitted to remain in the market. The position could be reviewed, if need be, by the Reserve Bank of India in April 1988.
4. The interest rate on inter – bank term deposits should also be determined by market forces.
5. The measures relating to the call money and inter-bank term deposit rates should be implemented with inception of the slack season at the end of April 1987.
6. There is no need for brokers to be re – introduced into the call money market. To the extent that broker services are felt necessary after the freeing of the call and inter – bank term deposit rates, the proposed Finance House could usefully provide this service.

Bills Rediscounting

7. There is need to take a number of positive measures of facilitate the emergence of a genuine bill culture.
8. The government should direct departmental undertakings and public sector organizations that payments for all credit purchases should be in the form of bills which should be strictly honoured on the due dates. Failure to pay a bill on the due date should attract a uniform penal rate of 2 percentage points above the maximum lending rate of banks. A similar procedure should be followed in the case of CAS parties. In the event of three instances of defaults on payment of bills, the working capital limits should be reduced suitably.
9. The working capital limits of large parties should be scaled down and the interest rates increased if bill acceptances are less than a stipulated percentage of credit purchases.
10. It would be necessary to move away form receivable financing to bill financing and accordingly a program commencing from April 1988 should be stipulated for phasing out receivable financing. Of the total receivable, the proportion of receivables eligible for financing under the cash credit / overdraft facilities should be 75 per cent from April 1, 1988, 50 per cent from April 1, 1989 and 25 per cent from April 1, 1990. The rest of the receivables should be financed only through demand / usance bill limits.
11. Within the CAS discipline, banks should be given the discretion to increase bills limits for temporary periods.
12. The stipulation on unsecured advances should be made applicable to bill financing.
13. The maximum discount rate on bills should be such that it does not exceed an equivalent effective interest rate of 16 per cent. This should be implemented at the end of April 1987 and after a year an assessment could be made as to whether the maximum discount rate could be freely determined by the banks.
14. As at the end of April 1987, the ceiling on the rediscount rate should be increased from 11.5 per cent to 12.5 per cent.
15. A review as to whether the ceiling on the discount rate should be removed could be undertake in April 1988.

16. Institution and other units such as companies, trusts etc. which can satisfactory demonstrate to the Reserve Bank that they have a resource surplus of a monthly average of at least Rs. 5 crores per annum should be allowed to participate in the bill rediscounting market.
17. Further rediscounting by the institutions should be freely permitted.
18. The producers for rediscounting bills should simplified by the end of April 1987.

Short- Term Commercial Paper

19. The time is appropriate for starting with a limited introduction of commercial paper. Initially. access to the commercial paper market should be given to 'A' rated companies.
20. The interest rate on commercial paper should be freely determined by market considerations.
21. The commercial paper market should function within the overall discipline of The Reserve Bank Should administer the entry in the market, the amount of each issue and the total quantum that be raised in a year.
22. There should be no restriction on the participants in the commercial paper market. The size of any single issue should not be Rs. 1 crore and the size of each note should not be less than Rs. 5 lakhs.
23. Commercial paper should be executed from the stipulations on unsecured advances in the case of banks.
24. The framework set out for developing a commercial paper market in India could be adopted and necessary legislative/ administrative changes should be completed so as to enable commercial paper to be operative by April 1, 1988. The authorities should take an early decision to commit themselves to a time 0 – bound introduction on commercial paper.

Government Paper

25. For an active secondary market in 182 Days Treasury Bills, it would be necessary for a large number of participants to bid regularly in the auctions and to build up a portfolio of varying maturities. Suitable measures need to be taken to ensure that the Treasury Bill rate remains flexible. The periodicity of the auction should be increased.
26. A Treasury Bill Refinance Facility should be introduced by the end of April 1987 and the refinance rate should be at least 1.5 percentage points above the prevailing Treasury Bill rate. In the event of the proposed facility being introduced, the stand-by refinance facility should be terminated.
27. Inter-bank transactions in dated securities on a buy-back basis should be encouraged and interest rates on such transactions should not be subject to interest rate control.
28. An autonomous public limited company called the Finance House of India should be set up jointly by the Reserve Bank, the public sector banks and the financial institutions to deal in short – term money market instruments. The finance house should have back-up facilities with banks and the Reserve Bank. In view of the schedule of other policy responses which are to be implemented in the slack season of 1987, the Finance House of India should be operative not later than July 1, 1987. Over period of time, there would be need for more than one finance house.

Development of New Instruments

29. There should be a continuing development and refinement of money market instruments. Each new instrument coming into the market must be specifically approved by the Reserve Bank.

Inter – Bank Participation Certificates

30. From the end of April 1987, inter – bank participation certificates should be introduced in modified form.

Certificate of Deposit

31. The introduction of Certificate of Deposit is not recommended at this stage. In the context of the various changes proposed by the Working Group and the introduction of the 182 Days Treasury Bill, the structure of short-term deposit rates up to one year as well as the number of maturities could be reviewed by the end of April 1987 and in the light of his review, the feasibility of introducing Certificates of Deposit could be reconsidered.

Factoring Services

32. The banks and private non-bank financial institutions should be encouraged to provide factoring services. A few Factoring Divisions should be set up by July 1, 1987.

Legislative Changes

33. In the interest of developing a strong financial and banking system, the government of India should take necessary measures to abolish the stamp duty on bills.
34. The viability of the new instrument of commercial paper would be better ensured if commercial paper is exempt from stamp duty.
35. Suitable amendments may need to be effected in the Reserve Bank of India Act to enable the Bank to provide refinance to the Finance House of India.

Time Frame of Implementation

36. While the measures recommended from an integrated package, there is a need for a well chalked out phased program and accordingly, a time schedule for implementing the Working Group's recommendations has been set out below.

III. REPORT OF THE COMMITTEE ON THE FINANCIAL SYSTEM (Narasimham Committee, November 1991)

1. The committee's approach to the issue of financial sector reform is to ensure that the financial services industry operates on the basis of operational flexibility and functional autonomy with a view to enhancing efficiency, productivity and profitability. A vibrant and competitive financial system is also necessary to sustain the ongoing reform in the structural aspects of the real economy. We believe that ensuring the integrity and autonomy of operations of banks and DFIs is by far the more relevant issue at present than the question of their ownership. SLR and CRR

2. The committee is of the view that the SLR instrument should be deployed in conformity with the original intention of regarding it as a prudential requirement and not be viewed as a major instrument for financing the public sector. In line with the Government's decisions to reduce the fiscal deficit to a level consistent with macroeconomic stability, the Committee recommends that the SLR be brought down in a phased manner to 25 per cent over a period of about five years, starting with some reduction in the current year itself.

3. As regards the cash reserve ratio (CRR), the Reserve Bank should have the flexibility to operate this instrument to serve its monetary policy objectives. The Committee believes that given the government's resolve to reduce the fiscal deficit, the occasion for the use of CRR to control the secondary expansion of credit should also be less. The Committee accordingly proposes that the Reserve Bank consider progressively reducing the CRR from its present high level. With the deregulation of interest rates there would be more scope for the use of open market operations by the Reserve Bank with correspondingly less emphasis on variations in the CRR.

4. The Committee proposes that the interest rate paid to banks on their SLR investments and on CRR in respect of impounded deposits above the basic minimum should be increased. As discussed

later, the rates on SLR investments should be progressively market – related while that on CRR above the basic minimum should be broadly related to bank's average cost of deposits. However, during the present regime of administered interest rates, this rate may be fixed at the level of bank's one year deposit rate.

Direct Credit

5. The committee recognizes that in the last two decades and credit policies have been deployed with a objective. However, the Committee believes that the pursuit of such objectives should use the instrumentality of the fiscal rather than the credit system. Accordingly, the Committee proposes that the directed credit programs should be phased out. This process of phasing out would also recognize the need that for some time it would be necessary for a measure of special credit support through direction. The Committee therefore, proposes that the priority sector be redefined to comprise the small and marginal farmer, the tiny sector of industry, small business and transport operators, village and cottage industries, rural artisans, and other weaker sections. The credit target for this redefined priority sector should henceforth be fixed at 10 per cent of aggregate credit which would be broadly in line with the credit flows to these sectors at present. The Committee also proposes that a review may be undertaken at the end of three years to see if directed credit programs need to be continued. As regards medium and large farmers, and the larger among small industries, including transport operators, etc. who would not now constitute part of the redefined priority sector, the Committee proposes that to further encourage banks to provide credit to these erstwhile constituents of the priority sector, the Reserve Bank and other refinancing agencies institute a preferential refinance scheme in terms of which incremental credit to these sectors would be eligible for preferential refinance subject to normal eligibility criteria.

Interest Rates

6. The committee is of the view that the present structure of administered interest rates is highly complex and rigid. This is so in spite of the recent moves towards deregulation. The Committee proposes that interest rates be further deregulated so as to reflect emerging market conditions. At the same time, the Committee believes that a reasonable degree of macroeconomic balance through a reduction in the fiscal deficit is necessary for successful deregulation of interest rates. Premature moves to market – determine interest rates could, as experience abroad has shown, pose the danger of excessive bank lending at high nominal rates to borrowers of dubious credit – worthiness, eventually creating acute problems for both the bank as well as the borrowers. Accordingly, the Committee recommends that for the present, interest rates on bank deposits may continue to be regulated, the ceiling in such rates being raised as the SLR reduced progressively as suggested by us earlier. Similarly, the interest rate on government borrowing may also be gradually brought in line with market – determined rates which would be facilitated by the reduction in SLR. Meanwhile, the Committee would recommend that concessional interest rates should be phased out. The structure of interest rates should bear a broad relationship to the Bank rate which should be used as an anchor to signal the Reserve Bank's monetary policy stance. It would be desirable to provide for what may be called a prime rate, which would be the floor of the lending rates of banks DFIs. The spreads between Bank rate, the bank deposit rates, the government borrowing rates and the prime rate may be determined by the RBI broadly in accordance with the criteria suggested by the Chakravarty Committee so as to ensure that the real rates of interest remain positive.

7. The inadequacy of capital in the banking system is a cause for concern. While progress towards BIS norms is desirable, the Committee recognizes that this will have to be phased over time. The committee suggests that the banks and financial institutions should achieve a minimum 4 per cent capital adequacy ratio in relation to risk weighted assets by March 1993, of which Tier 1 capital should be not less than 2 percent. The BIS standards of 8 per cent should be achieved over the period of the following three years, that is, March 1996. For those banks with an international presence it would be necessary to reach these figures even earlier.

8. The Committee believes that in respect of those banks whose operations have been profitable and which enjoy a good reputation in the markets, they could straight away approach the capital market for enhancement of their capital. The Committee therefore, recommends that in respect of such banks, issue of fresh capital to the public through the capital market should be permitted. Subscribers to such issues could include mutual funds, profitable public sector undertakings and employees of the institutions besides the general public. In respect of other banks, the government could meet the shortfall in their capital requirements by direct subscription to capital or by providing a loan which could be treated as subordinate debt.

9. Before arriving at the capital adequacy ratio for each bank, it is necessary that assets of the banks be evaluated on the basis of their realisable values. The committee proposes that the banks and financial institutions adopt uniform accounting practices particularly in regard to income recognition and provisioning against doubtful debts. There is need also for adopting sound practices in regard to valuation of investment on the lines suggested by the Ghosh Committee on Final Accounts.

Income Recognition

10. In regard to income recognition the Committee recommends that in respect of banks and financial institutions which are following the accrual system of accounting, no income should be recognized in the accounts in respect of non performing assets. An asset would be considered non-performing if interest on such assets remains past due for a period exceeding 180 days at the balance sheet date. The Committee further recommends that banks and financial institutions be given a period of three years to move towards the above norms in a phased manner beginning with the current year.

Provisioning

11. For the purpose of provisioning the Committee recommends that, using the health code classification which is already in vogue in banks and financial institution, the assets should be classified into four categories namely, Standard, Sub-standard, Doubtful and Loss Assets. In regard to Sub – Standard Assets, a general provision should be created equal to 10 per cent of the total outstandings under this category. In respect of Doubtful Debts, provision should be created to the extent of 100 per cent of the security shortfall. In respect of the secured portion of some Doubtful Debts, further provision should be created, ranging from 20 per cent to 50 per cent, depending on the period on for which such assets remain in the doubtful category. Loss Assets either be fully written off or provision be created to the extent of 100 percent. The Committee is of the view that a period of four years should be given to the banks and financial institutions to conform to these provisioning requirements. The movement towards these norms should be done in a phased manner beginning with the current year. However, it is necessary for banks and financial institutions to ensure that in respect of doubtful debts 100 per cent of the security shortfall us fully provided in the shortest possible time.

12. The Committee believes that the balance sheets of banks and financial institutions should be made transparent and full disclosures made in the balance sheet as recommended by the International Accounting Standards Committee. This should be done in a phased manner commencing with the current year. The Reserve Bank, however, may defer implementation of such parts of the standards as it considers appropriate during the transitional period until the norms regarding income recognition and provisioning are fully implemented.

13. The Committee suggests that the criteria recommended for non – performing assets and provisioning requirements be given due recognition by the tax authorities. For this purpose, the Committee recommends that the guidelines to be issued by the Reserve Bank if India under Section 43 D of the Income Tax Act should be in line with our recommendations for determining of non – performing assets. Also, the specific provisions made by the banks and institutions in line with our recommendations should be made permissible deductions under the Income Tax Act. The Committee further suggests that in regard to general provisions, instead of deductions under Section 36 (1) (viia) being restricted to 5 per cent of total income and 2 per cent of the aggregate

average advances by rural branches, it should be restricted to 0.5 per cent of the aggregate average non-agricultural advances and 2 per cent of the aggregate advance by rural branches. This exemption should also be available to banks having operations outside India in respect of their Indian assets, in addition to the deductions available under Section 36 (1) (viii)

Assets Reconstruction Fund

14. Banks, at present, experience considerable difficulties in recoveries of loans and enforcement of security charged to them. The delays that characterize our legal system have resulted in the blocking of a significant portion of the funds of banks and DFIs in unproductive assets, the value of which deteriorate with the passage of time. The committee, therefore, considers that there is urgent need to work out a suitable mechanism through which the dues to the credit institutions could be realized without delay and strongly recommends that Special Tribunals on the pattern recommended by the Tiwari Committee on the subject by set up to speed up the process of recovery. The introduction of legalization for this purpose is long overdue and should and should be proceeded with immediately.

15. While the reform of accounting practices and the creation of Special Tribunals are essential, the Committee believes that an arrangement has to be worked out under which at least part of the bad and doubtful debts of the banks and financial institutions are taken off the balance sheet so that the banks could recycle the funds realized through this process into more productive assets. For this purpose, the establishment, if necessary by special legislation, of an Asset Reconstruction Fund (ARF) which could take over from the banks and financial institutions a portion of the bed and doubtful debts at a discount, the level of discount being determined by independent auditors on the basis of clearly stipulated guidelines. The ARF should be provided with special powers for recovery somewhat boarder than those contained in Sections 29-32 of the State Financial Corporation's Act 1951. The capital of the ARF should be subscribed by the public sector banks and financial institutions.

Structure of Banking System

16. In regard to the structure of the banking system, the committee is of the view that the system should evolve towards a broad pattern consisting of:
    (a)   three or four large banks (including the State Bank of India) which could become international in character;
    (b)   eight to ten national banks with a network of branches throughout the country engaged in 'universal' banking;
    (c)   Local Banks whose operations would be generally confirmed to specific region; and
    (d)   Rural banks (including RRBs) whose operations would be confirmed to the rural areas and whose business would be predominantly engaged in financing of agriculture and allied activities.
    The Committee is of the view that the move towards this revised system should be market –driven and based on profitability considerations and brought about through a process of mergers and acquisitions.

17. The Committee is of the view that the structure of rural credit will have to combine the local character of the RRBs and the resources, skills and organizational / managerial abilities of the commercial banks. With this end in view the Committee recommends that each public sector bank should set up one or more rural banking subsidiaries, depending on the size and administrative convenience of each sponsor bank, to take over all its rural branches and, where appropriate, swap its rural branches with those of other banks. Such rural banking subsidiaries should be treated on par with RRBs in regard to CRR/SLR requirements and refinance facilities from NABARD and sponsor banks. The 10 per cent for directed credit which we have recommended as a transactional measure should be calculated on the basis of the combined totals of the parent banks and their subsidiaries. The committee purposes, that while RRBs should be allowed to engage in all types of

banking business, their focus should continue to be to lend to the target groups to maintain, at a minimum, the present level of their lending to these groups. With a view to improving the viability of their operations, the Committee proposes that the interest rate structure of the RRBs should be in line with those of the commercial banks. The committee would leave the option open to the RRBs and their sponsor banks as to whether the RRBs should retain their identity so that their focus on lending to the target groups is not diffused or where both the RRBs and the sponsor banks wish to do so they could be merged with the sponsor banks and the sponsor banks in such cases should take them over as 100 per cent subsidiaries by buying out the shares from other agencies at a token price, and eventually merge them with the rural banking subsidiaries which we have proposed. For those RRBs that retain their identity and whose viability would need to be improved, we propose that instead of investing in Government bonds as part of their SLR requirements, they could place the amounts stipulated under SLR as deposits with NABARD or some special federal type of agency that might be set up for this purpose. This would also be consistent with the statutory requirements in this regard and NABARD or this agency could pay interest on such balances by investing or deploying these funds to the best advantage on their behalf and thus help to augment the income of the RRBs.

18. The Committee proposes that government should indicate that there would be no further nationalization of banks. Such an assurance will remove the existing disincentive for the more dynamic among the private banks to grow. The Committee also recommends that there should be any difference in treatment between the public sector and the private sector banks. The Committee would purpose that there be no bar to new banks in the private sector being set up provided they conform to the start-up capital and other requirements as may be prescribed with regard to accounting, provisioning and other aspects of operations. This in conjunction with the relevant statutory requirements governing their operations would provide adequate safeguards against misuse of bank's resources to the detriment of the depositor's interests.

Branch Licensing

19. The Committee recommends that branch licensing be abolished and the matter of opening branches or closing branches (other that rural branches for the present) be left to the commercial judgement of the individual banks.

20. The committee also believes that, consistent with other aspects of Government policy dealing with foreign investment, the policy with regard to allowing foreign banks to open offices in India either as branches or, where the Reserve Bank considers it appropriate, as subsidiaries, should be more liberal, subject to the maintenance of minimum assigned capital as may be prescribed by the Reserve Bank and the statutory requirements of reciprocity. Joint ventures, between foreign banks and Indian banks could also be permitted, particularly in regard to merchant and investment banking, leasing and other newer forms of financial services.

21. Foreign banks when permitted to operate in India should be subjected to the same requirements as are applicable to domestic banks. If, in view of certain constrains such as absence of branch network, the foreign banks are unable to fulfil certain requirements such as directed credit (of 10 per cent of aggregate credit) the Reserve Bank should work out alternative methods with a view to ensuring a level playing field.

22. The Committee is of the view that the foreign operations of Indian banks need to be rationalized. In line with the structure of the banking system visualized above, there would seem to be scope for one or more of the large banks, in addition to the SBI, to have operations abroad in major international financial centres and in regions with strong Indian ethic presence. Pending the evolution of a few Indian banks with an international character, the Committee recommends as an interim measure that those Indian banks with the largest presence abroad and strong financial position could jointly set up or more subsidiaries to take over their existing branches abroad. The SBI operations abroad can continue and indeed be strengthened in course of time. The Government may also consider the larger banks increasing their presence abroad by taking over existing small banks incorporated abroad as a means of expanding their international operations.

23. The Committee believes that the internal organization of banks is best left to the judgement of the management of individual banks, depending upon the size of the bank, its branch spread and range of functions. However, for the medium and large national banks the Committee proposes a three-tier structure in terms of head office, a zonal office and branches. In the case of very large banks, a four – tier organization, as is the case with the State Bank, with head office, zonal office, regional and branch may be appropriate. Local banks may not need an intermediate tier between the branch and the central office.

Computerization

24. The Committee endorses the view of the Rajgarajan Committee on Computerization that there is urgent need of a far greater use of computerized system than at present. Computerization has to be recognized as an indisposable tool for improvement in customer service, the institution and operation of better control systems, greater efficiency in information technology and the betterment of the work environment for employees. These are essential requirements for banks to function effectively and profitably in the increasingly complex and competitive environment which is fast developing in the financial services segment of the economy.
25. The Committee believes that there has to be a recognition on the part of managements and trade unions that the system cannot hope to be competitive internally and be in step with the wide – ranging innovations taking place abroad without a radical change in work technology and culture and greater flexibility in personnel policies. We have been reassured to know that organized labour is as much convinced of the importance of enhancing the viability and profitability of the banking industry and providing efficient customer service. It is equally incumbent on management of banks to adapt forward looking personnel policies which would help to create a satisfying work environment.
26. The Committee recommends that the various guidelines directives issued by the Government of the Reserve Bank in regard to internal administration of the banks should be reviewed to examine their continuing relevance in the context of the need to ensure the independence and autonomy of banks. Such guidelines which relate to matters of internal administration such as creation and categorization of posts, promotion procedures and similar matter should be rescinded
27. The Committee believes that the Indian banking system, at present, is over-regulated and over – administrated. Supervision should be based on evolving prudential norms and regulations which should be adhered to rather than excessive control over administrative and other aspects of bank organization and functioning. The Committee would also like to place greater emphasis on internal audit and internal inspection systems of banks. The inspection by the supervisory authorities should be based essentially on the internal audit and inspection reports. Their main concern should be to ensure that audit and inspection machinery (which will cover the credit appraisal system and its observance) is adequate and conforms to well laid down norms.

Duality of Control

28. The Committee is firmly of the opinion that the control over the banking system between the Reserve Bank and the Banking Division of the Ministry of Finance should end and that the Reserve Bank should be the primarily agency for the regulation of the banking system. The supervisory function over the banks and other financial institutions, the Committee believes, should be hived off to a separate authority to operate as a quasi – autonomous body under the aegis of the Reserve Bank but which would be separate from other central banking functions of the Reserve Bank. The Committee recognizes that as long as the Government has proprietary interest in banks and financial institutions, it would be appropriate for the Ministry of Finance to deal with other Government departments and Parliament and discharge its other statutory obligations but not to engage in direct regulatory functions.
29. Central to the issue of flexibility of operations and autonomy of internal functioning is the question of depoliticising the appointment of the chief executive (CMD) of the banks and the board of the banks and ensuring security of tenure for the CMD. The committee believes that

professionalism and integrity should be the prime considerations in determining such appointment and while the formal appointments have to be made by Government, they should be based on a convention of acception the recommendations of a group of eminent persons who could be invited by the Governor of the Reserve Bank to make recommendations for such appointments. As regards the boards of public sector banks and institutions, as long as Government owns the banks, it would be necessary to have a Government director to take care of 'proprietorial' concerns but we believe that there is no need for the Reserve Bank to have a representative on the boards.

Development Financial Institutions (DFIs)

30. As regards development financial institutions, the main issue with regard to their operations are to ensure operational flexibility, a mearure of competition and adequate internal autonomy in matters of loan sanctioning and internal administration. The Committee proposes that the system recommended for commercial banks in the matter of appointment of chief executives and boards should also apply to DFIs. The present system of consortium lending has been perceived as operating like a cartel. The Committee believes that consortium lending should be dispensed with and, in its place, a system of syndication or participation in lending, at the instance not only, as now, of the lenders but also of the borrowers, should be introduced. The Committee also believes that commercial banks should be encouraged to provide term finance to industry, while at the same time, the DFIs should increasingly engage in providing core working capital. This will help to enhance healthy competition between banks and DFIs. The Committee proposes that the present system of cross holding of equity and cross representation on the boards of the DFIs should be dine away with. The Committee welcomes the removal of the tax concession enjoyed by IDBI as an important step in ensuring equality of treatment between various DFIs. As a further measure of enhancing competition and ensuring a level playing field, the Committee proposes that the IDBI should retain only its apex and refinancing role and that is direct lending function be transferred to a separate institution which could be incorporated as a company. The infected portion of the DFIs portfolio should be handed over to the ARF on the same terms and conditions as would apply to commercial banks.

New Institutions

32. In the last decade several new institutions have appeared on the financial scene. Merchant banks, mutual funds, leasing companies, venture capital companies and factoring companies have now joined hire purchase companies in expanding the range of financial services available. However, the regulatory framework for these new set of institutions has still to be developed.
33. The Committee recommends that the supervision of these institutions which form an integral part of the financial system should come within the purview of the new agency to be set up for this purpose under the aegis of the RBI. The control of these institutions should be principally confined to off-site supervision with the on-site supervision being restored to cases which call for active intervention. The SEBI which is charged with the responsibility of ensuring orderly functioning of the market should have jurisdiction over these institutions to the extent their activities impinge on market operations. In regard to mutual funds there is a good case for enacting new legislation on the lines obtaining in several countries with a view to providing an appropriate legal framework for their constitution and functioning. The present guidelines with regard to venture capital companies are unduly restrictive, and affecting the growth of this business and need to be reviewed and amended.
34. As in the case of banks and financial institutions there is need to lay down prudential norms and guidelines governing the functioning of these institutions. These prudential guidelines should relate, among other things, to capital adequacy, debt equity ratio, income recognition provisioning against doubtful debts, adherence to sound accounting and financial policies, disclosure requirements and valuations of assets. The eligibility criteria for entry, growth and exit should also be clearly stipulated so that the growth of these institutions takes place on proper lines.

Sequencing of Reforms

35. The Committee would like to emphasis that a proper sequencing of reforms is essential. Deregulation of interest rates can only follow success in controlling fiscal deficits. Asset reconstruction, institution of capital adequacy and establishment of prudential norms with a good supervisory machinery have to be proceeded with in a phased manner over the next 3 to 5 years but, we believe, it is important that the process must begin in the current year itself.
36. The Committee's approach thus seeks to consolidate the gains made in the Indian financial sector while improving the quality of the portfolio providing greater operational flexibility and most importantly greater autonomy in the internal operations of the banks and financial institutions so as to nurture a healthy, competitive and vibrant financial sector. This will above all else, require depoliticisation of appointments, implying at the same time a self-denial by Government and the perception that is has distanced itself from the internal decision making of the banks and the financial institutions. The proposed deregulation of the financial sector and the measure aimed at improving it health competitive vitality would, in the Committee's view, be consistent with the steps being taken to open up the Indian economy, enable the Indian financial sector to forge closer links with the global financial markets, and enhance India's ability to take competitive advantage of the increasing international opportunities for Indian trade, industry and finance.

IV. TASK FORCE ON MONEY MARKET MUTUAL FUNDS (MMMFs) (Basu Committee, Jnauary 1992)

1. To begin with, MMMFs be set up only by schedule commercial banks and public financial institutions as defined under Section 4A of the Companies Act, 1956 directly or through their existing mutual funds/subsidiaries engaged in funds management.
2. MMMFs can be set up either as a part of a bank in the form of a Division / Department, i.e. 'in house' MMMFs or it could be set up as a separate entity as a 'Trust'.
3. MMMFs Scheme canbe usually in two forms such as 'Money Market Deposit Account' (MMDA) or 'Money Market Mutual Funds' (MMMFs). MMDA Scheme can be operated either by issuing deposit receipts or through issue of a 'Pass Book'. The 'modus operandi' of the MMMF Scheme could be left to the individual institutions. The Pass Book Account Scheme should be without cheque book facility to being with.
4. MMMFs would have combined features of 'open' and 'close' ended schemes. However, if some banks/institutions like to formulate schemes of either 'close' or 'open' ended fund, adhering to the overall limit stipulated by the Reserve Bank of India, it should be left to their option to do so.
5. Smaller banks could be allowed to set up MMMFs jointly.
6. For setting up of MMMFs at the initial stage, prior authorization from the Reserve Bank of India is desirable. The Reserve Bank should, however, formulate guidelines which are transparent and, inter alia, based on financial, managerial and operational aspects of banks/financial institutions.

Mobilization of Resources by MMMFs

7. In case of MMMFs set up the banks, the limit for raising resources by MMMFs may be fixed on the basis of their overall deposit size. The limit for MMMF may be fixed at 2 per cent of the fortnightly average aggregate deposits of the bank concerned in the previous financial year of Rs. 50 crore, whichever is higher. The limit will apply to MMMFs set up by them directly or through their Mutual Funds / subsidiaries engaged in funds management. The norm for determining the size of MMMFs should be reviewed by the Reserve Bank periodically.
8. In case of public financial institutions the limit for MMMFs may be related to their total long-term domestic borrowing; the size could be specified at 2 per cent of long –term domestic borrowings as indicated in their audited balance sheet. As in the case of banks, this limit will apply also to MMMFs set up through their Mutual Funds / funds management subsidiaries.

9. As regards minimum size of investment by individuals or others in MMMFs, the Task Force suggests that no minimum size either for individual investors or other needs to be specified and the matter should be left to the discretion of MMMFs.
10. The minimum lock-in period for investment in MMMFs should be reduced from 3 months to 46 days. The Task Force would urge the Reserve Bank of India to examine the feasibility of further reducing or even removing the minimum lock – in period at a future date.

Investment Pattern of MMMFs

11. Liquidity consideration be given top priority by the MMMFs while deciding on the types of instruments for investment.
12. MMMFs should not deploy their funds in capital market instrument, even if maturing within a year, so that their investments are not exposed to under risks.
13. The Task Force feels that though dated Government securities are not money market instruments, considering the security aspects, MMMFs could be allowed to invest in dated. Government securities having an unexpired maturity of up to one year. Furthermore, MMMFs coule also be allowed to invest in dated Government securities on 'Repo' basis for a period not exceeding one month. The investments in dated Government securities including on 'Reop' Basis should not exceed 25 per cent of investible funds of MMMFs at any point of time.
14. The minimum investment in 182 Days Treasury Bills laid down in the guidelines should be raised from 20 per cent to 25 per cent, while the maximum investment in call / notice money market should also be raised from 20 to 30 per cent of total investible funds of MMMFs. In this context, the 'Task Force would urge the Reserve Bank of India to consider ways of increasing the yield on 182 Days Treasury Bills to enhance the attractiveness of this instrument.
15. The exposure to CP should not be more than 15 per cent of the total investible funds of the MMMFs and the exposure to CP issued by a particular company should not be more than 20 per cent of the investible funds of MMMFs in CP.
16. MMMFs should rediscount only those bills which are accepted or co – accepted by banks. For commercial bills accepted or co – accepted by banks too, the exposure should not be more than 20 per cent of the total investible funds so as to minimize any possible risk to MMMFs.
17. MMMFs may be allowed to invest/ trade in instrument of other MMMFs as underlying assets of all MMMFs would generally be of similar qualities and there would be no additional risk involved. A cap of 10 per cent of investible funds may be prescribed for investments by one MMMF in shares/units of others.

Management of MMMFs

18. In – house MMMFs should take adequate and effective measures to ensure that management, accounting and custody of their assets should be kept distinct and separate from those relating to the investments of the bank and accounts should be subjected to separate audit.
19. MMMFs should not give any guarantee to the public as to the rate of return on investments while announcing any scheme. MMMFs may distribute their net earnings either by way of periodic income distribution or by quoting appropriate bid prices or a combination of both.
20. MMMFs should calculate Net Assets Value (NAV) of each scheme and disclose the NAV of each of the schemes and the method of valuation for the benefit of the concerned subscribers. To start with, MMMFs may determine and disclose 'NAV' of Found once in a week. Thereafter 'NAV' may be determined more frequently.

Regulatory Measures

21. The MMMFs to be set up by banks, their subsidiaries, public financial institutions and non-bank institutions like the existing Mutual funds, be required to comply with the guidelines and directives that may be issued from time to time by the Reserve Bank of India only.

Legislative Changes

22 The provision of exemption from payment of income tax should be extended to MMMFs set up by private sector banks and subsidiaries of public sector banks and private sector banks by suitable amendment to sub-section (23D) of Section 10 of the Income Tax Act, 1961.
23. The Reserve Bank of India may consider exempting in – house MMFs set up by banks from a reserve requirements. To begin with, the Reserve Bank of India could prescribe that a statutory minimum SLR of 25 per cent under the Banking Regulation Act, 1949 be maintained by investment, inter alia, in 182 Days Treasury Bills as envisaged in the prudential investment guidelines.
24. The units/ shares of MMMFs may be exempted from stamp duty at the time of issue of instruments and at the time of transfer of instruments in the secondary market. This would provide impetus to the development of the secondary market for money market instrument. Accordingly, the Task Force suggests that the Reserve Bank of India should request the Government of India to remit stamp duty to such instruments.
25. The stamp duty chargeable in respect of all money market instruments, such as CDs, CPs, etc. be remitted as in the case of Commercial Bills and the Reserve Bank of India may take up this aspect with the Government of India.

V. WORKING GROUP ON NON-BANKING FINANCE COMPANIES (A.C. Shah Committee, September 1992)

1. Growth and diversification of non-banking financial companies (NBFCs) is an integral part of the development process of the financial market the economy. The approach of the Group revolves round the conviction that a thriving, healthy and growing non-banking financial sector is necessary for promoting the growth of an efficient and competitive economy. From the angle of depositors' protection and efficacy of monetary and credit policy, what is really required is a well – integrated regulatory framework which, while monitoring and supervising the operations of NBFCs, recognizes and even encourages the emergence of new types of financial services and products.
2. In the last two decades, non-banking financial sector has witnessed a marked growth. Some of the factors which have contributed to this growth have been, lesser regulation over this sector vis-à-vis the banking sector, higher deposit interest rates offered by this sector, higher level of customer orientation, the speed with which it caters to customer needs and so forth.
3. Number of NBFCs increased from 7,063 in 1981 to as much as 24,009 in 1900, thus registering compounded annual growth of about 14 per cent. Deposits with these companies grew ten fold during this period.
4. Non-bank deposits as a ratio of gross financial savings of the house – hold sector went up from 2 per cent in 1981-82 to 7.9 per cent in 1980-90. Although, the magnitude of deposits, with non-banking financial companies in relation to total bank deposits still forms a small percentage, there is enough evidence of acceleration in the growth of these deposits which underlines the need for effective regulation.
5. Although, the number of non-bank financial intermediaries, both in the organized and unorganized sector is very large, only about 1600 companies with constitute 21 per cent of the reporting companies account for as much as 97 per cent of total deposits.
6. The need for bringing NBFCs under the regulatory framework arises not only for ensuring their healthy growth but also improving the efficacy of the credit and monetary policy as well as for inculcating healthy financial discipline among both providers and users of credit.
7. The Group recommends dismantling of the category-classification of NBFCs and application of uniform regulation for all NBFCs.
8. The group recognizes the need for effective regulation of all deposit – taking entities, howsoever small they may be. However, due to the large number of operators in this filed and the limited size

9. of administrative infrastructure, the Group advocates that regulatory attention be confined to those large-size companies which account for a lion's share of total non – banking financial companies' deposits.
9. All the existing deposit – taking companies with net owned funds of Rs. 50 lakh and over should compulsory register with the regulatory authority. This cut-off point may be reviewed subsequently. Companies with net owned funds below this cut-off point may, if they so prefer, opt for registration. Registered companies will be allowed to accept public deposits up to a multiple of their net owned funds. Unregistered companies with net owned funds of less than Rs. 50 lakh will be allowed to accept public deposits at a lower level, i.e. in accordance with procisions of Section 58 A of the Companies Act, 1956.
10. The Group facours prescription of entry norms for all new NBFCs such as (a) minimum net owned fund of Rs. 50 lakh at the time of commencement; (b) registration with the regulatory authority; (c) restriction on deposit – acceptance activity at the level permitted to unregistered companies in first two full financial years of operation, and (d) permission for deposit acceptance at par with the existing registered companies after completion of this period, on the basis of track record, quality of management, methods of operation etc.
11. The Group is of the opinion that the function of registration and regulation be undertaken by the proposed High Powered Supervisory Board.
12. The Group advocates that the focus of NBFC – regulation be shifted from liability side to asset-side of NBFC balance sheet and is in facour of prescribing capital adequacy standard based on risk-weighted assets prescribed for commercial banks. The Group recommends that the regulatory authority; in co-ordination with the representatives of NBFCs, Self Organizations and the Institute of Chartered Accountants, may complete the exercise of computing risk weights and credit conversion factors by March 31, 1994 and that capital adequacy ratio at the rate of 8 per cent of the risk weighted assets and off-balance sheet items be introduced by March 31, 1995.
13. Until the time, capital adequacy framework is introduced, the existing limits on deposit acceptance may be continued subject, however, to an overall debt equity ratio of 15:1.
14. The Group recommends placing restrictions on the portfolio management activities of these companies.
15. In addition, the Group facours that NBFCs be required to (a) maintain liquidity ratio of 10 per cent of their total deposit liabilities, (b) limit their risk exposure to single and group borrowers to 15 and 25 per cent of their net owned funds respectively, (c) transfer at least 20 per cent of their net profit to reserves every year unit reserves equal the company's share capital, and (d) refrain from investing in certain undesirable activities as defined by the regulatory authority.
16. The Group favours that until the time commercial bank deposit interest rate are regulated, NBFC interest rate also continue to be regulated and that the latter be pegged two to three per cent above the former. The Group also favour that NBFCs be allowed to accept deposits for periods ranging between 12 to 84 months as against the existing range of 24 to 120 months.
17. The Group favours abolition of the existing distinction between the terms 'exempted' and 'regulated' deposits for the purpose of calculating the gearing ratio and instead suggests that a distinction be made between 'borrowings' and 'deposits'. The regulatory authority may, if it deems fir, create a distinction between 'exempted' and 'regulated' deposits for the purpose of tenor of deposit, rate of interest etc. Deposit insurance is not recommended at this stage.
18. The Group recommends making credit rating compulsory for all registered companies, not in the immediate future but after a period of five years. The Group also recommends relaxations in the Advertisement Rules.
19. The Group suggest prescription of norms regarding income recognition, disclosure or transparency of accounts, provision for bad and doubtful debts, etc. A committee may be constitute for formulating these norms. Suitable reporting formats may also be devised to that effective supervision may be undertaken by the regulatory authority.
20. The Group facvours assignment of greater role to auditors in the supervisory process. Periodical statements to be submitted by NBFCs to regulatory authorities will need certification by the auditors. Based on the rule of exception, NBFCs may be inspected by the regulatory authority.

21. The regulatory authority should be empowered to suspend/cancel registration of these companies and even move for winding up where it so deems necessary.
22. As regards unicorporated entities, apart form the existing restriction on the number of depositors, the Group recommends prescription of ceiling on the quantum of deposits they can accept. A Standing Advisory Committee may be constituted for reviewing regulatory requirements for these bodies.
23. The regulatory authority should publish the list of all NBFCs periodically.
24. The Group recommends that the regulatory authority and the self regulating organizations may initiate a public awareness program for educating the depositors about the risks associated in placing deposits with various kinds of non-banking financial companies.

VI. COMMITTEE ON CONSORTIUM LENDING
(J. V. Shetty Committee, August 1993)

1. The Committee recognizes the need to shift to market – driven banking from the present practices. Approach of the Committee has, therefore, been to ensure smooth transformation of the banking system during the current period of transition. The objectives behind the recommendations have, therefore, been to ensure financial discipline on the part of the borrowers together with improvement in the services offered by the banking system in the interregnum till the system completely switches over to market – driven banking. The Committee therefore, recommends introduction of syndication together with continuation of the existing consortium arrangement, in the case of consortium arrangement with substantial modifications to ensure that it becomes simpler and more flexible to meet quickly the credit needs of trade and industry.
2. In order to usher in market – driven banking the Committee recommends enhancement of the present threshold limit of Rs. 5 crors with immediate effect and to Rs. 25crore or above by March 31, 1996, for mandatory formation of a consortium when a borrower enjoys fund – based credit limits from more than on bank. The Committee also recommends that in the light of the experience gained the desirability of dispensing with the concept of threshold limit itself may be considered in due course.
3. The Committee recommends introduction of syndication for borrowers enjoying fund – based working capital limit of Rs. 25 crore or above from the banking system.
4. With the objective of ensuring financial discipline the Committee recommends that borrowers availing of credit facilities under multiple banking should submit details of credit facilities already availed of from different banks duly certified by their auditors, each time a fresh facility/ enhancement is sought for.
5. Considering the basic objective for forming consortium / syndication, i.e. dispersal of risks, the Committee recommends that banks can voluntarily form consortium even in cases where total limits are below the proposed enhanced threshold limits.
6. The need for expeditious disposal of credit proposals to meet the working capital requirements is well recognized and the following maximum time – frame has been prescribed for this purpose

	Maximum time frame for disposal of over-all credit proposals	Maximum time frame for disposal of export credit requirement
Proposal for sanction of fresh/enhanced credit limits	60 days	45 dyas
Proposal for renewal of existing credit limits	45 days	30 days
Proposal for sanction of ad-hoc credit limits	30 days	15 dyas

7. One of the main reasons for delay in arriving at decisions has been non – submission of data and information, particularly, the audited accounts. The Committee, therefore, recommends that banks

may review borrowal accounts during the first quarter of the current year (April to June) based on the audited statements for the year before last provisional statements for the last year, current year estimate and projections for the next year and consider releasing 50 per cent of the additional requirement of credit subject to submission of audited accounts at a later date for release of the balance account.

8. To expedite the process of disposal of proposals, banks should delegate sufficient power to their functionaries attending consortium meetings.

9. As a meaningful participation in a consortium should be determined based on the extent of share of a member in the credit limits rather than by limiting to total number of banks in a consortium should be dispensed with and banks should instead take a minimum share of 5 per cent of the fund – based working capital limits or Rs. 1 crore, whichever is more.

10. The set of documents under single window concept of lending for meeting the requirements of a borrower in a consortium has been revised and the same has been approved by the Managing Committee of Indian Bank's Association. The Committee recommends that the Reserve Bank of India may please adopt the revised set of documents and consider issuing of suitable instructions to this effect to the banks.

11. In order to ensure credit requirements of borrowers are met fully and within the maximum time – frame prescribed, borrowers will be free to induct new banks into a consortium. However, the entry of a new bank will be subject to its fulfilling certain procedural requirements to ensure financial discipline.

12. Banks will also have freedom to leave a consortium after a minimum period of two years subject to certain conditions. Further, it will be left to an individual bank in a consortium to decide about acceptance of its enhanced share for meeting additional credit requirements of a borrower.

13. The present discipline of banks being not permitted to extend any type of credit facility to borrowers, where they are not member of the consortia, or where such borrowers are not their regular constituents, will continue.

14. The terms and conditions governing the sanction of credit in a consortium should be uniformly applied by all members and are equally applicable to the rate of interest for different categories of advances.

15. At present of loans and advances by individual memner-banks in a consortium is not possible. With advent of market – driven banking and hence market – determined interest rates, it should be possible for banks to adopt independent pricing in due course. A beginning in this regard can be made now by adopting 'pricing' for facilities to be extended under syndication.

16. The lead bank should be vested with the responsibility of arranging for sanction and disbursal of credit (including documentation) as also for monitoring the account in the matter of advancing operative limits, verification of security, etc. The view of the lead bank and the bank having the next largest share will prevail in cases of disputes arising among members relating to terms and conditions of sanction.

17. The lead bank should have the freedom to sanction additional credit by a pre-determined percentage to meet emergent situations/ contigenicies.

18. The lead bank should be entitled to a fee, say 0.25 per cent of the limits per annum, to be borne by the borrower, for services rendered.

19. For assessment of credit requirements, borrowers having multi – division / multi product companies should be treated as one single unit, unless there is more than one published/ audited balance sheet and should be financed by one consortium. Similarly in the case of mergers one consortium should finance the merged unit.

20. The lending norms for arriving at the maximum permissible bank finance should henceforth be regarded as guidelines. Banks must have discretion to apply these norms with more flexibility.

21. Commercial paper should be made more popular by increasing its tenure to 360 days and developing an active secondary market for the instrument. CP should continue to be carved out of maximum permissible bank finance, as hitherto, as standby facilities / restoration of credit limits provide better investor confidence.

22. The legal framework permitting public limited and public sector companies to issue debentures for augmenting their long-term sources for working capital requirements to the extent of only 20

per cent of their gross current assets, loans and advances should be reviewed to consider raising this ceiling.
23. Inter – bank participation certificates could be made a more effective and popular money market instrument by marketing it freely transferable 'with risk' and/or 'without risk' as also permitting its issue on usance beyond 90 days. Further, an active secondary market for the instrument could be created by allowing money market mutual funds to invest in them.

VII. WORKING GROUP ON CASH CREDIT SYSTEM
(R. Jilani Committee, October 1993)

1. The existing borrowers enjoying fund – based working capital limits of Rs. 10 crore and more from the banking system should be subjected to a minimum current ratio of 1.5. The excess borrowings or the shortfall in the net working capital of the borrower arising out of the enhanced current ratio should be carved out of the cash credit account of the borrower and kept in a separate loan account. The balance in the loan account together with interest thereon should be repaid by the borrower within a period of three to five years, depending upon the cash generating potential and the capacity to service long – term debt.
2. The resultant MPBF to which the borrower is entitled should represent the cash credit (including packing credit) and / or bills limits or Commercial Paper.
3. Interest on both the components, i.e. the loan carved out of the original cash credit account as well as the resultant balance in the cash credit account should be charged at the same rate. In the case of default in repayment of the installments in respect of the newly created loan, banks should charge interest on the amount in default at a rate slightly above the normal rate of interest.
4. The borrowers enjoying working capital limits of Rs. 50 lakhs and above but below Rs. 10 crore should be subjected to a minimum current ratio of 1.5 in a phased manner within a period of three years.
5. In respect of the new borrowers availing themselves of fund based working capital limits of Rs. 10 crore and above from the banking system, a minimum current ratio of 1.5 should be insisted upon ab initio. All India Financial Institutions may be advised to take note of this while appraising the large projects.
6. When the current ratio of a borrowing unit is higher than 1.5 slip – back in the current ratio upon the level of 1.5 may be allowed provided tha bank is satisfied about the genuineness of the reasons.
7. To ensure proper end use of funds by the borrowers, utilization of funds should be strictly monitored on the basis of the quarterly information statements.
8. In the case of seasonal industries MPBF is at present calculated on the basis of maximum deficit in the monthly / quarterly cash budget. Under the proposed system, at least on – third of this deficit should be financed from the long – term sources of borrowers.
9. In view of the need boost exports, the existing facility of 100 per cent financing at the post – shipment stage should continue.
10. Steps should be take to promote bill culture to a greater extent in respect of both purchases and sales. Vigorous efforts should be made to persuade Government Departments, public sector undertakings and large industrial establishments to accept bill drawn on them.
11. The Group believes that with the emergence of several new money market instruments as adjuncts to bank credit in the last one decade and the gradual dismantling of the protective environment, the dependence of borrowers on bank credit is bound to show a diminishing trend in the coming years The lesser dependence of borrowers on bank credit will result in reduction of the quantum of advances granted by banks by way of cash credit. The Group, therefore, concludes that the measures recommended above, will help achieve better end use of funds, instill better financial discipline, improve the quality of bank advances, facilitate better management of bank's funds and will be in line with the reforms in the financial sector currently taking place.

VIII. COMMITTEE TO REVIEW IRDP

(D. R. Mehta Committee, November 1994)

1. The poor without skills and experience in handling assets should be segregated into a separate category by a committee comprising the representatives of blocks, Panchayats, lead banks, school masters, postmasters, prominent villagers and grass – root NGOs; such poor people should be initially provided wage employment under various schemes of State Governments and Jawahar Rozgar Yojana. They should also be supported by providing for greater social consumption expenditure. They would be provided with assistance under IRDP subject to their acquiring or upgrading their skills. The other segment of the poor, i.e. families above the poorest of the poor which has reasonable measure of skills and experience may be provided assistance under IRDP straight away. The relatively new entrants to job market may be provided training under TRYSEM or other programs followed by assistance under IRDP.
2. For doing away with leakages and malpractices, the Committee recommends switch over from front-end to back – end system of subsidy. The benefit of subsidy should also be available to borrowers who prefer to avail themselves of working capital finance.
3. For improving recovery, Government of Indian may consider liking of certain percentage of subsidy allocation to recovery performance. Special recovery officers may be appointed by Governments. Enactment of Model Bill as recommended by Talwar Committee by remaining State Governments may be expedited. Loan waivers may not be declared. DRDA, Vos and SHGs may help banks in recovery. Utilization – Reporter – cum – Recovery Facilitators may be appointed on commission basis.
4. The work relating to identification of investment opportunities and preparation of project profiles may be undertaken by district level Technical group to be set up by DRDAs.
5. DRDAs must prepare a perspective plan of infrastructure in consultation with DCC and BLBC. The limit of expenditure for setting up of infrastructure may be raised to 20 per cent of budgetary allocation. Atleast one mini ITI or Rural Polytechnic may be set up in each block for imparting training to poor rural youth. Private sector may be associated with the task of setting up such institutions. Additional shifts for TRYSEM should be opened in all it is and other training institutions.
6. Democratic character of IRDP should be restored and strengthened by ensuring greater involvement of Panchayats and village population as also by imparting to the process of identification of beneficiaries a greater degree or transparency.
7. Banks may be authorized to finalize targets in respect of IRDP under service area plans on the basis of previous years' actual figures after adding 10 per cent for cushioning, without waiting for targets from Government of India.
8. Banks should fix realistic repayment schedules and provide for gestation period where required. Working capital assistance in the form of cash credit limits may also be provided where necessary The repayment for IRDP loans should not be less than 5 years. Banks may encourage group loans for various activities under IRDP. The limit for non – obtention of mortgage may be fixed at Rs 25,000 for all activities under IRDP. Collateral security may not be insisted for loans up to Rs 50,000. Banks may be given freedom to select the beneficiaries from BPL list on a pilot basis.
9. The level of per family / enterprise investment under IRDP should be enlarged by providing larger credit as also higher amount of subsidy.
10. Non-farm, tiny/small enterprises and services sector may be further promoted under IRDP.
11. DRDAs must be recognized into compact teams of professional and technical experts.
12. Voluntary organizations and Self – Help Groups may be associated with the implementation of IRDP. In the case of projects approved by CAPART a few VOs can be on pilot basis given list of BPL families for identification of borrowers, ensuring availability of backward/forward linkages. as also verifying end use of credit.
13. Banks should provided loans under IRDP for acquisition of land.
14. Cash disbursement under IRDP may be extended throughout the country. Family Credit Plan Scheme should be further encouraged.
15. Supplementary does of assistance under IRDP may be provided to beneficiaries who have not crossed the poverty line with initial assistance.

16. Panchayti Raj Institutions at grass – root or middle levels should be involved in the implementation of IRDP.
17. A new dimension should be added to IRDP through Information Education and Communication for which a separate budget should be provided.

IX. COMMITTEE ON TECHNOLOGICAL ISSUES
(W. S. Saraf Committee, December, 1994)

1. An Electronic Funds Transfer (EFT) system be setup. The BANKNET communication network may be the carrier. The fund settlement may be effected at the originating and the destination centers through the accounts of banks, maintained at the banks managing the respective clearinghouses.
2. The ultimate goal of the EFT is to facilitate funds transfer between two bank branches. To start with, message transfers to the destination centers may be in a batch mode. High value institutional fund transfers (Rupees 10 million and above) may be batched every hour while the retail customers transfers may be batched at the end of the day.
3. The scheme may cover all important centers in a phased manner, starting with the 4 metropolitan centers.
4. For operationalizing the EFT scheme banks may install the necessary computer and communication infrastructure (a PC/AT, a printer, a modem and direct telephone line) at their Service/Main branches. They should also have connectivity to BANKNET.
5. Steps may be initiated by RBI to enact suitable legislation on the lines for Electronic Fund Transfer Act 1978 in the USA and Data Protection Act 1984 in UK.
6. A DVP System in SGL transactions may be introduced at the Public Debt Office, Bombay. This may later be extended to other major centers.
7. The DVP System will cover SGL accounts of all those institutions who are also having current accounts at the Reserve Bank (Deposit Accounts Departments).
8. Settlement may be on gross basis both for securities (i.e. SGL) transactions in the Public Debt officer and current account (i.e. funds) transactions in the Deposit Accounts Department.
9. Relevant provisions in Public Debt Act 1944, public Debt Rules 1946 and Bankers' Books of Evidence Act 1891 may be amended to empower RBI to revise the SGL transfer from and in due course introduce screen based reporting of such transactions.
10. The concept of 'Clearing Bank' may introduced for extension of DVP mode to all trading in Government Securities.
11. The "Clearing Bank" will be required to maintain a clear distinction between operations on its own account and those in behalf of its clients.
12. Once the DVP system stabilized, the system of screen based reporting of SGL transactions should be introduced. SGL Transfer Form may be replaced by electronic screen formats.
13. RBI may explore the feasibility of using NICNET for electronic reporting of currency chest transaction Dial-up connectivity through Modem may also be used.
14. The currency chest branches with STD facility may transmit the currency chest data to both the Issue Officer of RBI and their respective Link Officers either through NICNET (by dialing the local NICNET node) or through PSTN lines. The branches not having STD facility may report the data by telephone / telegram to their district headquarters branch, which in turn would transmit these data to the Issue Officer of the RBI and its Link Office.
15. Later, when STD facility becomes available at the remaining currency chest branches, all currency chest may transmit these data to the Issue Office of the RBI and its Link Office.
16. RBI will, on a daily basis, make available the currency chest data received during the day to the local Link Offices of the respective banks, before the closing hours.
17. Fund Settlement in respect of Government transactions may be delinked from submission of scrolls and documents (challans/paid cheques) to the Pay and Accounts Offices (PAO) of Government Departments. Reporting of transactions to RBI for fund settlement and forwarding of scrolls to PAO may take place simultaneously.

18. Bank branches undertaking Government business may communicate the net receipt and payment position by PC Modem/telex/telegrams to their respective focal point branches on the same day, for further communication of the consolidate figures electronically to their Link Cells at Nagpur. The link cells would consolidate and forward the data files on floppies, tapes or directly to the computer to CAS, Nagpur before a prescribed time of fund settlement. This will ensure a T+1 system.
19. Link Cells of all banks at Nagpur, all focal point branches, State Government link offices should be computerized.
20. Repetitive or low value transactions like interest, dividend, refund of primary issue subscriptions, salary, pension, etc. may be effected electronically, by introducing "Electronic Clearing Service (ECS)". The facility may be extended to all corporate bodies/Govt. Departments, Debit clearing should also be introduced for pre – authorized debits for payments like insurance premia, taxes, loan installments etc.
21. A "Bills Payment System" may be introduced which will enable the customers of utility services to pay their bills by debit to their accounts in the banks. The Utility service agencies may redesign the formats of their bills to enable automatic data capture of the paid bills at the debiting branch/bank level. The settlement may be effected at the RBI on the basis of the data supplied by banks. Suitable costing of the bank's services may be done for charging the utility ageincies.
22. Cheque clearing work may be decentralized by introducing "Clearing Bank" concept of efficient cheque processing. Member banks of clearing house may join one of the Clearing banks Group. Each Group may have its own in-house, cheque processing facilities and other infrastructure. At Bombay, there should be atleast three Clearing Groups while at other MICR centers, there should be two Clearing Groups.
23. "Clearing Banks" will provide mutual backup to each other in case of disaster at any cheque processing site.
24. All MICR instrument should be of a uniform size. MICR codeline should be modified to include an additional field to indicate minimum control information (e.g. the scroll number) of the presenting banks.
25. Banks should equip their Service Branches and other large branches with computer and communication infrastructure (PC/AT, printer, network software, dial – up capabilities etc.) so as to enable them to present and receive the cheque clearing data (both outward and inward) electronically.
26. At Bombay, all inter – bank payments which are now settled through inter – bank clearing at the end of the day should be settled by on – line computer links between RBI and the banks Such fund transfers may be on a gross basis.
27. Cheque Transaction System should be introduced initially for Intra – bank cheques of value up to Rs. 5000. In due course, it may be extended to inter – bank instruments. Suitable changes in the Negotiable Instruments Act and other relevant acts may be initiated.
28. MICR clearing should be introduced at Ahmedabad, Bangalore, Hyderabad, Pune, Baroda and Surat at the earliest and dependable back-up arrangements should be planned right from the beginning.
29. Cheque clearing centers should be financially self supporting.
30. All centers having more than 100 bank branches should be taken up for MICR clearing.
31. The system of "Floppy Input Clearing" may be introduced as an interim measure pending MICR clearing at these centers.
32. Clearing arrangements should be set up all centers with five or more banks.
33. National Clearing cells of RBI may use the BANKNET for reporting the particulars of unpaid items of inter – city clearing on the network to the originating centers and for sending the credit advises to the banks. The collection cycle in RBI's National Clearing service can further be reduced by adopting this system.
34. Coverage of RBI's National Clearing of inter – city cheques may be extended. To start with, the centers which are already connected in one way clearing may be linked for two way clearing.
35. State Bank of India may organize inter – city clearing at centers not served by RBI on the lines of National Clearing Services of RBI.]

36. Standard codeline structure should be prescribed for non – MICR cheques also to facilitate data processing of outstation cheques.
37. The physical reach of the network should be extended to all centers where the RBI has officers and also to other centers which have at least 100 bank offices.
38. Branches covered under Total Branch Computerization (TBC) and the Service branches of banks should be equipped with BANKNET nodes.
39. The 'COMET' (the communication software for BANKNET) should provide for the following additional functionalities:

    (a) Dial – up support;
    (b) File transfer – ASCII and BINARY
    (c) End – to end encryption/authentication of messages and files.
    (d) Adoption of CRC/XOR/Checksum feature to ensure data integrity;
    (e) PING (Packet Inter Groper) facility;
    (f) Notification for messages;
    (g) Split Screen Visual communication with remote user;
    (h) System and messages status log;
    (i) Screen Printer;
    (j) Batch Input/Output Interface;
    (k) BACKUP and RESTORE facility;
    (l) Bridge between BANKNET and SWIFT

40. Switchover from voice grade transmission to high speed transmission facilities like, VSAT technology, fiber, optics, radio frequency etc. may be targeted.
41. BANKNET users may keep the BANKNET machines powered up on all working days all the time to facilitate the Automode function of COMET to log in to the host IBM system at pre – set interval and collect the messages.
42. For enhancing the reliability of the Network, dependence on a particular IBM system to act as the message host may be overcome by providing the facility of automatic fall back on any other IBM system if one of them is down.
43. RBINET, the communication software developed inhouse at RBI may be installed at all RBI offices. All Central Office Departments / Divisions and Regional Offices nay be provided with RBINET nodes. Further all banks may use this software for their communication with the RBI as also with their major branches, controlling offices.
44. National Institute of Bank Management (NIBM), Pune may organize training capsules on BANKNET and RBINET or crash basis to train Bank officers in the user of network.
45. All banks and financial institution authorized by RBI to deal in foreign exchange business (84 at present) may join SWIFT. At present 41 authorized dealers have taken SWIFT membership
46. All 'A' category branches (181 in all) of banks authorized to deal in foreign exchanges may be linked to their respective SWIFT Operating Centers at Bombay. All 'B' category forex dealing branches (1918 in all) may also be connected to the respective SWIFT Operating Centers at Bombay in a phased manner.
47. Banks connected to SWIFT may utilize the network oprimally.
48. To meet the training gap on SWIFT operations, SWIFT may be requested to have tie up arrangements with one of the training institutions in India (preferably NIBM, Pune) for conducting training programs on a regular basis.
49. To promote acrd culture in India, a Society of Card Issuers may be constituted. The Indian Bank Association may take the initiative in forming such a Society. This Society could be useful to establish proper procedures on prevention of fraud, monitor merchant establishments and make card business more profitable.
50. For effective utilization of the resources of the proposed SPNS, the ATM card to be issued may be multipurpose card. Besides ATM card this network may also connect Point of Sale (POS) terminals, Branches Teller Machines (BRMs) and cash dispensers. The network should alsp provide connectivity to smart card as also other cards such as VISA. Mastercard and AMEX.

51. Electronic Fund Transfer at Point or Sale (EFTPOS) and use of smart cards may be promoted to develop at plastic money / electronic money culture.
52. Training at the work place should be organized for certain routine applications like copying / deleting of files, virus protection, E – Mail etc. Emphasis should be on local presence of the trainers.
53. In – house training institutions should be strengthened for higher technology inputs in all training programs by providing state of the art infrastructure and skilled faculty.
54. National Institute of Bank Management (NIBM), Pune may design intensive and specialized training programs of 4 to 6 months duration for EDP managers, database administrators and other specialists. National Center for Software Technology and National Informatics Center may also be requested to organize training programs, specially designed for bank personnel.
55. An institute on banking technology may be setup with the objective of imparting high – level technology training to the bankers. It may be an autonomous institute offering professional level courses.
56. Banks may sponsor high level academic courses in information technology with specialization in banking technology at the premier institute of learning such as IIT, IIM, ISI. Sabbaticals for acquiring IT qualifications may be encouraged.
57. NIBM may take lead in preparing self –learning video material on commonly used banking application packages.
58. IBA may start monthly magazine on banking technology.
59. A Standing Committee on Technology Uses in Banks should be set up under the aegis of RBI to periodically review the technology status in the Banking industry.

X. EXPERT GROUP ON FOREIGN EXCHANGE MARKETS (O. P. Sodhani Committee, June 1995)

Relaxations to Existing Regulations

1. Corporates should be permitted to take a hedge upon declaring the existence of genuine exposure.
2. The banks may be permitted to decide open position limits subject to their earmarking capital to the extend of 5 per cent of open exposure limit. The current cap of Rs. 15 crores on open exchange position may be withdrawn.
3. The discipline relating to aggregate gap limits, ideally, should encompass rupee transactions also. While this is the ultimate goal, to begin with, the banks should be permitted to fix their own gap limits based on capital, risk bearing capacity, etc.
4. Authorized dealers may on application to RBI be permitted to initiate cross currency positions overseas.
5. In order to impart depth and liquidity to the forward markets, banks should be allowed to lend or borrow short – term funds up to six months in the overseas markets up to specific limits.
6. The number of market participants should be increased by permitting financial institutions like IDBI, IFCI etc. to trade in the forex market.
7. Market intervention by RBI should be selective rather than continuous, Forex, swaps may be used as a tool by RBI to control the forward margins.
8. Banks should have the freedom to determine the interest rate and maturity period of FCNR (B) deposits subject to a cap being put in place by RBI.
9. Exporters should, subject to liquidation of outstanding advances, be permitted to retain 100 per cent of export earnings in foreign currency in India.
10. Inter – bank borrowings should be exempt from statutory pre – emptions to help the emergence of a rupee term money market and a deep and liquid debt / forex market.

Derivative Products, Risk Management and Accounting

11. Corporates should be permitted to cancel and re – book option contracts and hedge any genuine contingent exposure using options.
12. Banks should be permitted to offer lower cost option strategies like "range forwards" and "ratio range forwards"
13. Tax laws relating to withholding tax should be unambiguous and derivative transactions should not be subject to any withholding tax. This matter may be taken up with the Government of India.
14. Banks should have greater freedom to use derivative products for their own asset - liability management.
15. Banks can be given general permission to offer hedging products, like caps, floors, swaps etc. subject to post – facto reporting.
16. Corporates having EEFC accounts should be permitted to user amounts therein as margin for executing trades that will enable them access to hedging products overseas which are not available in India.
17. Subject to reforms the money market and permitting short-term investment / borrowings overseas, RBI may invite proposals from banks for offering rupee – based derivatives.
18. In the long run, authorized dealers may be permitted to offer all types of derivative products subject to their putting in place comprehensive risk management systems on the basis of RBI guidelines. A fresh set of guidelines for forex and derivative risk management should be framed by the RBI to replace the existing Internal Guidelines.
19. In view of the complexity of derivative products and attendant risks, an association of professionals or FEDAI should ensure that uniform documentation and market practices are followed by all the market participants.
20. The Group has apprehensions that some of the corporates have converted exposure management function into profit centre without having adequate control systems. It is there important that all market participants should put in place risk management policies and internal control systems before being allowed to transact in forex and interest rate derivative produucts.
21. Accounting of derivative transactions (including forwards) should specifically differentiate between its use for trading from for hedging.
22. Accounting standards for all market participants should be developed by the Institute of Charted Accountants of India (ICAI) for forex/derivative products to cover accounting and disclosure norms. As an interim measure, ICAI should issue a guidance note or statement of recommended practices (SORP) covering accounting and disclosure norms. In case an organisation does not adhere to the guidance note, the departure should be suitably commented upon by the auditor.
23. Proper disclosure of interest rate and forex rate risk should be made in the financial reports. The disclosure should include a clear statement on the risk management of derivatives and the company's accounting policy for derivatives.
24. The accounting practices recommended by the ICAI should be accepted by tax authorities for the determination of tax incidence.
25. All market participants may follow the recommended "best practices" for managing various risks while undertaking forex/derivative transactions. Boards of Directors of end-users should approve and implement a policy for the use of derivatives for financial risk management which sets the boundaries of their derivatives operations.
26. The netting of settlements and the related pre-settlement risk should be made legally enforceable. A study group may be set up to eximine the issue in all its ramifactions.

27. To ensure that banks and others contemplating derivatives dealing activity are not unprepared for the potential capital requirements for market price risks, as recommended should be followed by all the authorised dealers permitted to deal in derivatives.

Miscellaneous

28. RBI may set up a foreign exchange market committee to advise in on policy issues relating to foreign exchange, effecting improvement in the quality of risk management and preparing issue papers on specific market related topics.

29. Off-share banking units may be set up in Bombay.

30. RBI should take the initiative in collecting and publishing on a daily basis critical data on foreign exchange transactions.

31. The proposed Forex Clearing House in Bombay may be set up early considering the substantial benefits this transactions.

32. FEDAI's role may be reviewed and enalarged specifically to focus on training and preparing the stage for further relaxations in the forex/derivatives market.

33. With a view to offer the best possible exchange rates to smaller entities, banks should keep their forex dealing branches updated on rate variations or consider decentralising dealing operations.

APPENDIX-III

COMMITTEE ON TRADE FINANCIAL SERVICES
[GATs]

The following communication is circulated at the request of India to Members of the Committee on Trade in Financial Services.

1. India is pleased to submit the annexed revised draft conditional offer in financial services. This revised offer is an improvement to its 28th July 1995 schedule of commitments in financial service under the General Agreement on Trade in Services.

2. India reserves the right to modify, reduce or withdraw this offer in whole or in part... On the results of the negotiations on financial services.

3. India also reserves the right to make technical changes to the schedule and to correct any... Omissions or inaccuracies.

Modes of supply	1 Cross-border supply	2 Consumption abroad	3 Commercial presence	4 Presence of natural persons
Sector of Sub-sector Financial Services	Limitations of Market Access	Unbound	Limitations on National Treatment	Unbound
A. Insurance and Insurance-related services	Unbound	Unbound	Unbound	Unbound
Non-life, limited to Insurance of freight	Unbound	Unbound	Unbound	Unbound except as indicated in the horizontal section.
Reinsurance and retrocession	Unbound	Unbound	Unbound	Unbound except as indicated in the horizontal section.
Insurance intermediation, limited to reinsurance	Unbound	Unbound	Unbound	Unbound except as indicated in the horizontal section.

Modes of supply	1 Cross-border supply	2 Consumption abroad	3 Commercial presence	4 Presence of natural persons
B. Banking and other financial services (excluding insurance)	Unbound	Unbound	Unbound	Unbound
1.(I) Acceptance of deposits and other repayable funds from the public	Unbound	Unbound	1.(I) Foreign banks are required to constitute Local Advisory Boards consisting inter alia of professionals and persons having expertise in areas such as small-scale industry and exports. The Chairman and members of the Local Advisory Board must be resident Indian nationals except for the Chief Executive Officer who may be a foreign national. The appointment of chairman and members of the Board requires Reserve Bank of India approval	Unbound
(ii) Lending of all types, including consumer credit, mortgage, credit and financing of commercial transactions but excluding factoring	Unbound	Unbound	Foreign banks are required to publish consolidated financial statements of the Indian branches as at 31st March every year.	Unbound
(iii) All payment and money transmission services including credit, exchange and debt cards, travellers cheques and banker' drafts.	Unbound	Unbound	(iii) Public Sector enterprises can invest surplus funds in term deposits only with scheduled commercial banks incorporated in India.	Unbound
(iv) Guarantees and commitments	Unbound exceprt as indicated in the horizontal section	Unbound	Unbound	Unbound

Modes of supply	1 Cross-border supply	2 Consumption abroad	3 Commercial presence	4 Presence of natural persons
(v) Trading for own account of: (a) money market instruments (b) foreign exchange (c) transferable securities	Unbound exceprt as indicated in the horizontal section	Unbound	Unbound	Unbound
(vi) Protfolio management, custodial and trust services	Unbound exceprt as indicated in the horizontal section	Unbound	Unbound	Unbound
(vii) Clearing services for other banks for cheques, drafts and other instruments	Unbound exceprt as indicated in the horizontal section	Unbound	Unbound	Unbound
2. Participation in issues of all kinds of securities, including underwriting and placement as agent whether publicly or privately and provision of services related to such issues	Unbound	Unbound	Unbound	Unbound
3. Stock broking	Unbound exceprt as indicated in the horizontal section	Unbound	Unbound	Unbound

Modes of supply	1 Cross-border supply	2 Consumption abroad	3 Commercial presence	4 Presence of natural persons
4. Financial consultancy services, i.e. financial advisory services provided by financial advisers, etc. To customers on financial matters, investment and portfolio research and advice on acquisitions and on corporate restructuring and strategy	Unbound	Unbound	Unbound	Unbound exceprt as indicated in the horizontal section
5. Factoring	Unbound	Unbound	Unbound except for entties established in accordance with the limitations specified in the market access column.	Unbound exceprt as indicated in the horizontal section
6. Financial leasing	Unbound	Unbound	Unbound except for entties established in accordance with the limitations specified in the market access column.	Unbound exceprt as indicated in the horizontal section
7. Venture capital	Unbound	Unbound	Unbound except for entties established in accordance with the limitations specified in the market access column.	Unbound exceprt as indicated in the horizontal section

- **Unbound:** Implies no commitments have been undertaken by the country and there are no binding. In other words, the government is free to place any restriction if it wishes.

- **Limitations on Market Access:** Refers to the extent to which foreign companies can access the Indian market. When you read "unbound" under this column, it implies that restrictions to market access can be imposed at any stage. When you read "none" under this column, it implies that there are no restrictions on entry in this sector.

- **Limitations on National Treatment:** Refers to the conditions / requirements in which the country is discriminating against foreign firms. When you read " unbound" under this column it implies that the government is free to impose any conditions or discriminate against foreign firms in any way, at any stage. When you read " none" under this column, it implies that there is no discrimination against foreign firms.

The commitments in financial services are made in accordance with the General Agreement on Trade in Services and the Annex on Financial Services. All the commitments are subjects to entry requirements, domestic laws, rules and regulations and the rerms and conditions of the Reserve Bank of India, Securities and Exchange Board of India and any other competent authority in India.

Note:
The commitments in financial services are made in accordance with the General Agreement on Trade in Services and Annex on Financial Services. All the commitments are subject to entry requirements, domestic laws, rules and regulations and the terms and conditions of the Reserve Bank of India, Securities and Exchange Board of India and any other competent authority in India.

MARKETING OF FINANCIAL SERVICES

Abstract of

A Thesis Submitted to

The Maharaja Sayajirao University of Baroda

for

The Award of the Degree of

Doctor of Philosophy

in Business Administration

By
Umesh R. Dangarwala

Under the guidance of
Prof. B. S. Patel

Department of Commerce including Business Administration

Faculty of Commerce

The Maharaja Sayajirao University of Baroda,

Vadodara

September 1999

CONTENTS

CHAPTER – I
INTRODUCTION   01

CHAPTER – II
LITERATURE REVIEW AND A RATIONALE OF THE STUDY   06

CHAPTER – III
FINANCIAL SERVICES MARKETING   08

CHAPTER - IV
METHODOLOGY   11

CHAPTER - V
ANALYSIS AND INTERPRETATION OF DATA:
COMPARISON AND DIFFERENTIATION OF GROUPS   18

CHAPTER VI
ANALYSIS AND INTERPRETATION OF DATA: ASSOCIATION
BETWEEN GROWTH RATES AND MARKETING PRACTICES   23

CHAPTER VII
SUMMARY, IMPORTANT FINDINGS AND THEIR IMPLICATIONS   26

CHAPTER – I

INTRODUCTION

A recent FICCI paper avers that the service sector can contribute more than 50 per cent to the national GDP by AD 2000 provided it grows at a rate of 5.3 per cent annually. If this works out, the projected growth in this sector is going to surpass the growth in the agricultural and industrial sectors.

Finance plays an important role in shaping the economy of a country. The present study is concerned with the marketing practices of the financial service organizations. A review of the existing literature on the subject reveals that the marketing problem of the financial service organizations has remained a fairly unmapped area. The purpose of this study is to investigate to what extent the financial service organizations adopt the marketing concept in their marketing decisions, for the marketing concept holds, that, the key to achieving organizational goals consists in determining the needs and wants of target markets and delivering the desired satisfactions more effectively and efficiently than competitors.

In the present chapter, to begin with, a discussion on "Marketing and Economic Development" is undertaken. This is followed by "Developments in Marketing" and "Service Marketing". In the latter half of the chapter, the Nature and Scope, Limitations and Organization of the thesis are given.

1.1 MARKETING & ECONOMIC DEVELOPMENT

Marketing has a key role to play in the economic development of a country through its potential contribution to the process of economic development. Economic growth implies rise in gross National product through generation of additional income in various sectors of an economy such as agriculture, mining, industry and trade.

In this section of the chapter, following points are elaborated:

1.1.1 Role of Marketing in Economic Development
1.1.2 The Concept of A National Market in Developing Economies
1.1.3 Role of Marketing Functions in Economic Development

1.1.4 Coordinated Marketing Systems
1.1.5 Marketing and Economic Development – its Relevance to The Service Organizations in India

1.2 DEVELOPMENTS IN MARKETING

Initially, producers and manufacturers were concerned mainly with logistical issues – transporting and selling goods to widespread markets, often located far away from the point of production. The focus here was on production, with consumption and consumers being seen as the end result of a production and distribution chain. For as long as demand outstripped supply, which was generally the case as western counties started to go through periods of dramatic growth in economic activity and technological change, producers could all exist profitably simply by producing more efficiently and cutting costs. Little attention was given to the role of the consumer in exchange processes.

In the early twentieth century the realization that marketing was, in itself, an important part of the business process led to the founding of the American Marketing Association and the development of the earliest aspects of marketing theory and practice. It was much later, however, that the need for a marketing orientation was recognized, with a clear focus on the needs of the consumer.

In this section of the chapter, following points are highlighted:

1.2.1 Marketing Theory Developments
1.2.2 The Marketing Environment
1.2.3 Marketing Organizations
1.2.4 Marketing Today

1.3 SERVICES MARKETING

Marketing – driven organizations, whether in the manufacturing or service sectors, must have an intimate knowledge of the market in order to identify unfulfilled market needs and provide a marketing offering which will meet those needs, thereby satisfying both the customer, and the organization's objectives.

Market research, marketing planning, and the development of a set of marketing mix tools are equally important in services marketing and the marketing of physical goods.

In this section of the chapter following aspects pertaining to service marketing are covered in detail.

1.3.1 The Concept of Service
1.3.2 Reasons for Growth of The Service Sector
1.3.3 Marketing Mix
1.3.4 Special Characteristics of Services
1.3.5 The Nature of The Service Product
1.3.6 Areas Responsible For Problems and Key Issues in Services Marketing Management
1.3.7 Classification of Services

1.4 NATURE & SCOPE OF THE STUDY

A survey was undertaken to delve into the marketing practices of the financial service organizations and for the purpose of the study, the financial service organizations situated in the State of Gujarat were chosen. The study is a combination of exploratory, descriptive and casual research design. The data was collected from primary sources with the help of a structured questionnaire as well as from secondary sources available within and outside the financial service organizations.

In this study an attempt is made to ascertain the extent of association between input and output, the variable chosen for input are marketing practices and output is growth rate. Ideally, better marketing practices should lead to higher growth rate (which is the goal of financial service organizations). As the scale of operations of various financial service organizations differs, growth parameters i.e. advance growth rate, investments growth rate, deposits growth rate, commissions/fees growth rate have been used as output variable.

1.5 LIMITATIONS OF THE STUDY

The study was subject to certain limitations:

(i) Data on expenditure aspects could not be collected fully. As the financial service organizations were unwilling to divulge information pertaining to expenditure aspects.

(ii) The marketing practices of the financial service organizations concerning 'channel decisions' could not be analyzed in this study, as very few organizations (only 10 from the sample of 52 units) indicated that their they use 'channel' for generating business. It was felt that the results of these 10 respondents when analyzed might not conform to the realities of the situation.

(iii) The study examines the relationship between growth rate and marketing practices. However, there may be several other factors than marketing practices, which influence growth rate. (Other factors may be said to include role of Govt., market situation, rate of inflation etc.)

(iv) Due to constraints of time and finance, the study could not be broad based is confirmed to financial organizations situated in State of Gujarat.

1.6 ORGANIZATION OF THE STUDY – CHAPTERIZATION

Chapter I is an introductory chapter, which brings out the importance of marketing in economic development. The developments of marketing theory, the marketing environment, the development of the marketing concept, marketing mix and characteristics service products are also highlighted. The nature and scope of the study, as also the limitations of the study are brought out.

Chapter II highlights findings of a few studies. A case for a study on the marketing practices of the financial organizations is made out.

Chapter III is wholly devoted to the theoretical frame work of financial services, viz. special characteristics, competitive environment, financial services marketing mix, types of financial services etc. It also covers the role of regulatory authority in marketing of financial services. It also covers the rationale for a study on the marketing practices of financial service organizations.

Chapter IV describes the plan and procedure of the study in detail. This includes sample selection, development of the questionnaire, research objectives (hypothesis) and the statistical techniques used in analyzing data.

Chapter V is the first of the two chapters were the data collected was analyzed. Here, the level of performance of the different groups with respect to each of the marketing variables is discussed. The different groups are also compared and differentiated in terms of their marketing practices.

Chapter VI also deals with analysis and interpretation of data. The results accrued from the application of the step – wise regression technique are discussed the criterion variable being growth rate and predictor variable, the different marketing practices.

Chapter VII presents a summary of the study and highlights it major findings. The implications of the study are also discussed alongside.
Besides, there are appendices giving the questionnaire, the scoring key and some other related particulars.

CHAPTER – II

LITERATURE REVIEW AND A RATIONALE OF THE STUDY

2.1 INTRODUCTION

This chapter in brief provides the major findings of relevant important studies. The findings of these studies do suggest some definite basis on which further studies in the filed can be carried out. They are of considerable significance in the context of present study in as much as they provide excellent guidelines as well as important view points that are to be considered in the present investigation.

The present investigation is mainly concerned with marketing of financial services. Hence in this chapter an attempt is made to make a broad survey of the studies in the field of marketing of services.

2.2 A RATIONALE FOR THE STUDY

A fresh wave of economic liberalization and globalization has been sweeping most of the world since the 1980s, and India from 1990 onwards. Consequently the financial services scenario also has been undergoing a transformation, especially with regard to competition, technological advancement and innovation. Due to the competition from within and without, and the relentless improvement in the field of technology as applied to financial services, financial service organizations have been compelled to constantly innovate new products, new delivery techniques and convincingly attract customers. In addition, they have to make concerted efforts to retain them. To do this, they require sharp marketing skills.

Marketing is a well-researched subject. A large number of authoritative treatises are already available. Even the characteristic features of marketing in Indian context have been extensively analyzed.

A recent FICCI paper avers that the service sector can contribute more than 50 per cent to the national GDP by AD 2000 provided it grows at a rate of 5.3 per cent annually. It this works out, the projected growth in this sector is going to surpass the growth in the agricultural and industrial sectors. It is also noted that dissatisfaction with services rendered (be it banking, insurance, railways, health, tourism, postal services or whatever) is high. This may even be termed a period of service crisis. How to exploit growing opportunities in the services sector and heighten satisfaction with service delivery is an extremely typical issue for in-depth analysis. Financial services, as a crucial segment of the services sector, are today face-to-face with the issue. In a scenario like this, the discipline of financial services marketing is going to acquire critical importance in the foreseeable future, if it has not already.

Though product and services marketing are similar in many ways, there are some very crucial points of difference between them. For example, the intangible nature of service products and the strong presence of the human factor in services marketing. The need to view financial service marketing from the unique standpoint of services marketing is, therefore, obvious and strong.

Indian financial service is fundamentally different from financial services elsewhere. Features like low degree of technological sophistication, a highly unionized workforce and a cumbersome legal system mark it.

The inference is clear. Indian financial service marketing must develop its own body of concepts and principles revolving around distinctive characteristics of services marketing and tempered with the imperatives of the Indian situation. It must wriggle out of the stranglehold of product marketing influence. The long-term objective would be the development of a comprehensive theory of financial services marketing in the Indian Context, This study is an effort towards this objective. It endeavors to highlight the area of financial service marketing on the basis of peculiar features attendant to financial service marketing in India rather than a classical product marketing situation.

CHAPTER – III

FINANCIAL SERVICES MARKETING

3.1 INTRODUCTION

Marketing of financial services begins with the mightily problem in that the service designer to promote more or less a uniformed product, which unlike most packaged goods have intrinsic differences.

This chapter covers the theoretical aspects pertaining to financial services. Following aspects are covered in detail:

3.2 FINANCIAL SERVICES IN THE INDIAN CONTEXT
3.3 SPECIAL CHARACTERISTICS OF FINANCIAL SERVICES
3.4 THE MARKETING AND COMPETITIVE ENVIRONMENT
3.5 THE FINANCIAL SERVICES MARKETING MIX
3.6 FINANCIAL PRODUCTS (SERVICES) - THE OPTIONS AVAILABLE

In order to appreciate better the range of financial products available to us in the country we shall briefly discuss about their " providers" and that how financial services have come to blossom.

Here following financial product/service discussed at a length:

Some Typical Financial Products (Fund Based Services)

1. Savings & Recurring Account
2. Current Account
3. Fixed Deposits
4. Retail Loan Products
5. Commercial Loans
6. Leasing & Hire Purchase
7. Credit Cards
8. Venture Capital
9. Mutual Funds

Other Financial Products (Fee Based Services)

1. Underwriting
2. Broking
3. Custodial Services
4. Credit rating
5. Merchant banking
6. Loan syndication
7. Share registration services
8. Debenture Trusteeship
9. Insurance

Developing Financial Products:

1. Factoring
2. Forfaiting
3. Depository services
4. Commercial Paper
5. Treasury Bills
6. Derivatives

3.7 TECHNOLOGY POWER FOR FINANCIAL PRODUCTS

3.8 FINANCIAL SERVICES REGULATION AND LEGISLATION: IMPACT ON FINANCIAL SERVICES

All functions and responsibilities of financial service organizations (both Indian and foreign) are governed by the regulations stipulated by the Reserve Bank of India (RBI). For banks the two critical elements of Cash Reserve Ratio and Statutory Liquidity Ratio are fixed by RBI.

From time to time strictures are issued for matter such as revision of interest rates; change of policy ; foreign exchange regulations.

The Financial Services Regulations by SEBI & RBI are largely brought about to regulate the financial service organizations and protect the consumers. Financial Organizations including insurance companies have to abide by the regulations set down.

RBI has appointed various committees to carry out reforms in financial sector and have proper functioning and monitoring of financial service organizations as well as to protect the interest of consumers who avail services form financial service organizations.

All marketing efforts are financial service organizations have to be carried out within the boundaries of the recommendations of various committees. It may interest to take note of, while studying the marketing practices of financial service organizations, various recommendations made by various committees. Major recommendations of following committees are annexed with the study (as Appendix– III) to have an insight on marketing of financial service organizations.

1. Chakravarty Committee, 1985 (Committee to review the working of the monetary system)
2. Vaghul Committee, 1987 (Working group on the money market)
3. Narasimhan Committee, 1991 (Committee on the financial system)
4. Basu Committee, 1992 (Task force on money market mutual funds)
5. A. C. Shah Committee, 1992 (Working group on non-banking financial companies)
6. J. V. Shetty Committee, 1993 (Committee on consortium lending)
7. R. Jilani Committee, 1993 (Working group on cash credit system)
8. D. R. Mehta Committee, 1994 (Committee to review IRDP)
9. W. S. Saraf Committee, 1994 (Committee on technological issue)
10. O. P. Sodhani Committee, 1995 (Expert group of foreign exchange markets)

The role played by SEBI can also not be ignored while studying marketing of financial services. The Securities and Exchange Board Act of 1992 provides for the establishment of a Board to protect the interest of investors in securities and to promote the development and regulations of securities market. Various guidelines given by SEBI, for example, Guidelines for Debentures, Guidelines for Right Issues, Guidelines for Preferential Allotment, Guidelines (Norms) about Publicity and Issue Advertisement etc. are to be considered while studying / designing marketing strategies of financial service organizations.

CHAPTER - IV

METHODOLOGY

4.1 INTRODUCTION

This chapter describes how the research proposal came to be formulated and how the research was carried out.

A review of some studies on Marketing of Services and a case for a study on the marketing practices of financial services organizations has already been given in chapter II, hence the same is not being repeated.

(a) Statement of Problem :

As the study is concerned with marketing aspects only, the problem that is taken up for investigation is to find out how systematic and scientific are marketing practices of the financial service organizations.

(b) Research Objectives :

The objectives of the study are:
- i) to ascertain, the level of performance of the financial services organizations on the different marketing practices;

- ii) to ascertain, the existence of relationship and the extent of relationship between the performance variable, (growth rate), and predictor variables, (the marketing practices), both for the entire sample and for sub-samples. The marketing practices include are:

    - Competitive and demand practices (CDP),
    - Product/ Service practices (PDP),
    - New product/ Service practices (NPP),
    - Pricing Practices (PRP),
    - Promotion practices (PMP);

iii) to differentiate the various sub-groups in respect of their marketing practices. The sub-groups that are mutually exclusive are,
- "Risk taker" group – "Safe Player" group,
- "Professionally Managed" group–"Traditionally managed" group,
- "Fund Based Services" group– "Fee Based/Advisory Services" group,
- "Private Organizations" group – "Nationalized Organizations" group.
- "Consumer Finance" group – "Industrial Finance" group

(c) Focus of research

The focus of research in the present study is concerned with relationship among the characteristics of the objects, (here the objects are the financial service organizations and characteristics are the different variables under study).

The research design, for acquiring the information needed is inclusive of exploratory, descriptive and casual studies. An 'experience survey' was undertaken by the investigator in an attempt to obtain information on the strengths and weaknesses of financial service organizations with special reference to the marketing aspects.

Further, three financial service organizations situated in Baroda were chosen at random for the purpose of pilot study.

4.2 SAMPLING

(a) Sample Frame

Thus the sampling frame consisted of 522 financial service organizations included in the study population. These units were then classified on the basis of the two broad categories of services they render namely viz. Fund/Asset based services and Fees based / Advisory services.

(b) Sample Size :

It was decided that 10% of the study population would be drawn as the sample size. This works out to 52 financial service organizations, which was considered to be an expedient size from all practical aspects.

(c) Sampling Technique

Having decided on the sample size, the next aspect to be considered is the method of drawing the sample. As indicated earlier the 522 financial service organizations of the study population do provide different financial service groups. Therefore, it was decided to go in for 'Stratified Random Sampling'.

(d) Sample Selection

The sampling units included in the study population were grouped into different strata and then each of organizations of each strata was numbered serially, and, 'Table of Random Numbers' was referred to select the sample.

The extent of the sample was confined to the State of Gujarat

The time when the sample was drawn is January 1997.

The elements in the sample were to comprise either the fund based financial service organizations of fee based / advisory service organizations.

4.3 INSTRUMENTATION – QUESTIONNAIRE

To carry out the survey, a questionnaire had to be developed. This was necessitated since the means of obtaining information from respondents was through 'Structured – Direct Interviews' (Please refer appendix-I for questionnaire).

Pre-testing of the questionnaire was done in two stages. In the first stage the 'Delphi Method' was used.

The second stage in the pre-testing of the questionnaire was done in the field itself.

4.4 SCORING TECHNIQUE

Three types of scoring were adopted in assigning scores to the various questions. They were, namely –
- Equal scoring,
- Unequal scoring, and
- Frequency.

The detail of score of each question is given in annexure.

4.5 DATA COLLECTION

The questionnaire after having passed through all the stages enumerated above was pressed into the field. The investigator personally interviewed the respondents and collected the data.

4.6 DATA ANALYSIS

In marketing the choice of the appropriate statistical technique, the objectives of the study were given due consideration.

To fulfill objective (i) of para 4.1 b above, simple techniques such as arithmetic mean, standard deviation, co-efficient of variation and percentages were used.

In trying to fulfill objective (ii) of para 4.1 b outlined above the following aspect had to be considered i.e. the nature of assumed prior judgements on how the data matrix is to be partitioned in terms of the number of sub-sets, and also, the number of variables in each of these partitioned sub-sets the criterion versus predictor variables. Taking all these aspects into account the statistical technique chosen for the fulfillment of the objective is the 'step-wise multiple regression technique'. This would help in bringing out which of the predictor variable are of importance and their order of importance / contribution to the criterion variable.

The third objective outlined in para 4.1 b above involves the differentiation of the sub-groups in terms of marketing practices. One way of accomplishing the same is through the use of discriminate analysis, which helps in determining weather differences in average score profiles for two or more groups are statistically significant. This can be done by undertaking group classifications. Thus it is possible to discriminate between two groups (as in the present study) on the basis of a few variables (in the present study it would be marketing practices).

4.7 CLASSIFICATION OF RESPONDENTS ORGANIZATIONS

For the purpose of analysis the respondent organizations were divided into groups on the basis of following different criteria, each of them is examined below.

(i) "Risk Taker" group (RTG) – "Safe Player" group (SPG)
(ii) "Professionally Managed" group (PROF.MG.)- "Traditionally Managed" Group (TRAD.MG.)
(iii) "Fund Based Services" Group (FBSG) – "Fee Based/Advisory Services" Group (ABSG)
(iv) **Private Organizations Group (POG) – Nationalized Organizations Group (NOG)**
(v) **Consumer Finance Group – Industrial Finance Group**

4.8 VARIABLES IN THE PRESENT STUDY

The different aspects covered each of the variables are described below:

a) **Variable 1**
The first variable stands for growth rate, i.e. the overall growth rate in terms of deposits/funds mobilized and revenue/income generated in a year.

b) **Variable 2**
The second variable stands for marketing concept adoption in competitive and Demand practices. This is covered in section II of the questionnaire and concerns the following aspects:
- Knowledge of target market
- Information on competitors and their strategies;
- Estimation of total demand and market share etc.

c) **Variable 3**
This variable denotes marketing concept adoption in the sphere of product/service practices. It has been dealt with in section III of the questionnaire and includes aspects such as,
- Customer's preferences / requirements in the particular product/service;
- Estimation of growth rate (i.e. growth rate forecast)
- Practice of sales analysis;
- Knowledge of product/service life cycle and the ensuing product/service innovation;
- Constraints on the product/service etc.

d) **Variable 4**
The fourth variable is also a marketing variable and denotes marketing concept adoption in new product (service) decisions. This is covered in section IV of the questionnaire and is inclusive of-
- Introduction of new products (services);
- Genesis of new products (services);
- Costing of new products (services);
- Production (servicing) capacity for new products (service) etc.

e) **Variable 5**
Variable 5 denotes marketing concept adoption in pricing practices and section V of the questionnaire includes aspects such as –
- Objectives in pricing;
- Number of parameters considered in pricing
- Limitation in price fixation;
- Break-even analysis and its applications.

f) **Variable 6**
This is the last of the marketing variables and stands for marketing concept adoption in promotion decisions. Section VI of the questionnaire covers this variable and the different aspects considered in this section are –
- The necessity to communicate with target market;
- Purpose of advertising
- Methods of sales promotion used;
- Publicity;

- Responses sought through communication etc.

The data thus collected was processed on the computer,

CHAPTER - V

ANALYSIS AND INTERPRETATION OF DATA: COMPARISON AND DIFFERENTIATION OF GROUPS

5.1 INTRODUCTION

This is the first of the two chapters in which the data collected are analyzed, interpreted and discussed.

In the present chapter, the different groups are compared and differentiated with respect of each of the marketing variables. In section I (5.2 to 5.6), the level of performance of the groups in each marketing practice is highlighted. Also, the variability in the practice of each of marketing decisions for each of the groups is discussed. The statistical techniques for analyzing the data utilized here are, arithmetic mean, standard deviation, co-efficient of variation and percentages.

In section II (5.8 to 5.12) of the present chapter, each dichotomous classification is taken up for discussion at a time, and the groups are differentiated on the basis of marketing practices. The grouped t test is applied to test the difference between the two means. At first the F test is applied for testing the quality of variance, next either the pooled variance estimate t test or the separate variance estimate t test is applied (depending on the F value). Thus the two groups are discriminated on the basis of various marketing practices.

5.7 CONCLUDING REMARKS IN SECTION I

The performance of the financial service organizations on the different marketing practices is summarized in the following paragraphs.

(i) The performance of the financial service organizations on competitive and demand practices may be said to be average.
The financial service organizations can improve upon their competitive and demand practices by taking into account certain aspects, such as,

- knowledge of the competitors is a MUST,
- the financial services organizations must endeavor to create new customers i.e. searching new market segments.
- they must be able to recognize, who, where and why of their customers.
- Competitive strategies may be used to penetrate substitute's gaps or penetrate directly the competitors position(s),
- Also, they must anticipate the extent of the market, so that they may not have to incur unnecessary cost.

(ii) The performance of the small financial service organizations on product/service practices ranges between average and good. This is the only variable where by and large most of the financial service organizations have better performance (in comparison to other marketing practices). It goes without saying that every financial service organizations must know the strengths and weakness of their product/service and must endeavor to match their product/service with the market.

(iii) The performance of the financial service organizations on new product practices may be said to be poor. A few indicators that may be borne in mind while making product/service choice are:
- absolute market share,
- market concentration,
- trends in market size,
- trends in market share,
- trend in the price of the product,
- competitive trends,
- productivity (sales per employee),
- trend in material cost,

(iv) The performance of the financial service organizations on pricing practices may be said to be low.

Often the so-called best pricing, from the view point of maximizing profit may not be the best selling price for the product/service. Where to fix higher prices or lower prices depends on the pricing criteria, to cite a few examples,
- when a firm goes in for little promotion the product/service may be low priced;
- when coverage is intensive, the product/service may be low priced;
- when turnover is fast, then the product/service may be low priced, and when it is slow it may be high priced;
- when the market is mature, the product/service may be low priced, and when new/declining it may be high priced, etc.

(v) The performance of the small financial service organizations on promotion practices may be considered to be low.

Promotion may be used to stimulate non-users, light users, and increase frequency of usage of services.

Regarding the performance in the different groups the following is stated:

(vi) The RTG group secured an overall average of 53% in marketing practices, while the SPG group secured 34% . the difference in the level of performance is 19%. Therefore, it may be said that the marketing practices of the RTG group are definitely better than those of the SPG group.

(vii) The PROF.MG. group secured and overall average of 49% in marketing practices and TRAD.MG. group secured an average of 42% the difference between the two means is 7%. Although the mean of PROF.MG. group is higher than that of the TRAD.MG. group, the difference may be considered to be marginal.

(viii) The FBSG group secured an overall average of 44% in marketing practices and ABSG group an average of 49%. The mean of the ABSG group is higher than that of the FBSG group by 5%. The difference in the performance level of both groups may be said be nominal.

The POG group secured an overall average of 50% in all marketing practices and that of the NOG group is 45%. The difference in the performance level is 5%, and this may be considered to be nominal.

5.13 CONCLUDING REMARKS

The entire discussions in section I and section II of this chapter is concluded here.

i) The maximum adoption of the marketing concept is found in product/service practices. This is followed by competitive and demands practices. In respect of other practices, the adoption of the marketing concept has been either low or poor.

ii) The RTG was on the top in so far as the adoption of the marketing concept was concerned. All other groups were either low or poor in this respect.

iii) Of the four classification in this study the groups in each of the two classifications, namely, FBSG – ABSG and POG-NOG, do not differ in terms of adoption of the marketing concept in marketing practices.

In the marketing remaining two classifications, it is found that differences are significant in respect of adoption of the marketing concept in marketing practices. The RTG-SPG groups may be differentiated in the practice of competitive and demand decisions, product/service decisions, new product/service decisions, pricing decisions and promotion decisions. The PROF.MG.-TRAD.MG. group may be differentiated on the basis of their growth rate, and competitive and demand practices.

iv) The exercise on differentiation of groups has brought to the light two aspects that are or importance to financial services organizations namely,

- Risk Takers Organization, & Safe Players Organizations.
- Professionally & Traditionally Managed Organizations.

Regarding the first, risk takers is found conductive to better adoption of the marketing concept in marketing decisions. The second aspect indicates that professionally managed organization is preferable, as it is conductive to higher growth rate.

In the next chapter, the technique of step-wise regression is used to ascertain the association between growth rate and marketing practices.

CHAPTER VI

ANALYSIS AND INTERPRETATION OF DATA: ASSOCIATION BETWEEN GROWTH RATES AND MARKETING PRACTICES

6.1 INTRODUCTION

In the present chapter that analysis and interpretation of data are undertaken with the help of regression technique. An attempt is made to explain the variance of growth rate in relation to the marketing practices. That is, measure the overall strength of association between growth rate and the full set of marketing practices. As the analysis of regression is undertaken stepwise, the contribution of each of the marketing variables to total explained variation in growth rate is described.

The approach used here is, to first of all ascertain the presence of relationship between the criterion (growth rate) and predictor variables (marketing practices), and then proceed towards prediction. The former is established by correlation and the latter by regression.

Before going on to describe and interpret the data, the symbols indicating the different variables need to be clarified to avoid any confusion. In the present chapter, the following are used:

- Y : Criterion variable: Variable 1: Growth rate.

- X_1 : independent variable: Variable 2: marketing concept adoption in competitive and demand practices (CDP)

- X_2 : independent variable: Variable 3: marketing concept adoption in product/service practices (PDP).

- X_3 : independent variable: Variable 4: marketing concept adoption in new product/service practices (NPP).

- X_4 : independent variable: Variable 5: marketing concept adoption in pricing practices (PRP).

X_5 : independent variable: Variable 6: marketing concept adoption in promotion practices (PMP)

a : Constant (intercept)

b_1 : regression co-efficient or beta weight for the first predictor variable X_1

b_5 : regression co-efficient or beta weight for the fifth predictor variable X_5.

The alpha reading in the regression equation is merely a constant, which determines the general level of the line. The b co-efficient gives the slope of the regression line and denotes a ratio. It tells how many units Y increases with every increase of one unit in X. It needs to be note here that the value of multiple R has been examined for its significance. This is done with the help of F-ratio test.

While interpreting the results, the levels of confidence arbitrarily fixed by the investigator are .01 and .05 levels of significance, and all the results are adjusted to the relevant degrees of freedom.

The analysis and interpretation of data is described in two sections. In the section-I (6.2 to 6.5) the regression technique is applied to the data pertaining to the entire sample and the significant predictor variables are drawn out. In the present study marketing variables CDP and PMP have been found to be significant and contributing to explaining the variation in growth rate. Therefore in the next section i.e. section-II (6.5), each of the groups is taken up for analysis at a time and regression technique applied, to find out, to what extent these variables, i.e. CDP and PMP, contribute in explaining the variation in growth rate.

CONCLUDING REMARKS

The maximum contribution of marketing variables CDP and PMP in explaining the variation in growth rate is found in the POG group (61%) followed by PROF.MG. group (34%). This helps us to draw a conclusion that in private organizations group and professionally managed group there is greater adherence to the marketing concept (with respect to CDP and PMP) as contribution to explaining variation in growth rate is a lot higher in these groups than other groups.

The ratio of growth rate to marketing practices in the sphere of competitive and demand decisions is best in the POG group (3.14 : 1) followed by ABSG group (1.45 : 1) and RTG group (1.34 : 1).

The ratio of sales to promotion practices are better in FBSG group (0.6 : 1) followed by RTG and POG groups (0.5 : 1).

Marketing variables CDP and PMP are not significant in SPG and TRAD.MG. groups.

CHAPTER VII

SUMMARY, IMPORTANT FINDINGS AND THEIR IMPLICATIONS

7.1 SUMMARY OF THE STUDY:

The marketing practices of the financial services organizations is by and large an unmapped area, and the present study is an investigation on the same.

In the first chapter the role of marketing in the economic development of a country and its special relevance in financial service organizations are discussed. Besides this, the developments of marketing theory, the marketing environment, the development of the marketing concept, marketing mix and characteristics of service products are also highlighted. The nature and scope of the study, as also the limitations of the study are also brought out.

The second chapter is devoted to a review of some studies on the financial service organizations. The findings of selected studies are enumerated. The findings of all these studies indicate the presence of marketing problems. The extent of the marketing problem in the financial service organizations is brought out. Besides this, allied problems of financial service organizations are pointed out. Further, a case for a study on the marketing practices of financial service organizations is made out.

This is followed by a discussion on the population (Gujarat) from which the sample for the study was drawn.

The plan and procedure of the study are enumerated in the chapter on methodology. At first, the statement of the problem, the research objectives and focus of research are spelt out. The specific objectives of the study are:
 (i) to ascertain the level of performance of the financial services organizations on the different marketing practices.

 (ii) To ascertain the existence of relationship and extent of relationship between the performance variable – growth rate and predictor variables- the different marketing practices, both for the entire sample and for sub-samples and

(iii) To differentiate the various sub-groups in respect of their marketing practices.

For the purpose of the study a questionnaire on the various marketing practices was developed and a system of scoring the responses was formulated. Two other aspects are dealt with in this chapter. First, the classification of respondent organizations was done into mutually exclusive groups for the purpose of study and analysis. The dichotomous groups are, risk taker & safe player groups; professionally & traditionally managed groups; fund based services group & Fee Based/Advisory Services groups; private organizations & Nationalized organizations groups. Second, the different marketing variables on which the financial service organizations are examined to competitive and demand practices, product/service practices, new product/service practices, pricing practices, and promotion practices.

Chapter V is the first of the two chapters on analysis and interpretation of data. For comparing the different groups on their performance on the various marketing practices, simple statistical techniques such as, arithmetic mean, standard deviation and co-efficient of variation were applied.

The differentiation of the groups was undertaken by discriminating them on the various marketing practices, which involved grouped t tests, where first the F-test for quality of variances was determined.

Chapter VI attempts stepwise regression analysis. The entire sample was at first subject to regression analysis and the significant variables were drawn out. Next, regression was applied to each of the groups to ascertain the contribution of the significant marketing variables in explaining the variation in growth rate.

7.2 FINDINGS AND THEIR IMPLICATIONS:

Major conclusions reached in this study are presented in a tabular form and these are subsequently discussed in this chapter.

Table VII-1
Major Findings.

Particulars	Significant results / findings
Marketing practices considered as a whole	The RTG group conductive to marketing concept adoption.
Maximum adoption of marketing concept	Product/service Practices.
Minimum / least adoption of marketing concept	New product/service Practices.
Low/adoption of marketing concept	Pricing Practices
Significant in explaining growth rate	Competitive & demand practices. Promotion Practices.
Growth rate	PROF.MG. conducive to sales.
Groups	CDP & PMP good in POG SPG and TRAD.MG. poor performers. Practically no difference between (A) FBSG – ABSG groups and (B) POG – NOG groups.

Considering all the marketing practices together, from the survey it was found that the risk taker group is more conducive to marketing concept adoption in its various marketing decisions. This group secured the highest group average. These findings bring out the relevance of a financial service organizations being risk takers and also the priority that needs to be given to customers overall other functional areas.

The maximum adoption of the marketing concept was found in respect of product/service practices. Also, greater homogeneity was found in decisions regarding product/service. The average scores of the groups indicate that most of them are average or good in the marketing variable relating to product/service decisions.

The least adoption of the marketing concept is found with respect to new product/service practices. It was also found that there was greater heterogeneity among the financial services organizations in the practices relating to new product/services. This implies that the financial service organizations do not adopt appropriate practices when they think of introducing new product/service in the market. This points out to the need for systematic approach by financial service organizations. Market information centers may be set up by financial service organizations.

It has been found that marketing concept adoption in pricing practices has been relatively low. It may be said that the financial service organizations are shrewd and know their profits, but it has happened may times that out of the many services they rendered only a few may be doing very badly but overall profits are good they never get to know it. The financial service organizations need to be trained and aware of the gains that can be accrued from proper book keeping and also from adopting other measures of pricing than full cost pricing.

Marketing practices relating to competitive and demands decisions and promotion decision have come out as the only two significant variables that contribute towards explaining the variation in growth rate. This implies that every financial service organization should take care to adhere to the marketing concept when they take decisions regarding competition and demand and promotion practices. By doing this they may improve the growth rate/commission/ revenue of their organization.

The only classification where growth rates turned out to be a significant differentiating factor is professionally - traditionally managed groups. From this, it may be said that professionally managed group is conducive to higher growth rate. Also is this classification, one other marketing variable is significantly differentiated and there is competitive and demands practices.

The risk taker group and safe player group differ significantly in all their marketing decisions. This means that there is a lot of differences in the way the financial service organizations of both these groups as functioned.

The poor performers are safe player and traditionally managed group. The style of working of these organizations is not in conformity with the marketing concept.

In the private organizations group, it is found that decisions relating to competition, demand and promotion are taken in greater adherence to the marketing concept as the regression results prove that the two variables contribute a lot in explaining the variation in growth rate.

Finally, in the two classifications namely, FBSG-ABSG and POG-NOG there is almost no difference in respect of marketing practices.

7.3 SUGGESTIONS FOR IMPROVING MARKETING OF FINANCIAL SERVICES

a) **Carrying out Customer Analysis**

Financial service organizations should profile threir current customer base to identify which segments of the market they come from and identify any common characteristics and buying behavior patterns, which might help future segmentation or marketing tactics. It is also necessary to assess their customers on following aspects:
- Who are they?
- Who is involved in the purchase decision?
- What motivates their behaviour?
- Which customers are worth most?

b) **Assessing Consumer Satisfaction**

Faced with global competition financial service organizations will have to redefine approaches and attitudes towards distribution and promotion of financial services. Growths should be sought by reinforcing brand equity and developing competitive advantage through distribution equity. Reaching out effectively, efficiently and economically to an ever increasing population spread through the length and breadth of a vast geography is becoming the service marketing mantra of today. In service sector, blue prints for growth are therefore becoming synonymous with strategies for customer satisfaction. Measurement of customer satisfaction involves developing a survey design tailor-made to individual context that would encompass amongst others and following steps:
1. Determining who is the customer: Multi – individual involvement, the processes of the sale mind set of the company's operating managers have to taken into account.

2. Determining what constitutes customer satisfaction: Identify parameters through pilot studies at senior levels – the complex interaction between them – and adopt indexed data collection approach to reduce subjectivity.

3. Designing the scale on which customer satisfaction would be measured: Simple coding of customer category (Government, corporate, private) and assigning relative importance to them by considering variables such as company's market presence business compulsions, growth directions and market complexions.

4. Measuring current levels of customer satisfaction: Qualitative personal interview data from various clients' department.

5. Trend analysis and painters for management of customer satisfaction: Data statistically analyzed, benchmarking and developing top – down models (based on the correct systems) and Bottom – up models (based on improving individuals customer satisfaction).

Each financial services organization should have to find its own path, which depends upon the kinds of financial service the organization offer and their relative strength, weakness and also on different macro and micro environmental (economic – physical) factors.

c) Offer Product Packages

No Customer comes to a financial service organization merely for a fixed deposit or for a loan. He comes essentially to get his problems solved and his need satisfied. Customer needs are varied, complex and multi dimensional. For the satisfaction of these multi dimensional needs, financial service organizations should offer product packages rather than stand-alone products. Financial organizations have very few product packages to offer. Some such packages are being offered to corporate customers, but not many to household segment customers. Even in the case of product packages for the corporate segment, marketing of package under a single brand name and in an integrated manner is not much in evidence.

d) Construct Perceptual Maps

To device effective marketing strategy the financial services organizations must use the perceptual mapping techniques:

- i) to measure similarity or dissimilarity between pairs of services
- ii) to measure performances between services of two competitive organizations
- iii) to have ratings of different services on various attributes

e) Be Innovative

In coming years, it would become impossible to survive and prosper unless organizational skills are effectively channelised towards innovating new ideas, new services and new strategies for winning over and retaining the customer.

A typical situation in Indian financial service organizations is that one organization floats a new product idea or a new marketing strategy and in no time ten other organizations rush to follow suit. This type of "me-too" strategy would be a recipe for mediocre marketing. Successful organizations of the future should scrupulously avoid practicing this " me-too" strategy. Innovation should be their main weapon.

Before concluding this chapter it seems worthwhile to briefly identify some related aspects – areas on which research needs to be undertake.

7.4 DIRECTION FOR FURTHER RESEARCH

Based on the findings of survey, a few suggestions for further research are indicated. It may be worthwhile to undertake a study on any of the following:

   (i) Marketing concept adoption in the sphere of new product/service practices has been rather poor. Therefore an intensive study on new product/service practices beginning with product/service idea generation up to say for a period of two years after its introduction in the market may be taken up.

(ii) By and large it was found that financial service organizations went in for full cost pricing. It may be worthwhile to find out if any other system of pricing is prevalent among financial service organizations, if not, why? Is it because of their lack of awareness of the subject or else what would be the reason for the same?

(iii) Investigation of the specific marketing practice of the financial service organizations regarding collection of information – data on competitors and demand analysis may be revealing.

(iv) As day by day, new financial services e.g. depository services, derivatives etc., are being invented and avenues are opening for establishing "Financial Super Market" and the India has already agreed to sign on General Agreement on Trade in Financial Services. (GATs) (list of financial services are annexed as appendix-III.) It is necessary to device marketing strategies keeping in the mind the global environment. The study in this line will be very useful to financial service organizations for marketing effectively their financial service.

This chapter is followed by Bibliography (Books & Articles and Websites and following appendices):

Appendix-I	Questionnaire on "Marketing of Financial Services"
Appendix – II	Major Recommendations of Selected Committees (1985-95)
Appendix-III	Committee on Trade Financial Services [Gats]

CPSIA information can be obtained
at www.ICGtesting.com
Printed in the USA
BVHW031209120822
644458BV00009B/491